AF323302

Cool Restaurants Sydney

teNeues

Imprint

Editor: Aurora Cuito

Introduction: Cristian Campos

Research: Marta Casado

Photography: 3R Design (pages 72–73, 84–87, 100–105 and 106–111), Murray Fredericks (pages 10–15, 16–23, 24–27, 44–49 and 112–117), Matteo Piazza (pages 56–61), Sharrin Rees (pages 76–79, 118–123, 124–127, 128–133), Marian Riabic (pages 80–83), Shania Shegedyn (pages 32–37, 50–55, 62–67, 68–71, 84–87 and 94–99). All other photos by the restaurants.

Layout & Pre-press: Emma Termes Parera

Translations: Antonio Moreno (English), Tanja Fontane (German), Caroline Rouquet (French), Maurizio Siliato (Italian)

Produced by Loft Publications
www.loftpublications.com

Published by teNeues Publishing Group

teNeues Book Division
Kaistraße 18
40221 Düsseldorf, Germany
Tel.: 0049-(0)211-994597-0
Fax: 0049-(0)211-994597-40
E-mail: books@teneues.de

teNeues Publishing Company
16 West 22nd Street
New York, NY 10010, USA
Tel.: 001-212-627-9090
Fax: 001-212-627-9511

teNeues Publishing UK Ltd.
P.O. Box 402
West Byfleet
KT14 7ZF, Great Britain
Tel.: 0044-1932-403509
Fax: 0044-1932-403514

teNeues France S.A.R.L.
4, rue de Valence
75005 Paris, France
Tel.: 0033-1-55766205
Fax: 0033-1-55766419

teNeues Ibérica S.L.
c/ Velázquez, 57 6.° izda.
28001 Madrid, Spain
Tel.: 0034-657-132133

teNeues Representative
Office Italy
Via San Vittore 36/1
20123 Milano, Italy
Tel.: 0039-(0)347-76 40 551

Press department: arehn@teneues.de
Phone: 0049-2152-916-202

www.teneues.com

ISBN-10: 3-8327-9027-6
ISBN-13: 978-3-8327-9027-1
© 2006 teNeues Verlag GmbH + Co. KG, Kempen

Printed in Italy

Bibliographic information published by Die Deutsche Bibliothek.
Die Deutsche Bibliothek lists this publication in the Deutsche Nationalbibliografie; detailed bibliographic data is available in the Internet at http://dnb.ddb.de.

Average price reflects the average cost for a dinner main course without beverages.
Recipes serve four.

Contents   Page

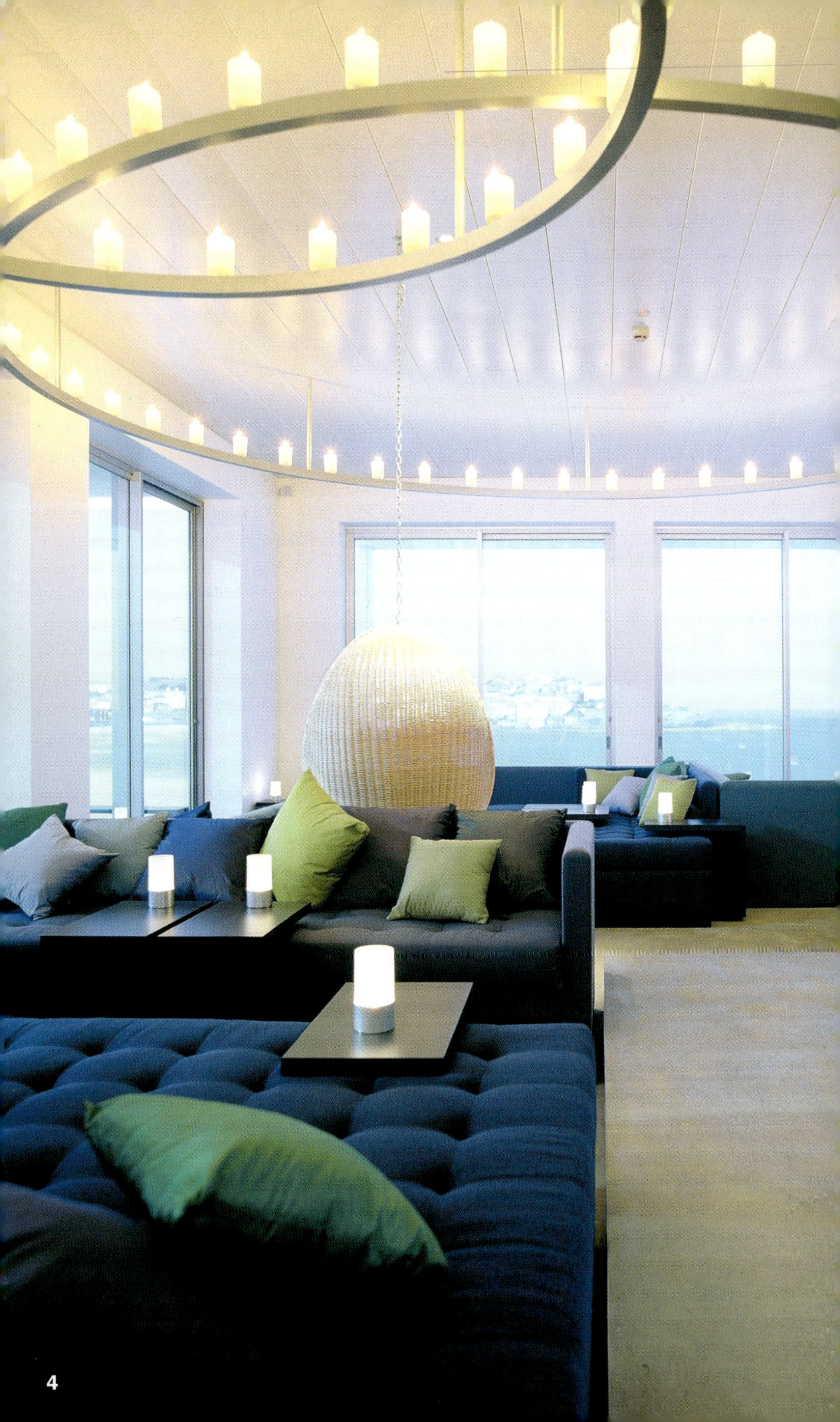

Introduction

From its early history as a British penal colony to the eviction and resettlement of many aboriginal tribes—whose names live on in some neighborhoods—Sydney has made a habit of reinventing itself. Today, Sydney is amongst the world's most vibrant and dynamic cities. On several occasions, the city was able to triumph in the face of adversity, as for instance when a drastic decline in population occurred due to the mid-19th century Gold Rush, or at the time of the Great Depression after World War I. In the early 20th century, thanks to its wool industry, the city's economy was booming and Sydney attracted many mainly European immigrants. Economic growth permanently left its marks on the city, such as Harbor Bridge in the bay area and opened in 1932, and Sydney Opera House, which opened in 1973. Perhaps the single most important event in recent years was the 2000 Olympic games. The Olympics played a deciding role in the creation of new infrastructure connecting the suburbs with the city center. Nowadays, Sydney is a metropolis, which sprawls mainly southwards, incorporating the beaches, bays and natural parks along Australia's eastern coast. Sydney's diversity is visible in the vitality, shops and the variety of the city's culinary repertoire. Sydney's restaurants are characterized by the simplicity of their geometric forms, their large and luminous interiors and, in keeping with the city's architecture, the interiors and exteriors are harmonized. Sydney's cuisine is an exciting blend of flavors, which Australia has imported through several generations of Italian, Lebanese, Chinese, Greek and, obviously, English immigrants.

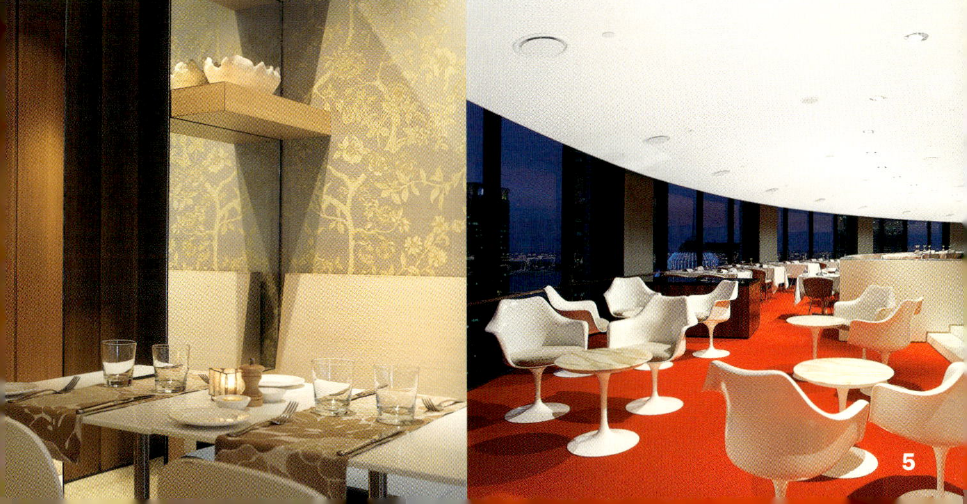

Einleitung

Seit der Entstehung der britischen Strafkolonien und nach der Vertreibung und Umsiedelung vieler Stämme der Aborigines, von denen heute noch die Namen einiger Stadtteile zeugen, hat Sydney im Laufe seiner Geschichte immer wieder sein Gesicht verändert. Heute ist es eine der brodelnsten und dynamischsten Städte der Welt. Mehrere Male war man hier in der Lage, bedrohliche Situationen zu überstehen, wie zum Beispiel den drastischen Bevölkerungsrückgang Mitte des 19. Jahrhunderts durch den Goldrausch oder die große Depression nach dem Ersten Weltkrieg. Anfang des 20. Jahrhunderts begann, dank der Wollindustrie, der wirtschaftliche Aufschwung Sydneys, der viele, in erster Linie europäische Immigranten anzog. Das Wirtschaftswachstum hat unauslöschliche Spuren in der Stadt hinterlassen, wie die 1932 eingeweihte Harbour Bridge oder die Oper, die ihre Türen 1973 öffnete. Aber das wohl größte Ereignis der letzten Jahre waren die Olympischen Spiele 2000. Sie waren der Anlass für die Entstehung einer Infrastruktur zur Anbindung der Außenbezirke an die Innenstadt. Inzwischen ist Sydney eine Metropole, die sich vor allem in Richtung Süden ausbreitet und dadurch zunehmend Strände, Buchten und Naturparks entlang der australischen Ostküste einschließt. Die Vielfalt Sydneys findet ihren Niederschlag in der Vitalität der Stadt, in ihren Läden und in ihrem vielseitigen kulinarischen Angebot. Ein Charakteristikum der Restaurants von Sydney ist eine gewisse Schlichtheit durch einfache geometrische Formen sowie große und helle Räume, mit großen Teilen der übrigen Stadtarchitektur haben sie die enge Verbindung zwischen Innen- und Außenraum gemein. Die Küche Sydneys ist eine aufregende Kombination dessen, was mehrere Generationen Italiener, Libanesen, Chinesen, Griechen und unverkennbar Engländer nach Australien mitgebracht haben.

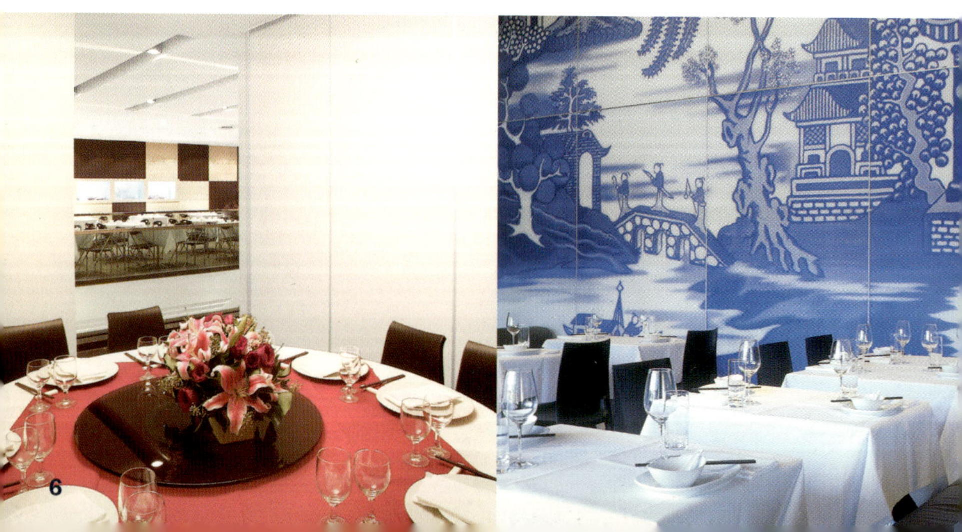

Introduction

Depuis ses origines de colonie britannique (terre de déportation pour les détenus) et suite à l'expulsion et au déplacement de nombreuses tribus aborigènes dont les témoignages qui subsistent aujourd'hui sont les noms de quelques quartiers, Sydney s'est constamment redéfinie au cours de son histoire et est devenue aujourd'hui l'une des villes les plus effervescentes et les plus dynamiques du monde. À plusieurs reprises, elle a été capable de surmonter des situations adverses, comme la drastique diminution de sa population au milieu du XIXème siècle due à la ruée vers l'or ou à la grande dépression ayant précédé la Première Guerre Mondiale. Au début du XXème, se produisit l'explosion économique de Sydney grâce à l'industrie lainière, attirant de nombreux immigrants, principalement européens. La croissance économique a laissé dans la ville des traces ineffaçables comme le pont sur la baie, inauguré en 1932, ou l'Opéra, qui ouvrit ses portes en 1973. Cependant, l'événement le plus important de ces dernières années reste les Jeux Olympiques de l'an 2000. Les Jeux influèrent en effet de manière déterminante sur la construction de grandes infrastructures qui renforcèrent la connexion entre le centre ville et les quartiers périphériques. Désormais, Sydney est une grande métropole qui s'étend principalement vers le sud et qui a englobé des plages, des baies et des parcs naturels tout au long de la Côte Est australienne. La vitalité mythique de Sydney peut être également perçue au travers de son activité urbaine, de ses locaux commerciaux et de son offre culinaire particulièrement variée. En général, les restaurants de Sydney se caractérisent par la simplicité de leurs formes géométriques, des volumes spacieux et lumineux et l'étroite relation entre les intérieurs et l'extérieur, caractéristique que ces restaurants partagent avec la grande majorité des œuvres architecturales de la ville ; la cuisine qu'ils proposent est un amalgame sensationnel de saveurs importées en Australie par de nombreuses générations d'immigrants italiens, libanais, chinois, grecs et, bien sûr, britanniques.

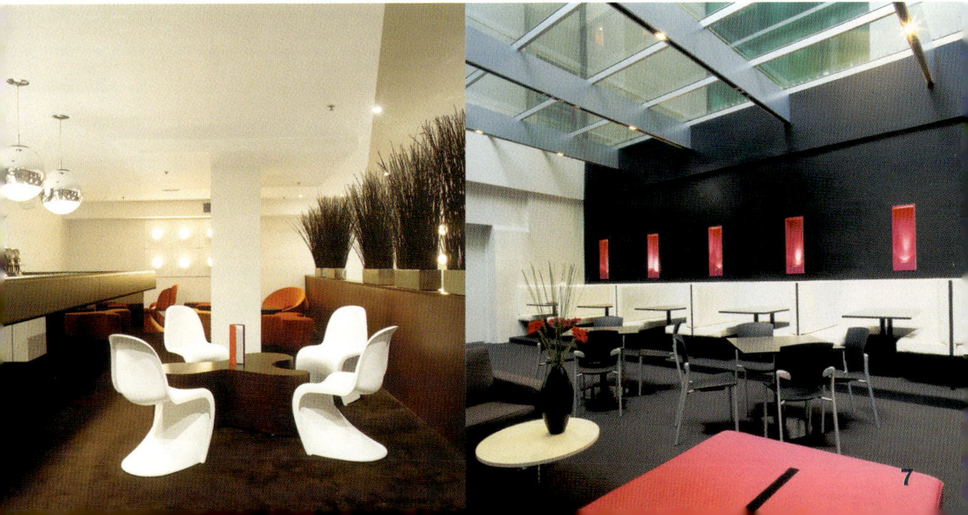

Introducción

Desde sus orígenes de colonia penal británica y tras la expulsión y el desplazamiento de muchas tribus aborígenes de las que hoy quedan testimonios en los nombres de algunos barrios, Sydney se ha reinterpretado constantemente a lo largo de su historia y es hoy una de las ciudades más efervescentes y dinámicas del mundo. En varias ocasiones ha sido capaz de sobreponerse a situaciones adversas, como la disminución drástica de su población a mediados del siglo XIX a causa de la carrera del oro o la gran depresión posterior a la Primera Guerra Mundial. A principios del siglo XX, gracias a la industria de la lana, se produjo la explosión económica de Sydney, que atrajo a muchos inmigrantes, principalmente europeos. El crecimiento económico ha dejado en la ciudad huellas imborrables como el puente Harbour sobre la bahía, inaugurado en 1932, o la Ópera, que abrió sus puertas en 1973. Pero quizá el acontecimiento más importante de los últimos tiempos haya sido el de los Juegos Olímpicos del 2000. De hecho, los Juegos influyeron de modo determinante en la construcción de grandes infraestructuras que reforzaron la conexión entre el centro de la ciudad y los barrios periféricos. Ahora Sydney es una gran metrópoli que se extiende principalmente hacia el sur y que ha incorporado playas, bahías y parques naturales a lo largo de la costa este australiana. La mítica vitalidad de Sydney puede percibirse también en su actividad urbana, en sus locales comerciales y en su variada oferta culinaria. Los restaurantes de Sydney se caracterizan por la simplicidad de sus formas geométricas, por unos espacios amplios y luminosos, y por la estrecha relación entre los interiores y el exterior, característica que comparten con gran parte de las obras arquitectónicas de la ciudad; la cocina de Sydney es una excitante amalgama de sabores importados a Australia por varias generaciones de inmigrantes italianos, libaneses, chinos, griegos y, obviamente, británicos.

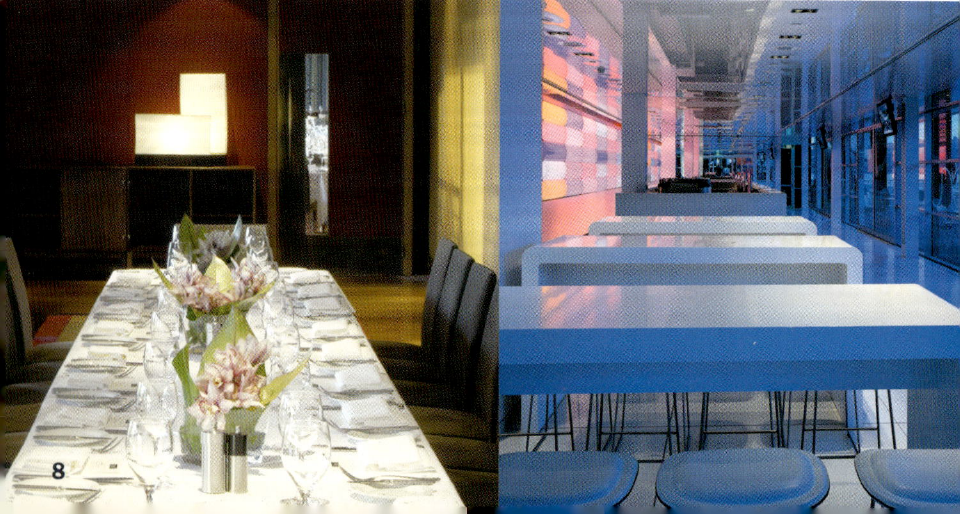

Introduzione

Sin dalle sue origini di colonia penale britannica e in seguito all'espulsione e allo spostamento di molte tribù aborigene – di cui rimane ancora testimonianza nei nomi di alcuni quartieri – Sydney si è costantemente reinventata nel corso della storia, fino a diventare oggi una delle città più effervescenti e dinamiche del mondo. Più volte ha dimostrato di saper superare situazioni avverse: il calo drastico della sua popolazione verso la metà del XIX secolo a causa della corsa all'oro, per esempio, o la grande depressione che fece seguito alla prima guerra mondiale. Agli inizi del XX secolo, grazie all'industria della lana, Sydney fu protagonista di un vero boom economico che attrasse molti immigranti, soprattutto europei. La crescita economica ha lasciato nella città tracce indelebili come il famoso ponte sulla baia, inaugurato nel 1932, o l'Opera House, che aprì i battenti nel 1973. Ma l'evento sicuramente più importante degli ultimi anni è rappresentato dai Giochi Olimpici del 2000, in occasione dei quali sono state realizzate grandi infrastrutture che hanno migliorato i collegamenti tra il centro della città e i suoi quartieri periferici. A tutt'oggi Sydney è una metropoli che si sta sviluppando principalmente verso sud, e il suo territorio va così estendendosi a spiagge, baie e parchi naturali lungo la costa orientale australiana. La vitalità di Sydney si può percepire nella realtà urbana, nei negozi e nella ricca offerta culinaria. La caratteristica tipica dei ristoranti di Sydney è la sobrietà dettata da forme geometriche semplici, spazi ampi e luminosi nonché ispirata ad un'armoniosa interazione fra interni ed esterni, peculiarità quest'ultima che contraddistingue anche gran parte delle opere architettoniche della città. La cucina della capitale è uno stimolante amalgama creatosi con l'avvicendarsi delle generazioni di immigranti italiani, libanesi, cinesi, greci, ed ovviamente britannici che hanno importato in Australia i sapori di casa.

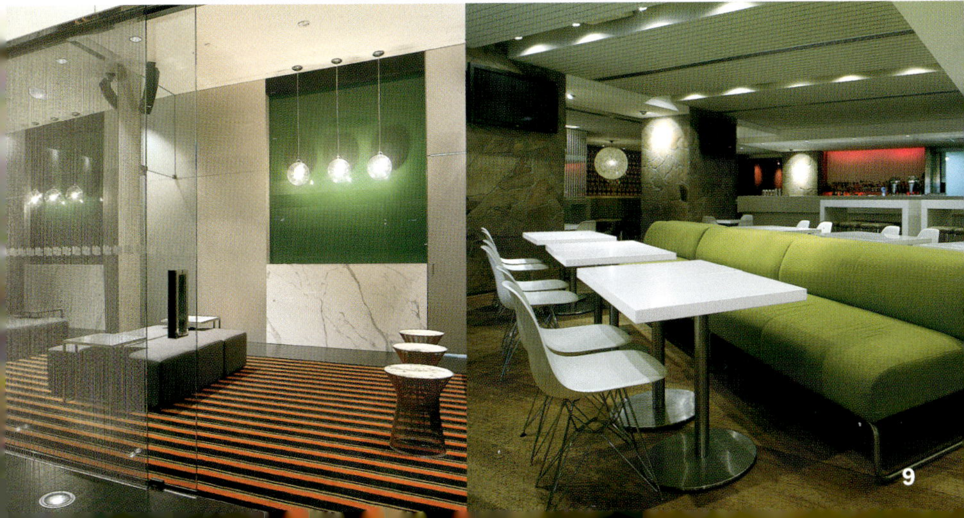

Arena Bar & Bistro

Design: McConnell Rayner | Chef: Graeme Jones

212 Bent Street, Entertainment Quarter | Sydney, 2021 | Moore Park
Phone: +61 2 9361 3833
www.arenabistro.com.au
Opening hours: Every day from noon until late
Average price: Starters A$ 18, main courses A$ 28
Cuisine: Modern Australian and French
Special features: Host to celebrity film premieres

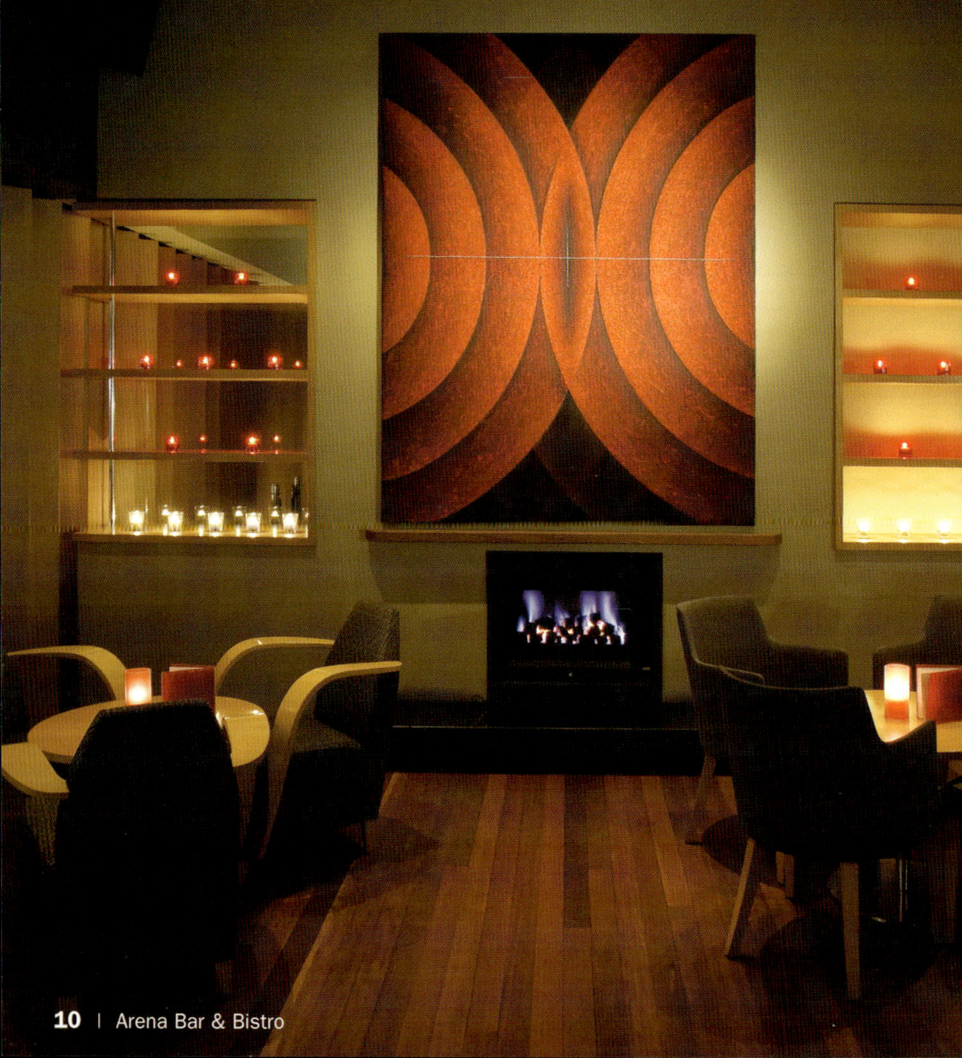

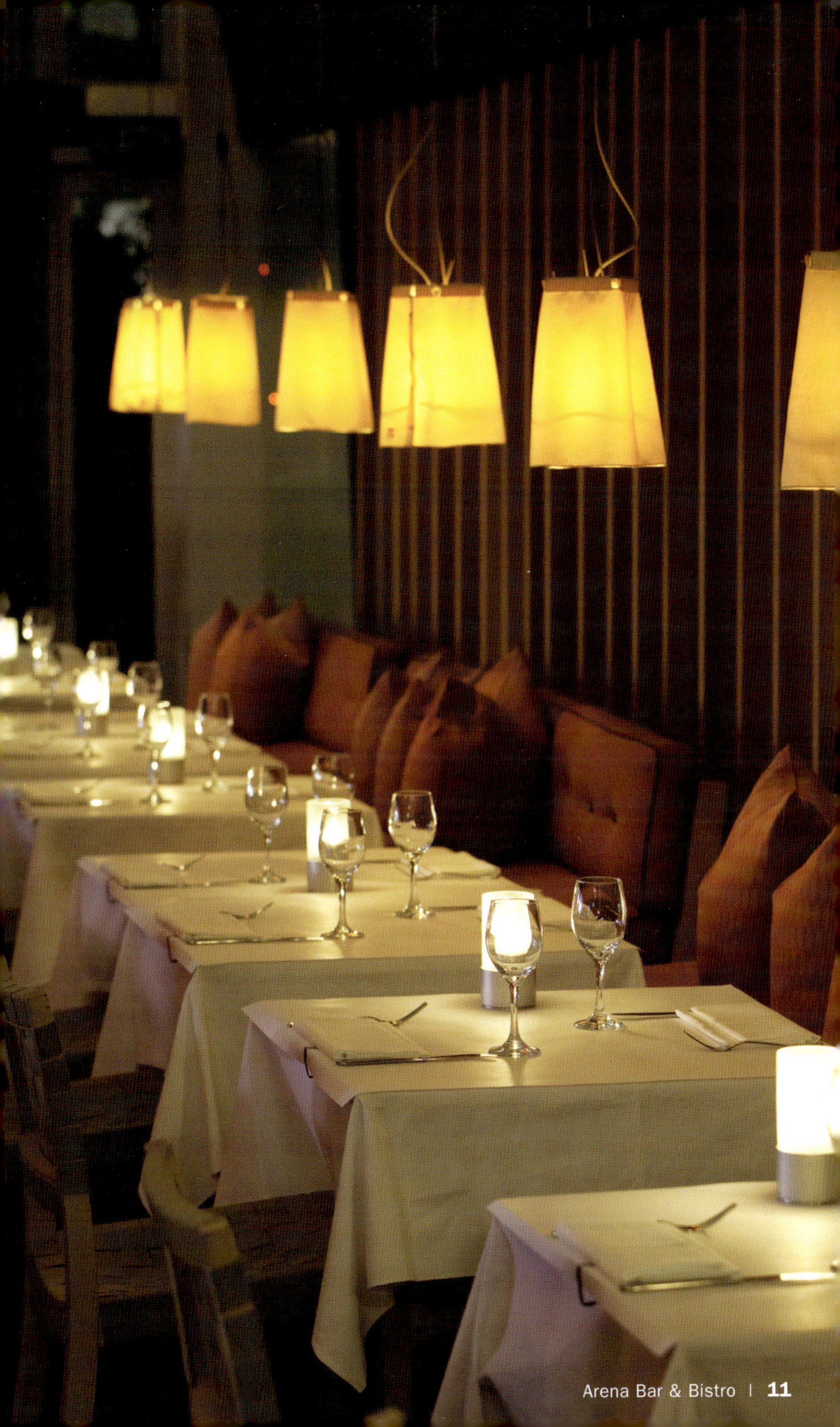

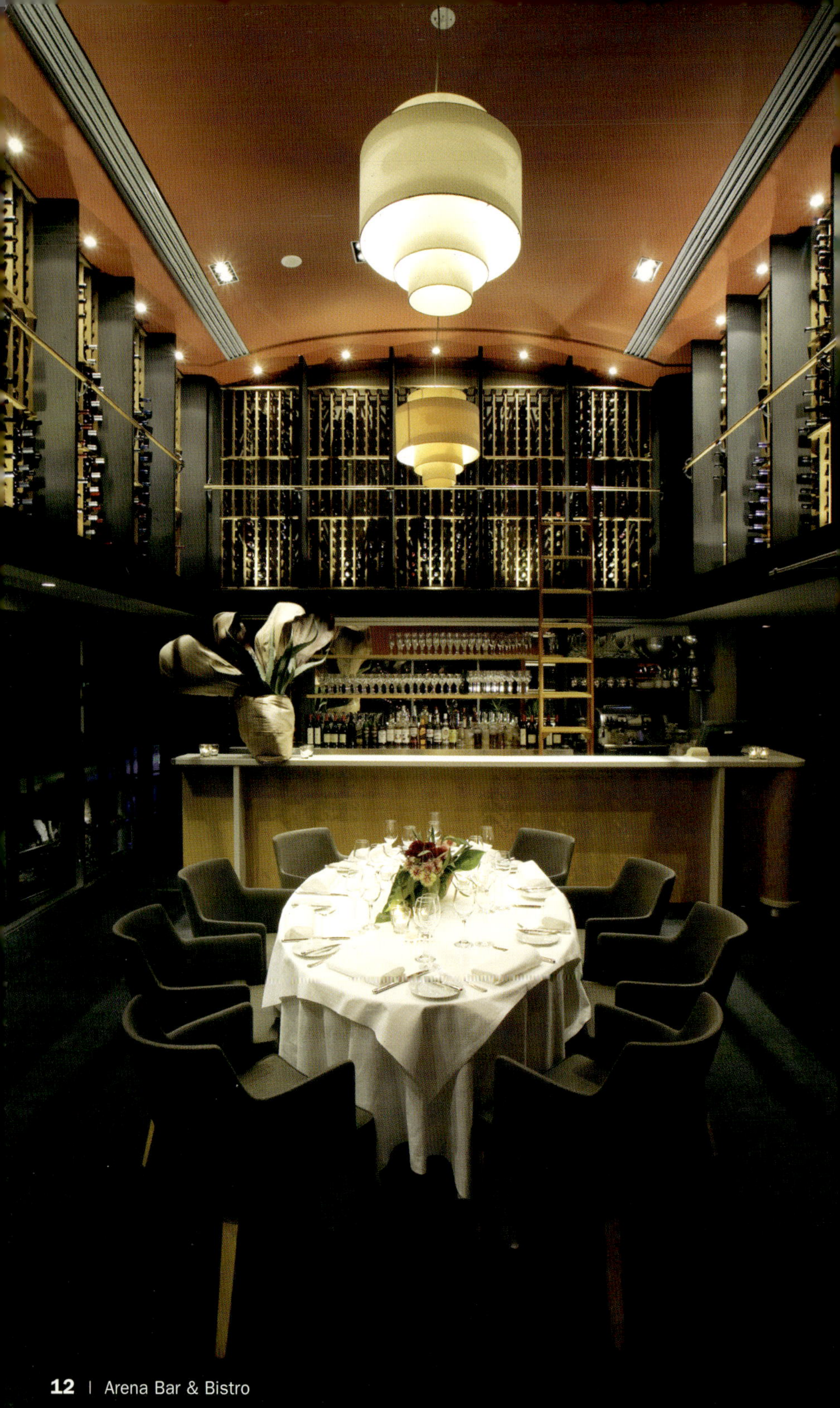

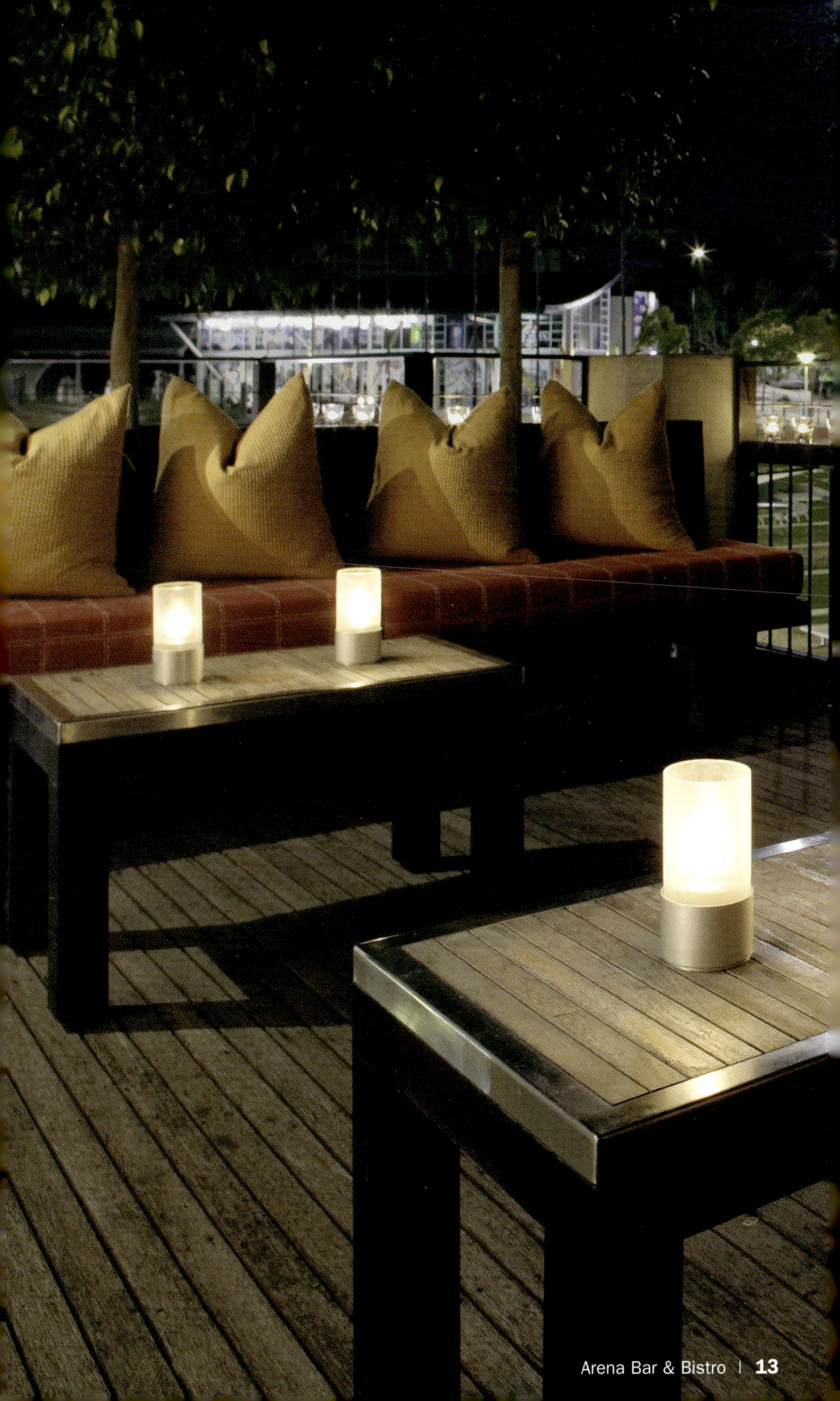

Crispy Tomato
and Parmesan Tortilla

Tomatentorte mit knusprigem Parmesan

Tarte à la tomate et au parmesan doré

Tarta de tomate y parmesano crujiente

Torta di pomodoro e parmigiano croccante

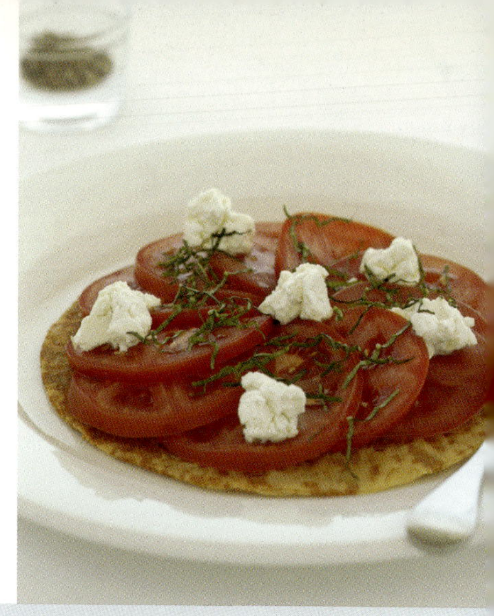

6 medium size tomatoes
1/5 oz sea salt
2 3/5 oz unbleached flour
2 3/5 oz wheat flour
2 3/5 oz butter
3 1/2 oz grated parmesan
50 ml olive oil
Basil

Preheat the oven to 350 °F. Slice the tomatoes and dry with paper towel, salt and set aside. Mix the two types of flour, butter and 2 1/10 oz parmesan and work until the mix acquires a sandy texture. Add 30 ml water and knead until the dough becomes sticky. Spread the dough on a tray and refrigerate for 15 minutes. Spike the dough with a fork, cover with aluminum foil and bake for 15 minutes. Afterwards, remove the aluminum foil and bake for another 10 minutes. Remove from the oven and dust with the remaining parmesan.
Cover the tort with the tomato slices, sprinkle with olive oil and garnish with some basil leaves.

6 mittelgroße Tomaten
5 g Meersalz
75 g ungebleichtes Mehl
75 g Weizenmehl
75 g Butter
100 g geriebener Parmesan
50 ml Olivenöl
Basilikum

Den Ofen auf 175 °C vorheizen. Die in Scheiben geschnittenen Tomaten mit Küchenkrepp trocknen, salzen und beiseite stellen. Die verschiedenen Mehle mit der Butter und 60 g Parmesan so lange vermengen, bis eine sandartige Textur entsteht. 30 ml Wasser hinzufügen und zu einem Teig verkneten. Den Teig auf einem Blech ausbreiten und für 15 Minuten im Kühlschrank kaltstellen. Mit einer Gabel den Teig anstechen, mit Alufolie abdecken und 15 Minuten im Ofen backen. Danach die Alufolie entfernen und weitere 10 Minuten backen. Aus dem Ofen nehmen und mit dem restlichen Parmesan bestreuen.
Die Torte mit den Tomatenscheiben bedecken, mit Olivenöl beträufeln und mit einigen Basilikumblättern garnieren.

6 tomates de taille moyenne
5 g de sel marin
75 g de farine non raffinée
75 g farine de blé
75 g de beurre
100 g de parmesan râpé
50 ml d'huile d'olive
Basilic

Préchauffer le four à 175 °C. Sécher les tomates coupées en rondelles dans du papier absorbant, saler et réserver. Mélanger les deux sortes de farines, le beurre et 60 g de parmesan et malaxer jusqu'à obtention d'une texture sablée.

Ajouter 30 ml d'eau et pétrir. Étaler la pâte sur une plaque et laisser refroidir au réfrigérateur pendant 15 minutes. Piquer la pâte avec une fourchette, la recouvrir avec du papier aluminium et glisser au four pendant 15 minutes. Ôter ensuite le papier aluminium et glisser au four pendant 10 minutes. Retirer du four et saupoudrer du parmesan restant.
Couvrir la tarte de rondelles de tomates, arroser d'huile d'olive et décorer de quelques feuilles de basilic.

6 tomates de tamaño mediano
5 g de sal marina
75 g de harina no blanqueada
75 g de harina de trigo
75 g de mantequilla
100 g de parmesano rallado
50 ml de aceite de oliva
Albahaca

Precalentar el horno a 175 °C. Secar los tomates cortados en rodajas con papel de cocina, salar y reservar. Mezclar los dos tipos de harina, la mantequilla y 60 g de parmesano, y amalgamar hasta que la mezcla adquiera una textura

arenosa. Añadir 30 ml de agua y amasar hasta que el preparado adquiera una consistencia pegajosa de masa. Extender la masa en una bandeja y dejar enfriar en la nevera durante 15 minutos. Pinchar la masa con un tenedor, cubrirla con una hoja de papel de aluminio y hornear durante 15 minutos. Luego quitar el papel de aluminio y hornear durante 10 minutos más. Sacar del horno y espolvorear con el parmesano que haya quedado.
Cubrir la tarta con las rodajas de tomate, rociar con aceite de oliva y decorar con unas hojas de albahaca.

6 pomodori medi
5 g di sale marino
75 g di farina non sbiancata
75 g di farina di grano
75 g di burro
100 g di parmigiano grattugiato
50 ml di olio d'oliva
Basilico

Preriscaldare il forno a 175 °C. Asciugare i pomodori tagliati a rondelle con della carta da cucina, salare e mettere da parte. Mescolare i due tipi di farina, il burro e 60 g di parmigiano e amalgamare fino ad ottenere un impasto dalla

consistenza sabbiosa. Aggiungere 30 ml d'acqua e continuare ad impastare fino ad ottenere una consistenza appiccicosa. Stendere l'impasto su un vassoio e lasciarlo raffreddare in frigo per 15 minuti. Forare l'impasto con una forchetta, coprirlo con un foglio di carta stagnola e cuocere in forno per 15 minuti. Dopodiché togliere la carta stagnola e cuocere per altri 10 minuti. Togliere dal forno e spolverizzare con il parmigiano rimasto.
Coprire la torta con le rondelle di pomodoro, spruzzarvi sopra un po' d'olio d'oliva e decorare con alcune foglie di basilico.

Aria

Design: Alexander Tzannes | Chef: Matthew Moran

1 Macquarie Street | Sydney, 2000 | East Circular Quay
Phone: +61 2 9252 2555
www.ariarestaurant.com
Opening hours: Mon–Fri lunch from noon to 2:30 pm, pre-theater from 5:30 pm to 7 pm, dinner from 5:30 pm to 11 pm, supper from 10 pm to 11:30 pm, Sat pre-theater from 5 pm to 7 pm, dinner from 5 pm to 11:30 pm, supper from 10 pm to 11:30 pm, Sun dinner from 6 pm to 10:30 pm, supper from 10 pm to 10:30 pm
Average price: Seven course dinner tasting menu A$ 135
Cuisine: Modern Australian
Special features: Exclusive desserts and pastries

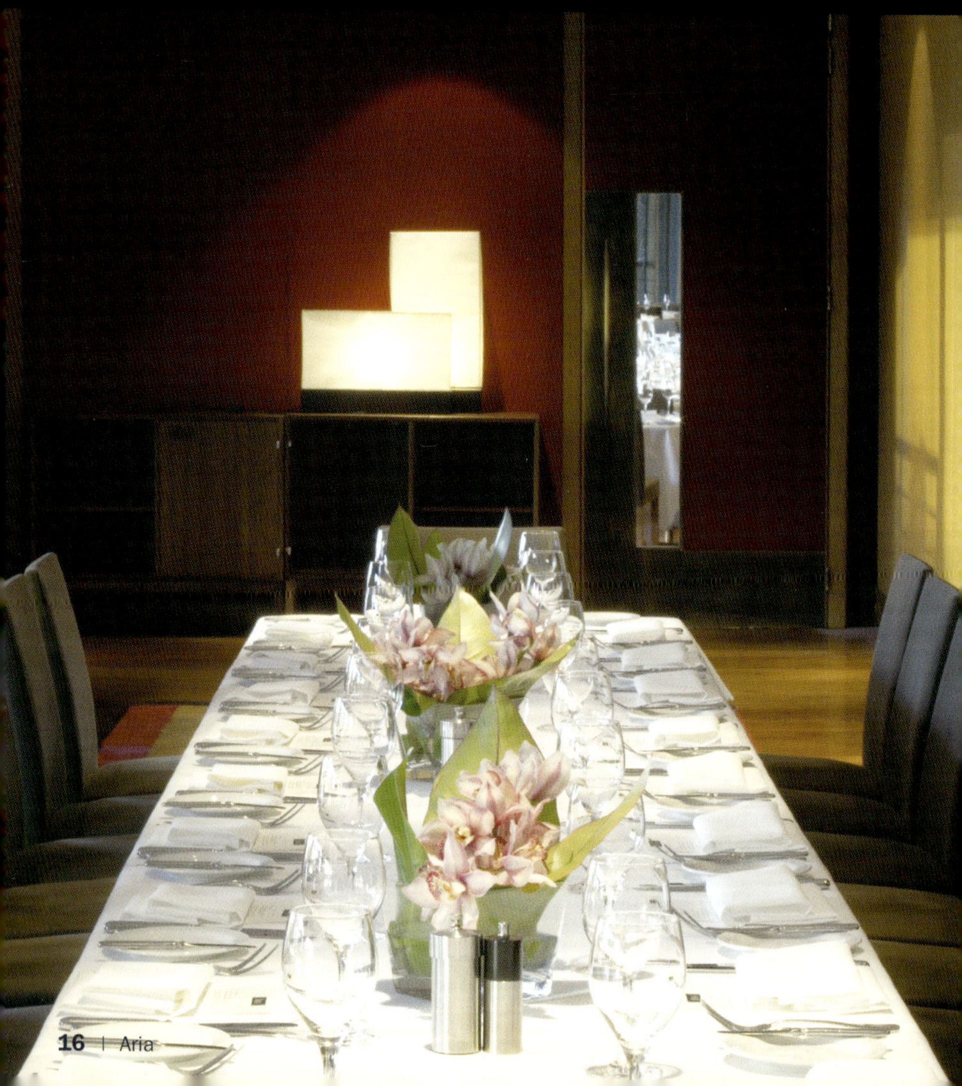

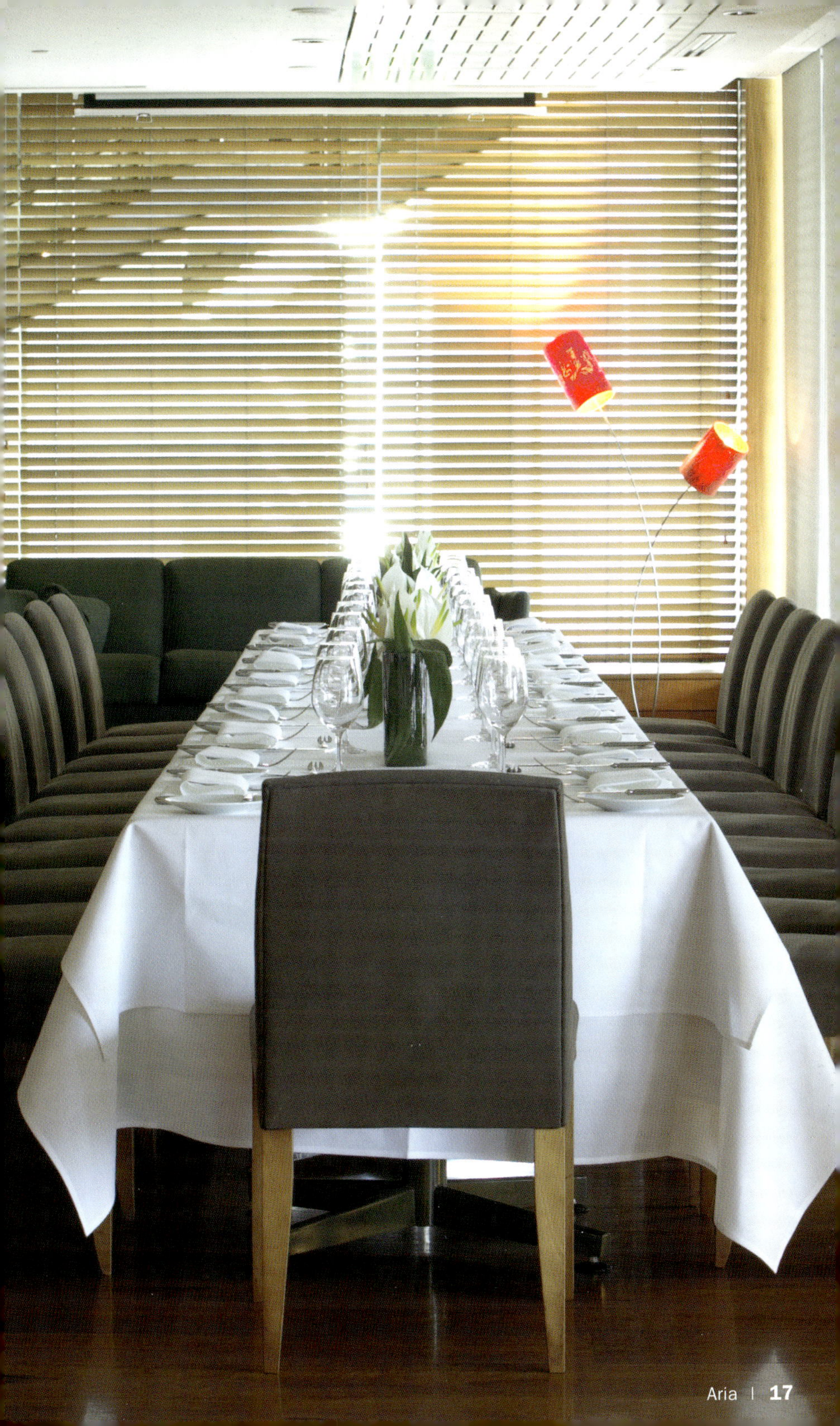

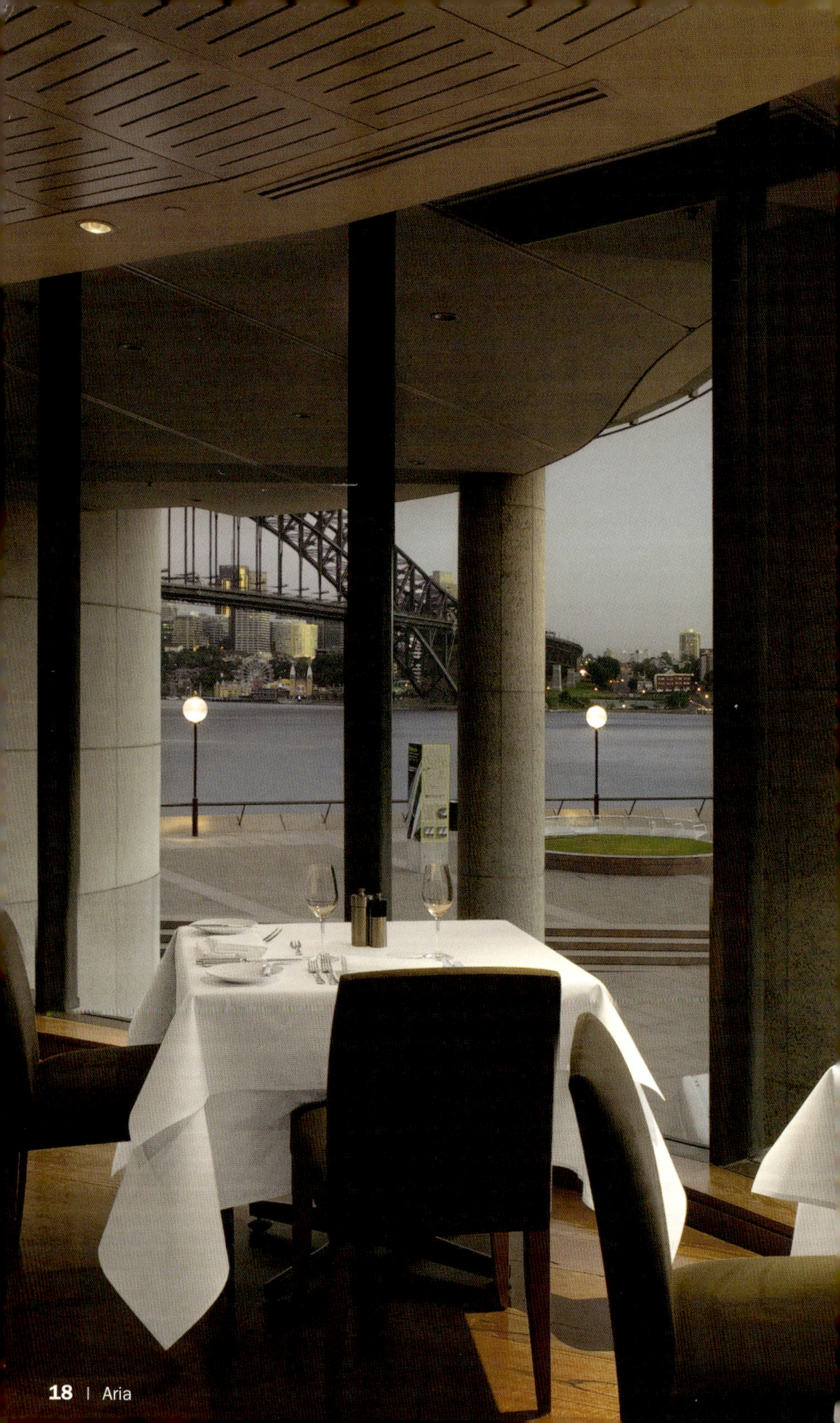

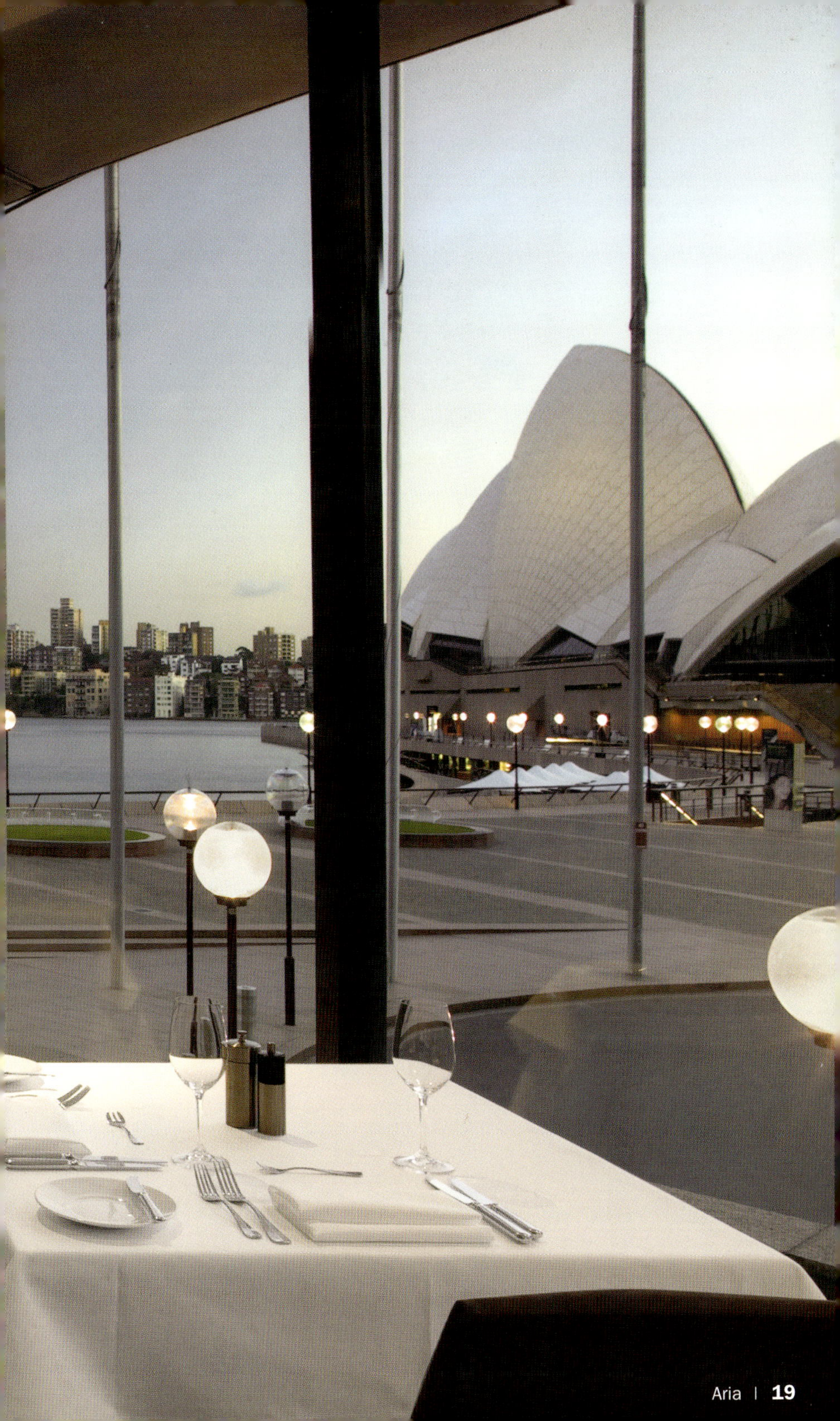

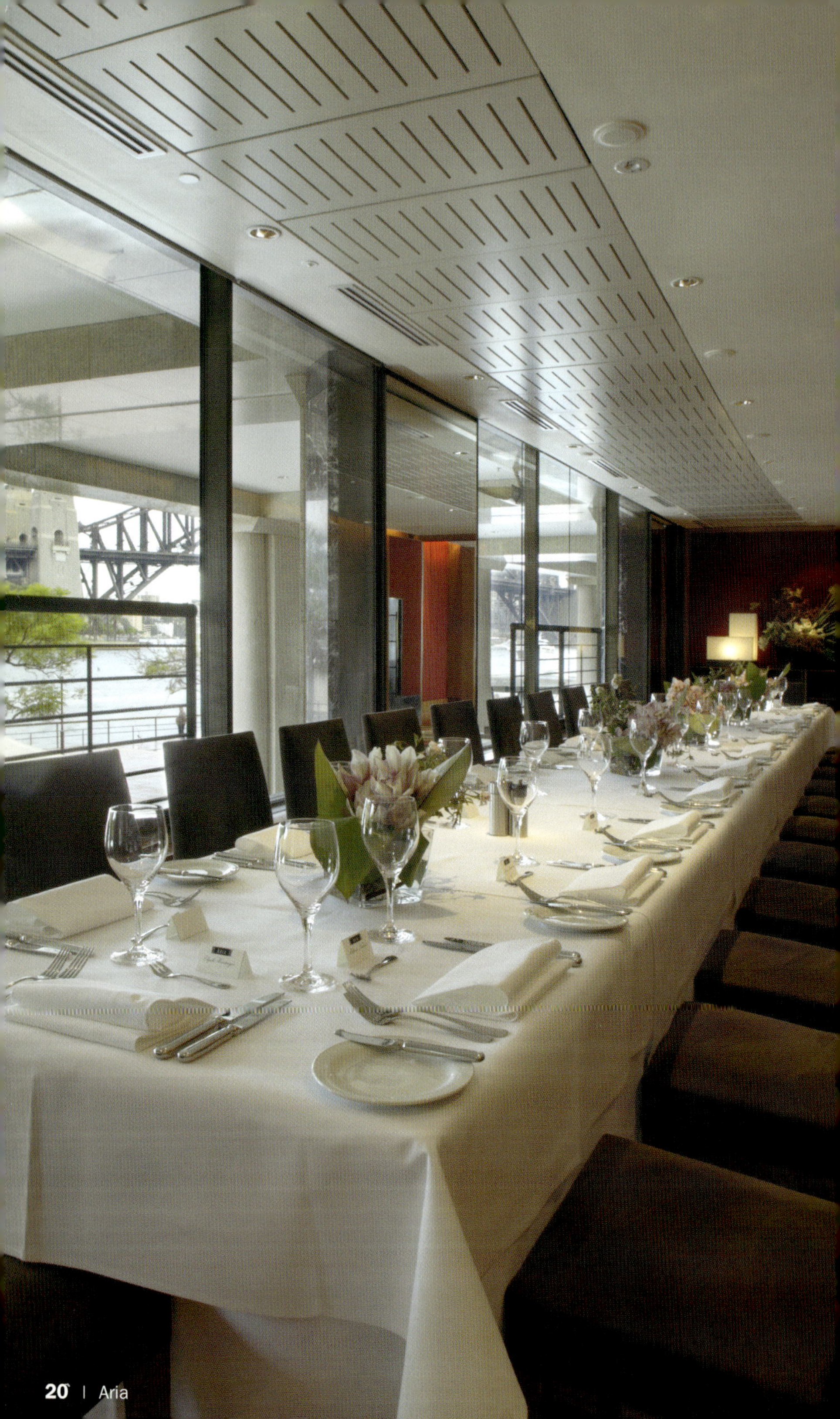

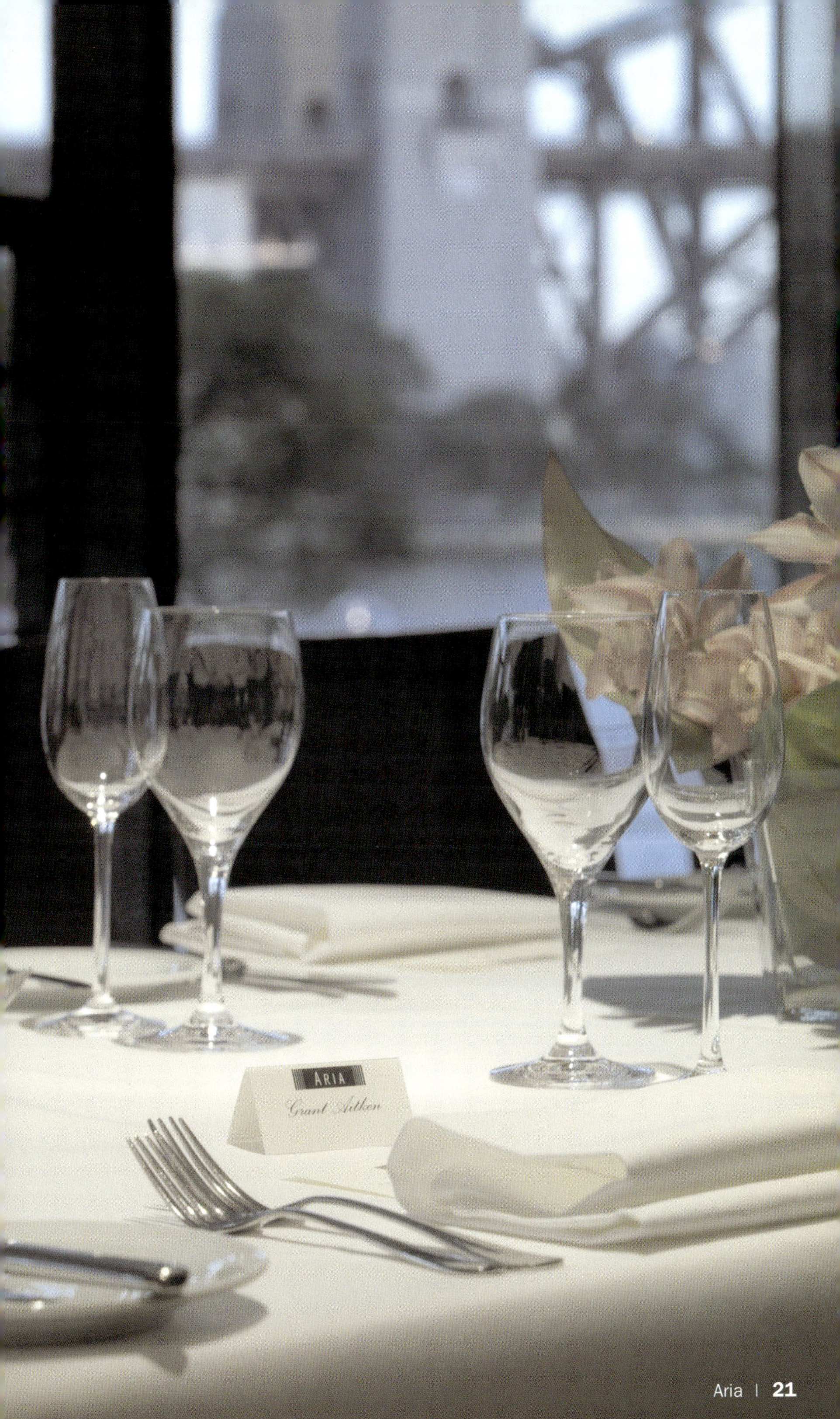
ARIA
Grant Aitken

Baked Lamb

with Spicy Eggplant

Gebratenes Lamm mit Auberginen in
Gewürzen

Agneau rôti avec aubergine aux épices

Cordero asado con berenjena en especias

Agnello al forno con melanzana alle spezie

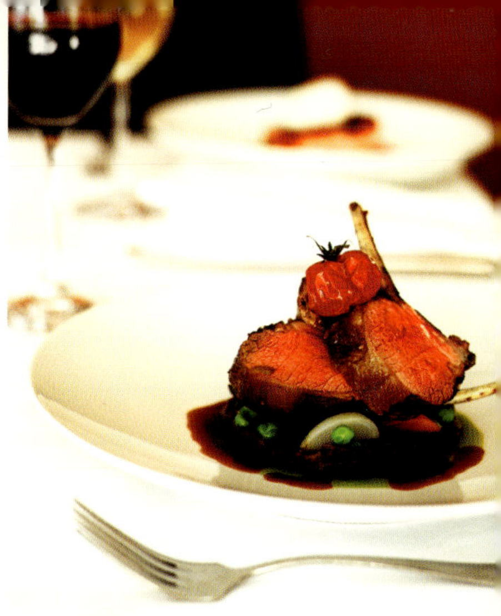

3 servings lamb ribs
1 eggplant
1 3/4 oz mango chutney
1 red chili
1/14 oz ground cumin
1/14 oz ground coriander
2 1/10 oz peas
2 1/10 oz sliced turnips
50 ml herb oil
1 tomato
Salt
Pepper
1 fried tomato

Wash, prick and bake the eggplant for 30 minutes. Cut in half; remove the pulp until the outer skin resembles a bowl-shape. Dice the fleshy pulp and mix with the mango chutney, diced chili, cumin and coriander. Season the mixture with salt and pepper and spoon into the eggplant skins. Set aside. Wash and boil the peas and turnips for 20 minutes; drain and sprinkle with the herb oil. Set aside. Season the lamb with salt and pepper and bake for 20 minutes. Place the eggplant skins on a dish, garnish with peas and turnips and top with the meat. Decorate with 1 fried tomato.

3 Portionen Lammkarree
1 Aubergine
50 g Mango-Chutney
1 rote Chilischote
2 g gemahlener Kreuzkümmel
2 g gemahlener Koriander
60 g Erbsen
60 g Steckrüben in Scheiben
50 ml Kräuteröl
1 Tomate
Salz
Pfeffer
1 gebratene Tomate

Die Aubergine waschen, anstechen und im Ofen 30 Minuten backen. Halbieren und das Fruchtfleisch herausnehmen, bis die Schale einen Napf ergibt. Das Fruchtfleisch kleinhacken und mit dem Mango-Chutney, der gehackten Chilischote, Kümmel und Koriander mischen. Die Mischung salzen und pfeffern und in die beiden Auberginenhälften füllen. Beiseite stellen. Erbsen und Steckrüben waschen und 20 Minuten kochen, abtropfen lassen und mit Kräuteröl würzen. Beiseite stellen. Lamm salzen und pfeffern und 20 Minuten im Ofen backen.
Die Auberginenschalen auf einem Teller anordnen, mit Erbsen und Steckrüben versehen und mit dem Fleisch krönen. Mit 1 gebackenen Tomate verzieren.

3 portions de carré d'agneau
1 aubergine
50 g de chutney de mangue
1 chili rouge
2 g de cumin en poudre
2 g de coriandre en poudre
60 g de petits pois
60 g de navet coupé en rondelles
50 ml d'huile d'herbes
1 tomate
Sel
Poivre
1 tomate braisée

Laver, piquer l'aubergine puis la glisser au four pendant 30 minutes. La couper en deux et ôter la pulpe des deux moitiés pour leur donner une forme de ramequin. Réserver les deux moitiés. Hacher la pulpe et la mélanger avec le chutney, le chili haché, le cumin et la coriandre. Saler, poivrer et remplir les ramequins avec le mélange. Réserver. Laver et faire bouillir les petits pois et les navets pendant 20 minutes ; égoutter et assaisonner avec l'huile d'herbes. Réserver. Saler, poivrer l'agneau et glisser au four pendant 20 minutes.
Disposer les coques d'aubergine sur une assiette, couvrir avec les petits pois et les navets et couronner avec la viande. Décorer avec 1 tomate braisée.

3 costillas de cordero
1 berenjena
50 g de chutney de mango
1 chile rojo
2 g de comino molido
2 g cilantro molido
60 g de guisantes
60 g de nabos en rodajas
50 ml de aceite de hierbas
1 tomate
Sal
Pimienta
1 tomate asado

Lavar, pinchar la berenjena y hornearla durante 30 minutos. Cortarla por la mitad y sacar la pulpa hasta obtener una cáscara en forma de cuenco. Picar la pulpa y mezclarla con el chutney, el chile picado, el comino y el cilantro. Salpimentar y rellenar las dos mitades de berenjena con la mezcla. Reservar. Lavar y hervir los guisantes y los nabos durante 20 minutos; escurrir y condimentarlos con el aceite de hierbas. Reservar. Salpimentar el cordero y hornearlo durante 20 minutos.
Disponer las cáscaras de berenjena en la base del plato, cubrir con los guisantes y los nabos y coronar con la carne. Decorar con 1 tomate asado.

3 porzioni di costole d'agnello
1 melanzana
50 g di chutney di mango
1 peperoncino piccante rosso
2 g di cumino tritato
2 g di coriandolo tritato
60 g di piselli
60 g di rape a rondelle
50 ml di olio alle erbe
1 pomodoro
Sale
Pepe
1 pomodoro cotto

Lavare, forare la melanzana e cuocerla in forno per 30 minuti. Tagliarla a metà, estrarre la polpa fino a che la buccia rimasta non sia simile a una scodella. Mettere da parte le due parti di melanzana svuotate della polpa. Tritare la polpa e mescolarla con il chutney, il peperoncino tritato, il cumino e il coriandolo. Salare e pepare e riempire le due ciotole di melanzana con il composto ottenuto. Mettere da parte. Lavare e cuocere i piselli e le rape per 20 minuti; scolare e condirli con l'olio alle erbe. Riservare. Condire l'agnello con sale e pepe e cuocerlo in forno per 20 minuti.
Sistemare le due ciotole di melanzana al centro del piatto, coprire con i piselli e le rape e in ultimo sistemarvi sopra la carne. Decorare con 1 pomodoro cotto.

Bayswater Brasserie

Design: Rachel Lacy | Chef: Robert Hodgson

32 Bayswater Road | Sydney, 2011 | Kings Cross
Phone: +61 2 9357 2177
www.bayswaterbrasserie.com.au
Opening hours: Mon–Sat from 5 pm until late, Fri from noon, Sun from 5 pm to 10 pm
Average price: A$ 60–90
Cuisine: Brasserie, Modern Australian
Special features: The Rear Conservatory, Private Dining Room, and Courtyard are all
available for parties with a choice of fixed menus, including canape menus and
tailored cocktails

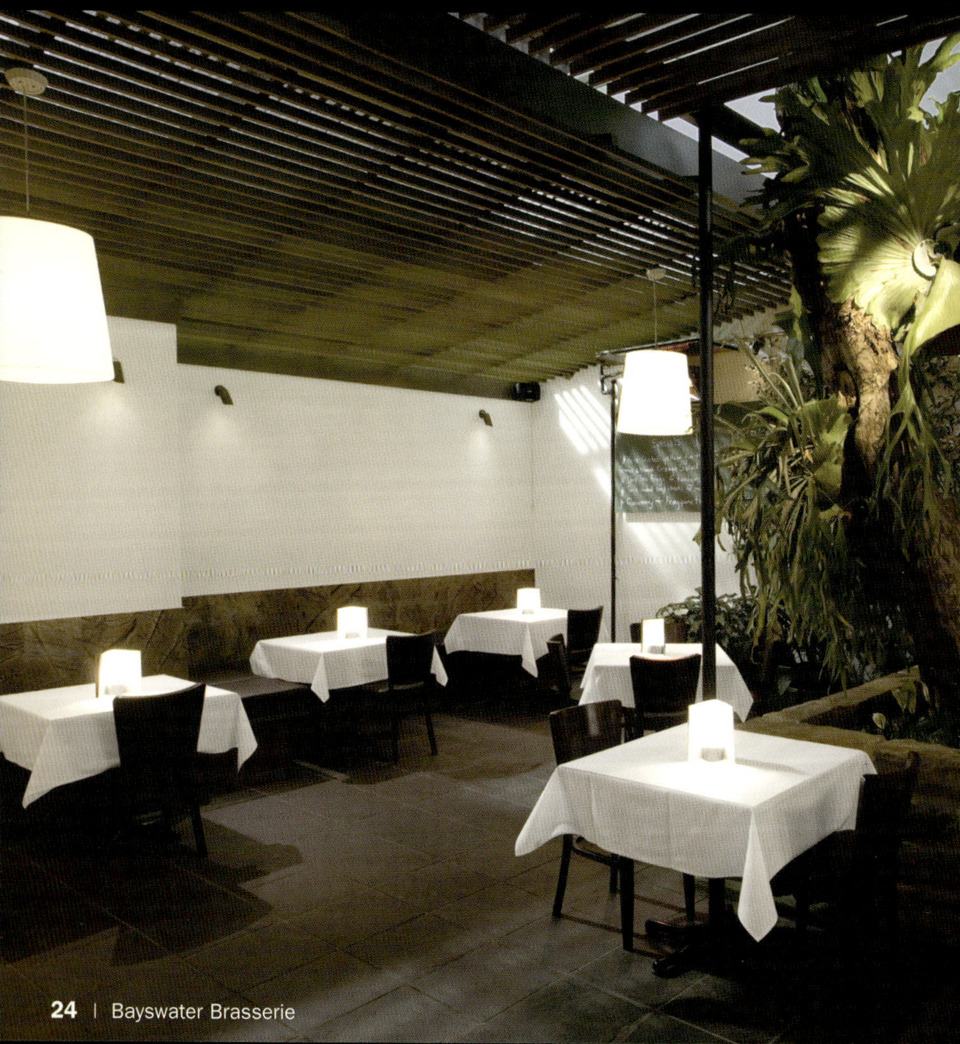

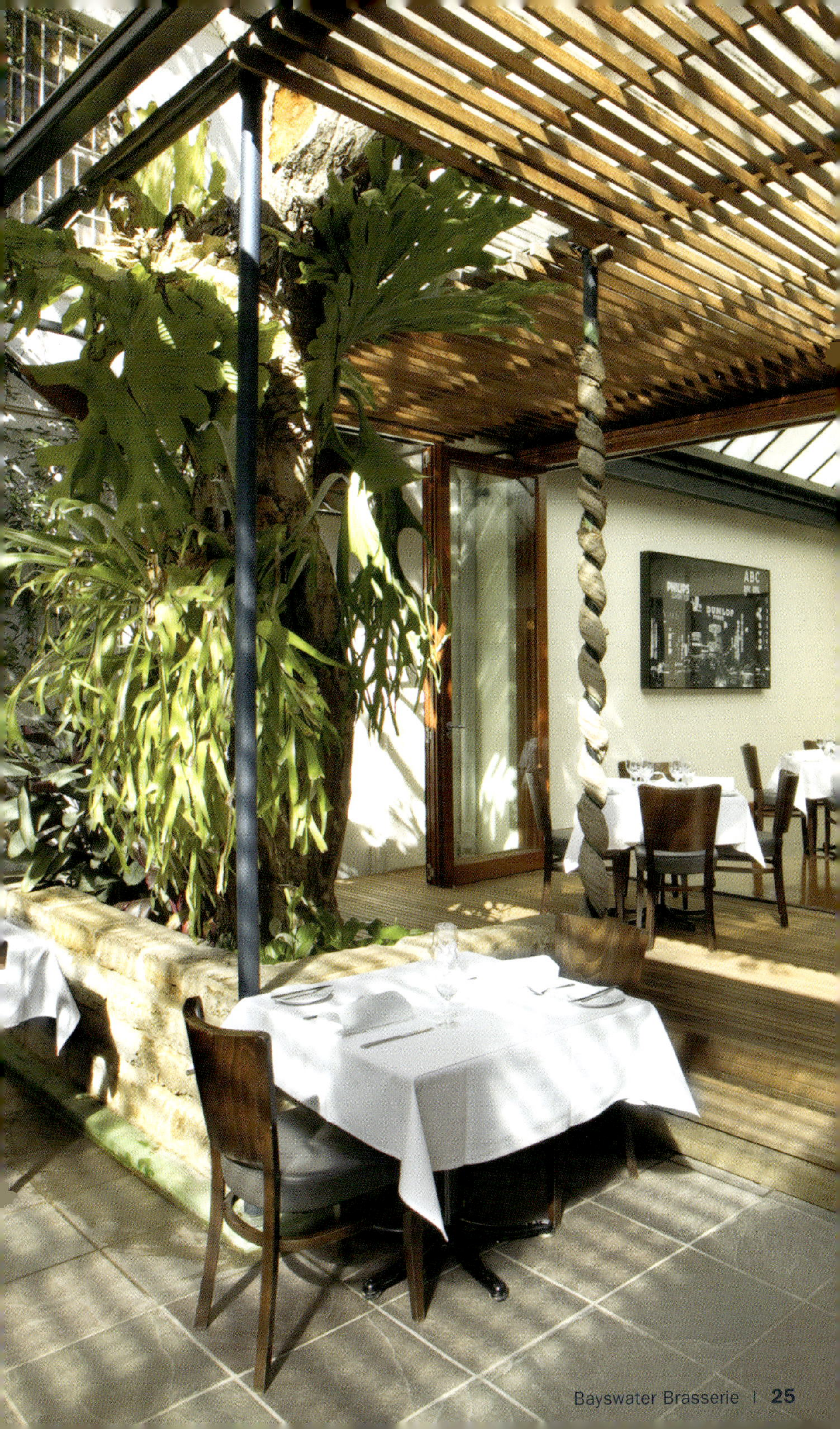

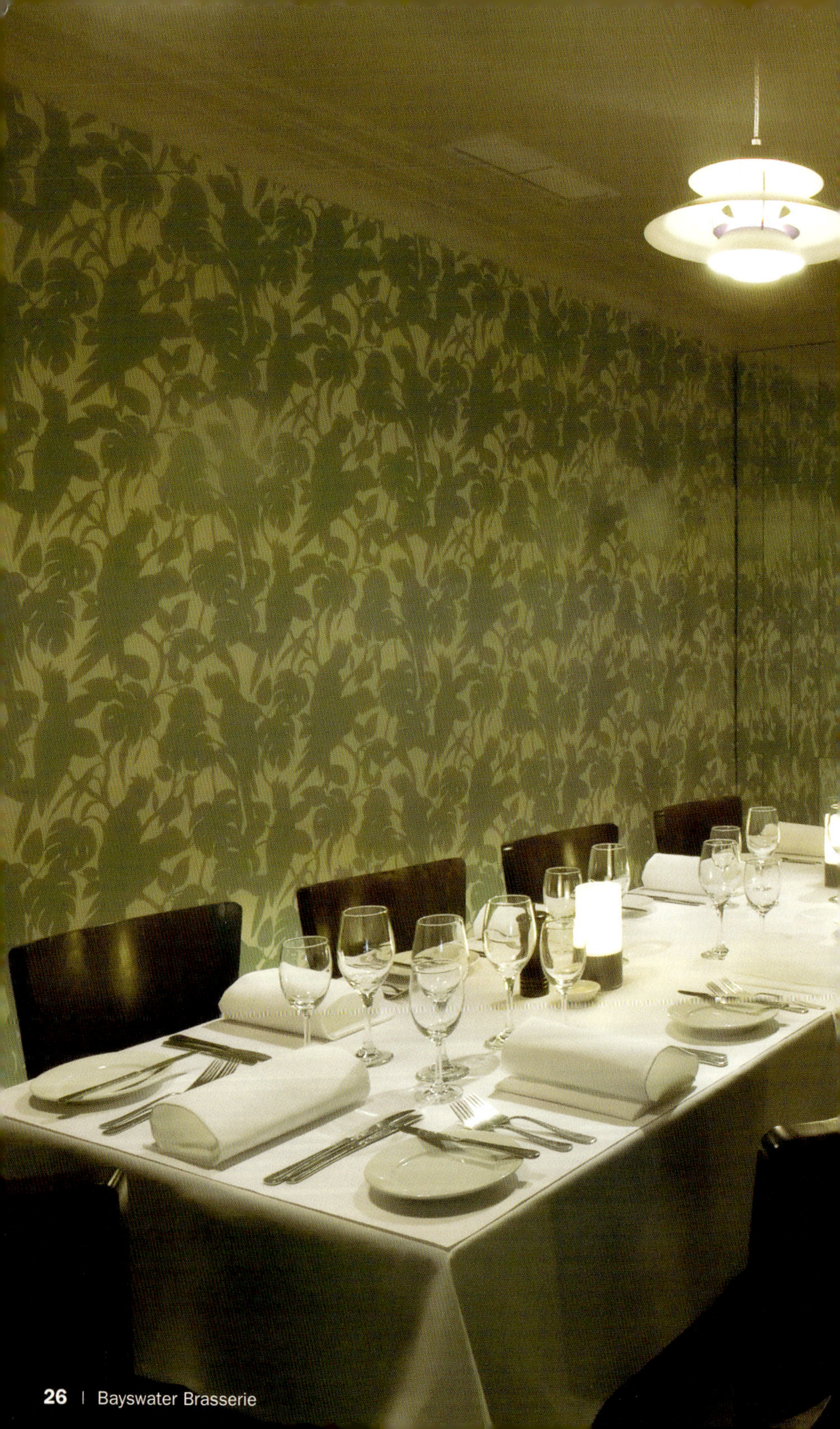

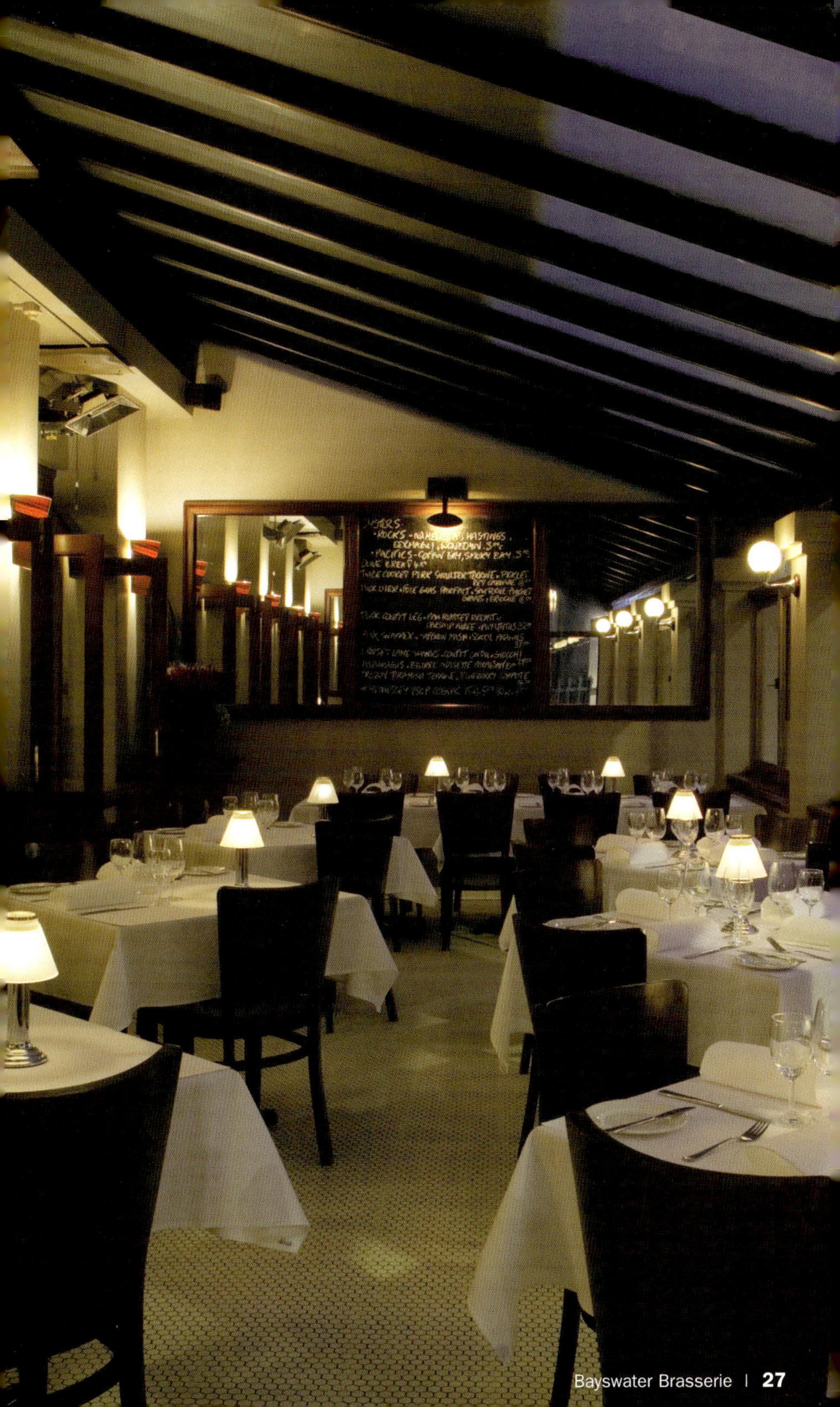

cherriJam

Design: Kim Akimovic | Chef: Karl Friederich

16–18 Cross Street | Sydney, 2028 | Double Bay
Phone: +61 2 9363 0555
www.cherrijam.com.au
Opening hours: Wed–Sun from 6 pm to 3 am
Average price: Starters A$ 16–24, main courses A$ 26–35, desserts A$ 12–20
Cuisine: Modern Oriental
Special features: Cocktails like Harem Nights or Flying Carpets in this Arabian Nights-inspired location

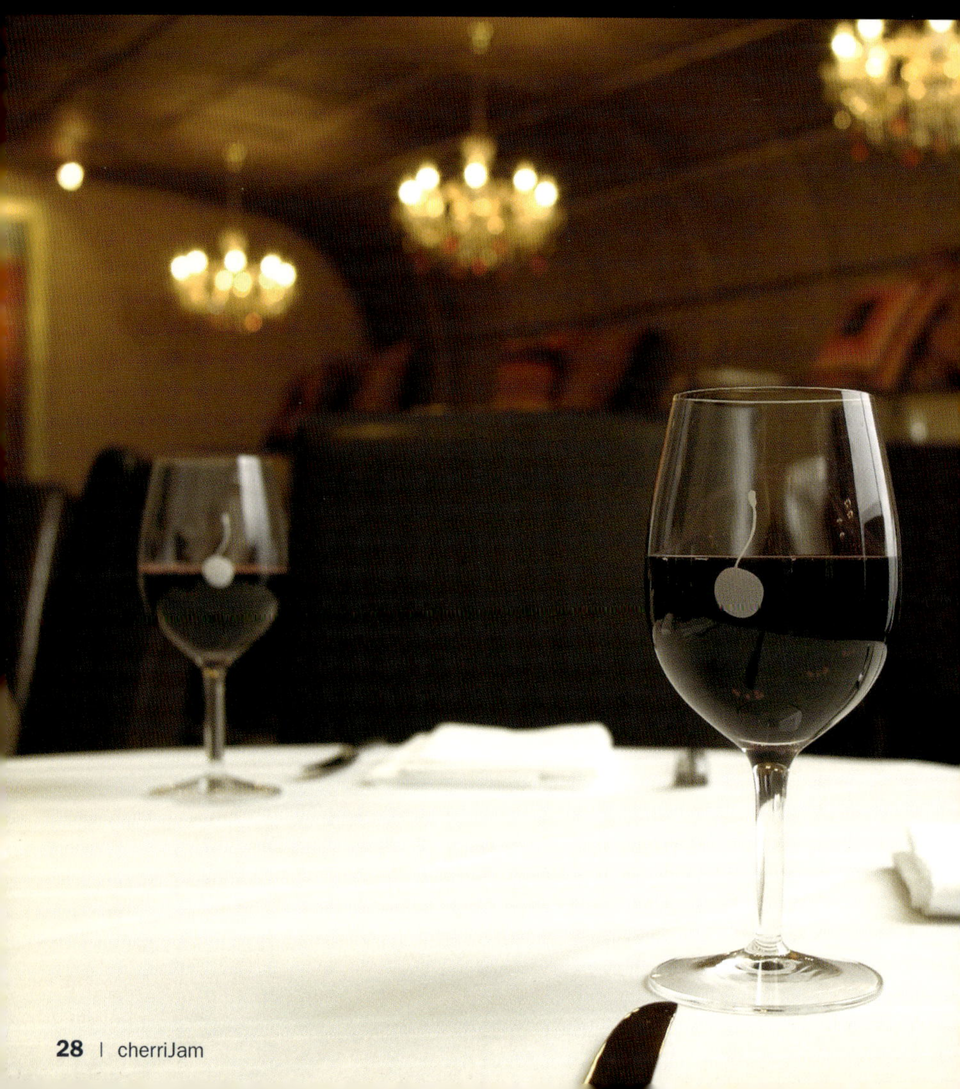

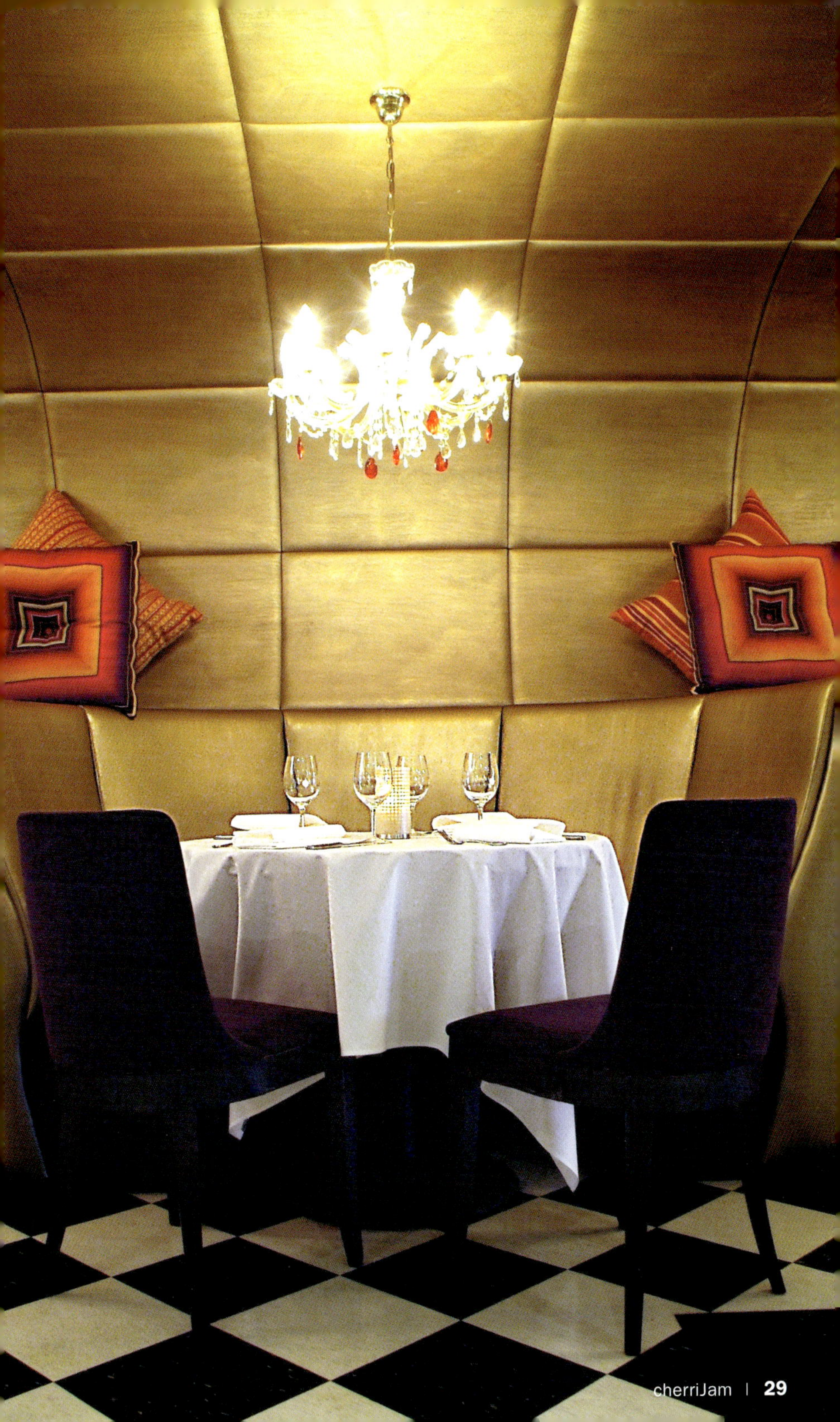

Cod with Peas

and Sweet Spicy Sauce

Kabeljau mit Erbsen und süßer
Gewürzsoße

Morue aux petits pois et sauce douce
aux épices

Bacalao con guisantes y salsa dulce
de especias

Baccalà con piselli e salsa dolce alle
spezie

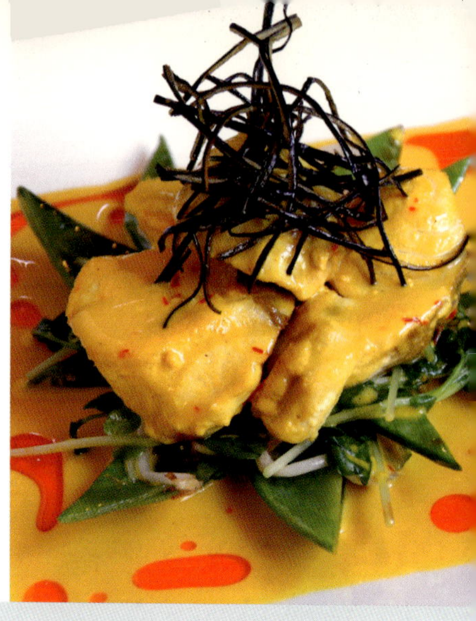

6 oz cod fillets
2 4/5 oz shallots
1 3/4 oz butter
20 ml coconut milk
40 ml water
150 ml white wine
400 ml consommé
1/5 oz curry, 1 pinch of saffron, 1/5 oz cumin
500 ml pouring cream
1 ginger root
1/4 red pepper
1/2 zucchini
2 1/10 oz peas
1 3/4 oz soy shoots
7/10 oz shiitake mushrooms
70 ml olive oil
Salt and pepper

For the sauce, crush the shallots with the butter in a bowl. Add the coconut milk and water and boil in a casserole dish. Add the wine and reduce.
Afterwards, add the consommé, curry, saffron and cumin. Allow to reduce again and then add the pouring cream. Simmer over a low heat for 3 minutes and season to taste. Reheat the mixture and fold in the grated ginger, finely chopped red pepper and zucchini. Braise the pieces of cod fillet in the sauce for 5 minutes and set aside. Sauté the peas and soy shoots and, in another frying pan, sear the finely chopped shiitake mushrooms.
Arrange a layer of peas and soy shoots on a dish, placing the cod fillets on top and season with the sweet sauce. Top with mushrooms.

170 g Kabeljaufilets
80 g Schalotten
50 g Butter
20 ml Kokosmilch
40 ml Wasser
150 ml Weißwein
400 ml Consommé
5 g Curry, 1 Prise Safran, 5 g Kreuzkümmel
500 ml flüssige Sahne
1 Ingwerwurzel
1/4 rote Paprika
1/2 Zucchini
60 g Erbsen
50 g Sojasprossen
20 g Shiitake-Pilze
70 ml Olivenöl
Salz und Pfeffer

Für die Soße die zerstampften Schalotten mit der Butter vermischen. Kokosmilch und Wasser zufügen und in einer Kasserolle kochen. Wein zugeben und reduzieren lassen.
Später die Consommé, Curry, Safran und Kümmel zugeben. Nochmals reduzieren lassen und dann die flüssige Sahne zugießen. 3 Minuten schmoren lassen und nach Geschmack würzen. Die Masse nochmals erhitzen und nun den geriebenen Ingwer, die Paprika und Zucchini, in kleine Stücke geschnitten, damit vermischen. In der Soße die in Stücke geschnittenen Kabeljaufilets 5 Minuten garen und beiseite stellen. Erbsen und Sojasprossen dünsten und in einer anderen Pfanne die feingeschnittenen Shiitake-Pilze anbraten.
Auf dem Teller aus den Erbsen und Sojasprossen eine Basis anrichten; darauf die Kabeljaufilets legen und mit der süßen Soße würzen. Mit den Pilzen krönen.

170 g de filet de cabillaud
80 g d'échalote
50 g de beurre
20 ml de lait de coco
40 ml d'eau
150 ml de vin blanc
400 ml de consommé
5 g de curry, 1 pincée de safran, 5 g de cumin
500 ml de crème liquide
1 racine de gingembre
1/4 de poivron rouge
1/2 courgette
60 g petits pois
50 g de pousses de soja
20 g de champignons shiitake
70 ml d'huile d'olive
Sel et poivre

Pour la sauce, mélanger dans une terrine l'échalote hachée avec le beurre. Ajouter le lait de coco et l'eau et porter à ébullition dans une casserole. Ajouter le vin et laisser réduire.
Rajouter ensuite le consommé, le curry, le safran et le cumin. Laisser à nouveau réduire et ajouter la crème liquide ; faire bouillir à feu doux pendant 3 minutes et assaisonner à volonté. Refaire chauffer la préparation et la mélanger avec le gingembre râpé, le poivron et la courgette coupés en petits morceaux. Cuire les filets de morue coupés dans la sauce pendant 5 minutes et réserver. Faire sauter les petits pois et les pousses de soja puis, dans une autre poêle, faire frire les champignons shiitake finement coupés.
Dresser une assiette en préparant une base avec les petits pois et les pousses de soja ; disposer dessus les filets de morue et assaisonner avec la sauce douce. Couronner avec les champignons.

170 g de filetes de bacalao
80 g de chalota
50 g de mantequilla
20 ml leche de coco
40 ml de agua
150 ml de vino blanco
400 ml de consomé
5 g de curry, 1 pizca de azafrán, 5 g de comino
500 ml de nata líquida
1 jengibre
1/4 de pimiento rojo
1/2 calabacín
60 g de guisantes
50 g de brotes de soja
20 g de setas shiitake
70 ml de aceite de oliva
Sal y pimienta

Para la salsa, mezclar en un cuenco la chalota machacada con la mantequilla. Añadir la leche de coco y el agua y hervir en una cazuela. Añadir el vino y dejar reducir.
Luego agregar el consomé, el curry, el azafrán y el comino. Dejar reducir nuevamente y añadir la nata líquida. Hervir a fuego lento durante 3 minutos y sazonar al gusto. Calentar de nuevo el preparado y mezclarlo con el jengibre rallado y el pimiento y el calabacín cortados en pequeños trozos. Cocer los filetes de bacalao troceados en la salsa durante 5 minutos y reservar. Saltear los guisantes y los brotes de soja y, en otra sartén, freír las setas shiitake cortadas finamente.
Presentar en el plato preparando una base con los guisantes y los brotes de soja; disponer encima los filetes de bacalao y aliñar con la salsa dulce. Coronar con las setas.

170 g di filetti di baccalà
80 g di scalogno
50 g di burro
20 ml di latte di cocco
40 ml d'acqua
150 ml di vino bianco
400 ml di consommé
5 g di curry, 1 pizzico di zafferano, 5 g di cumino
500 ml di panna liquida
1 zenzero
1/4 di peperone rosso
1/2 zucchina
60 g di piselli
50 g di germogli di soia
20 g di funghi shiitake
70 ml di olio d'oliva
Sale e pepe

Per la salsa, in un recipiente mescolare lo scalogno schiacciato con il burro. Aggiungere il latte di cocco, l'acqua e far cuocere in una pentola. Aggiungere il vino e lasciare ridurre.
Quindi unire il consommè, il curry, lo zafferano e il cumino. Far ridurre nuovamente e aggiungere la panna liquida; cuocere a fuoco lento per 3 minuti e condire secondo i gusti. Riscaldare di nuovo il preparato e mescolarlo con lo zenzero grattugiato, il peperone e la zucchina tagliati a pezzetti. Cuocere i filetti di baccalà tagliati a pezzi nella salsa per 5 minuti e mettere da parte. Saltare i piselli e i germogli di soia e, in un'altra padella, friggere i funghi shiitake tagliati finemente.
Presentare il piatto preparando una base con i piselli e i germogli di soia; sopra adagiarvi i filetti di baccalà e condire con la salsa dolce. Coronare il tutto con i funghi.

China Doll

Design: Ian Halliday | Chef: Frank Shek

6 Cowper Wharf Road, Shop 4 | Sydney, 2011 | Woolloomooloo
Phone: +61 2 9380 6744
www.chinadoll.com.au
Opening hours: Mon–Sat lunch from noon to 3 pm, dinner from 6 pm to 10:30 pm,
Sun from noon to 8:45 pm
Average price: Starters A$ 15–25, main courses A$ 30–35, desserts A$ 12
Cuisine: Modern Asian
Special features: Outside dining area, upstairs private area, modern cocktails
by Linden Pride

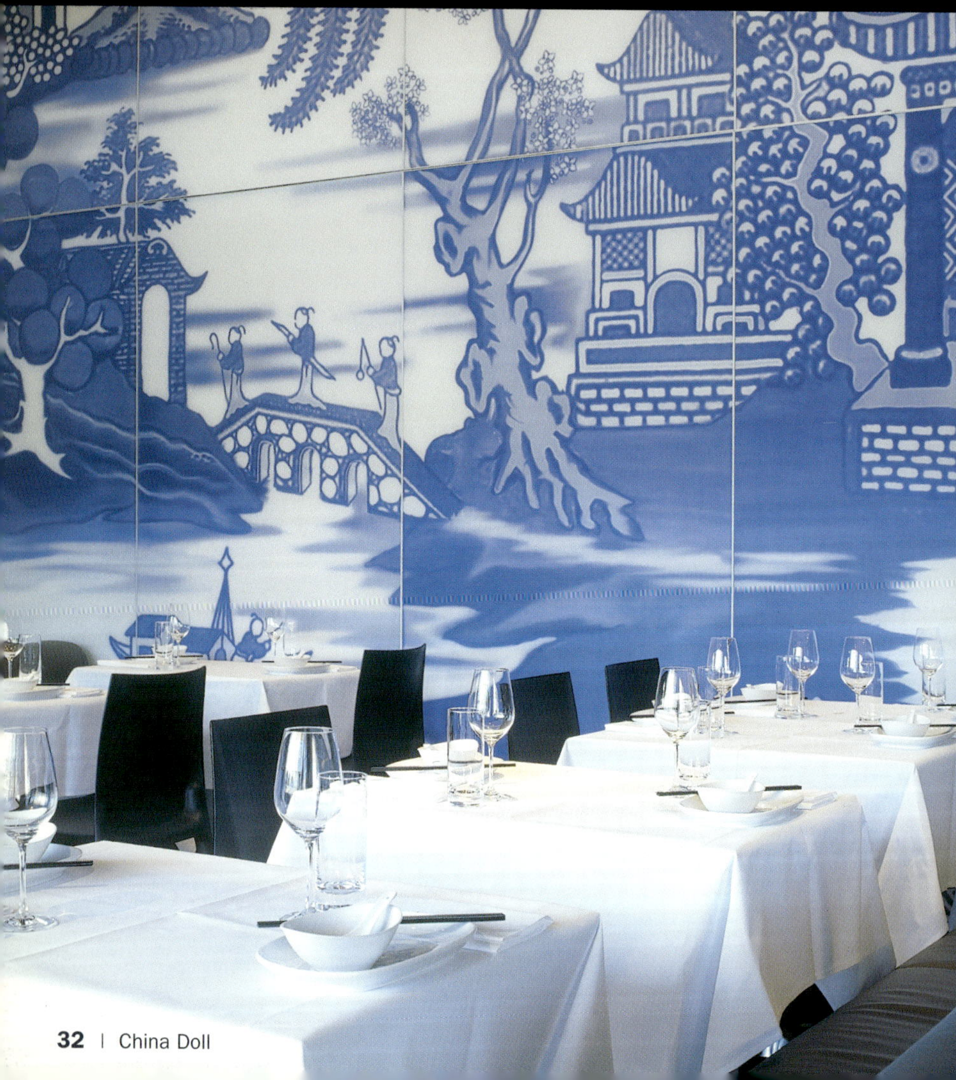

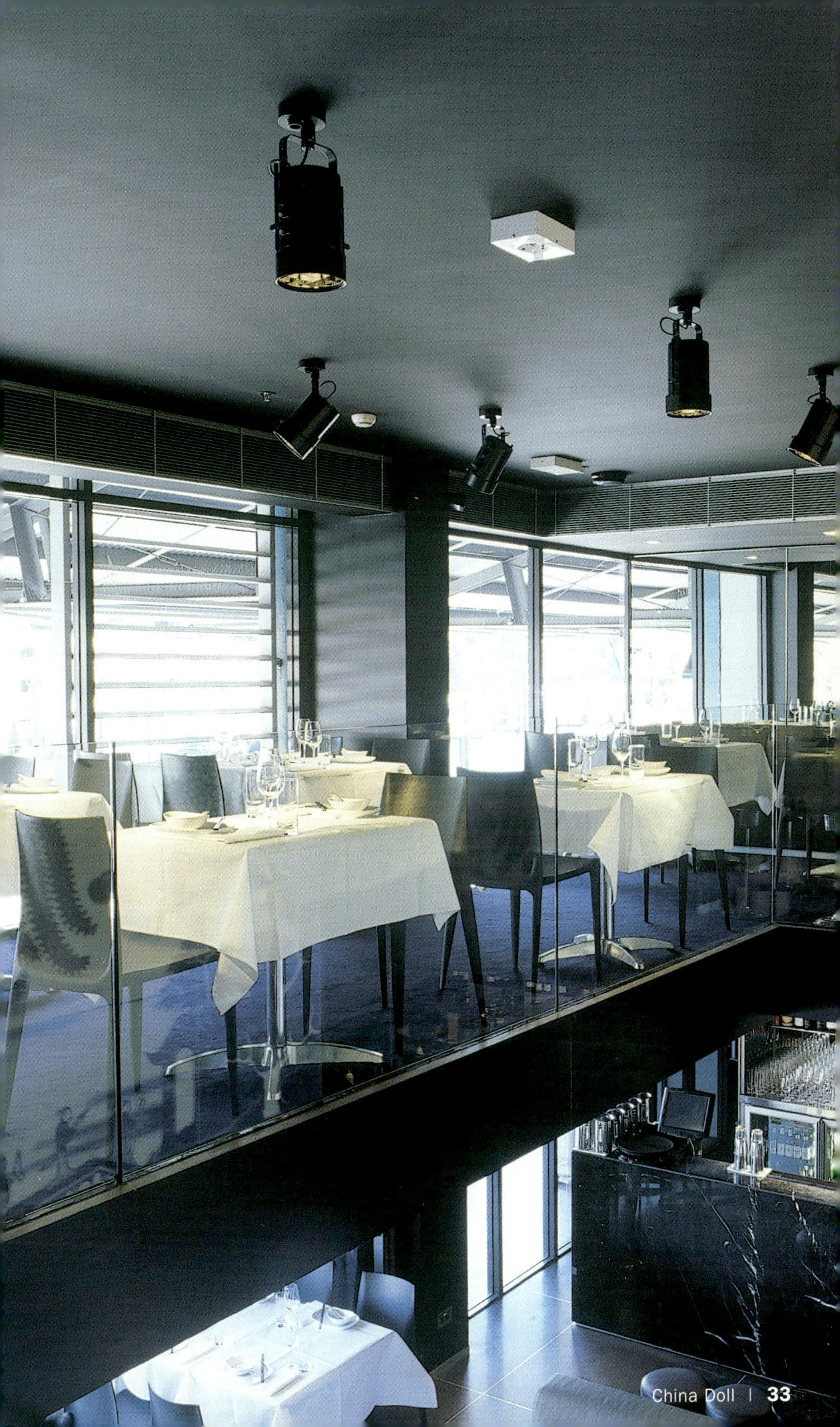

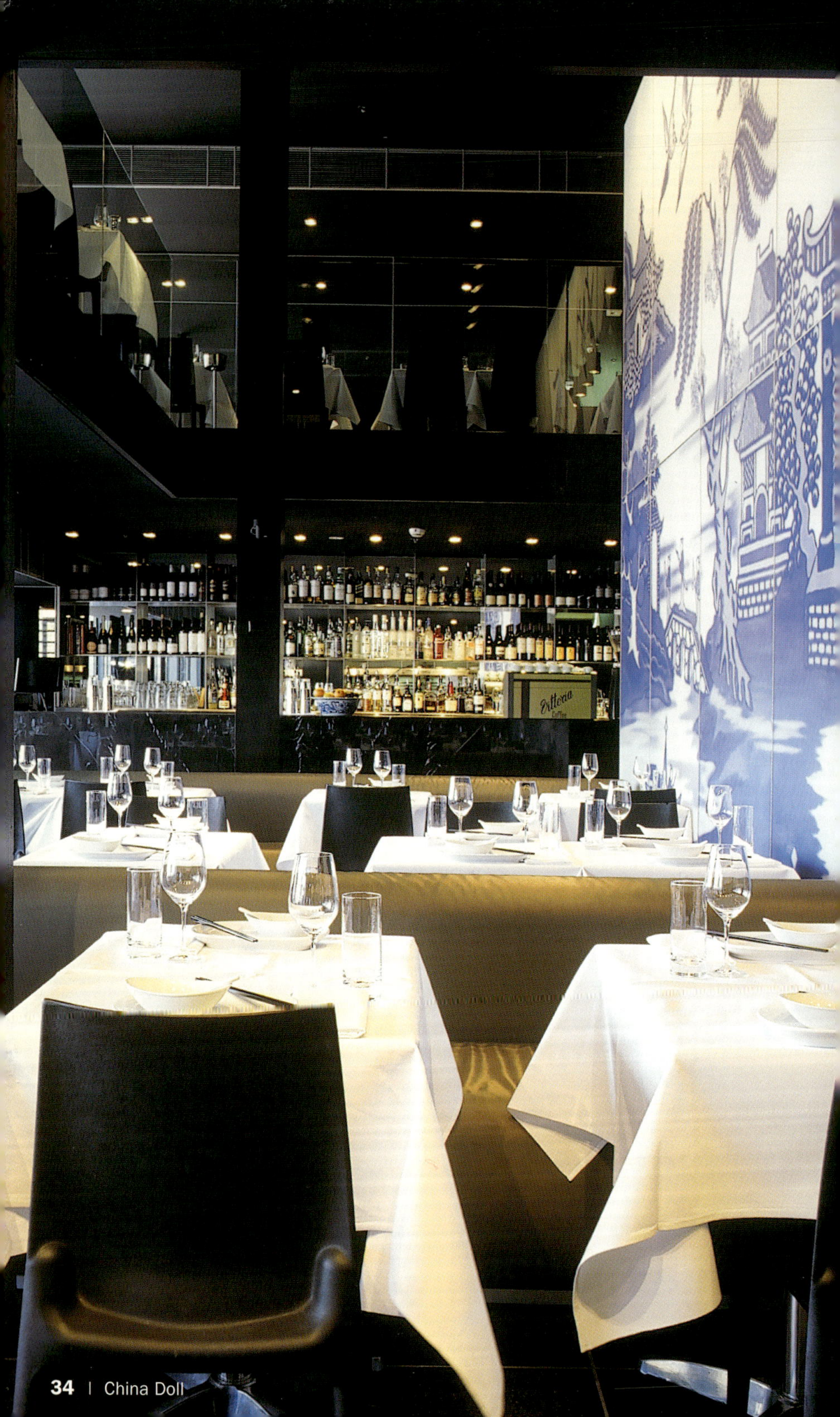

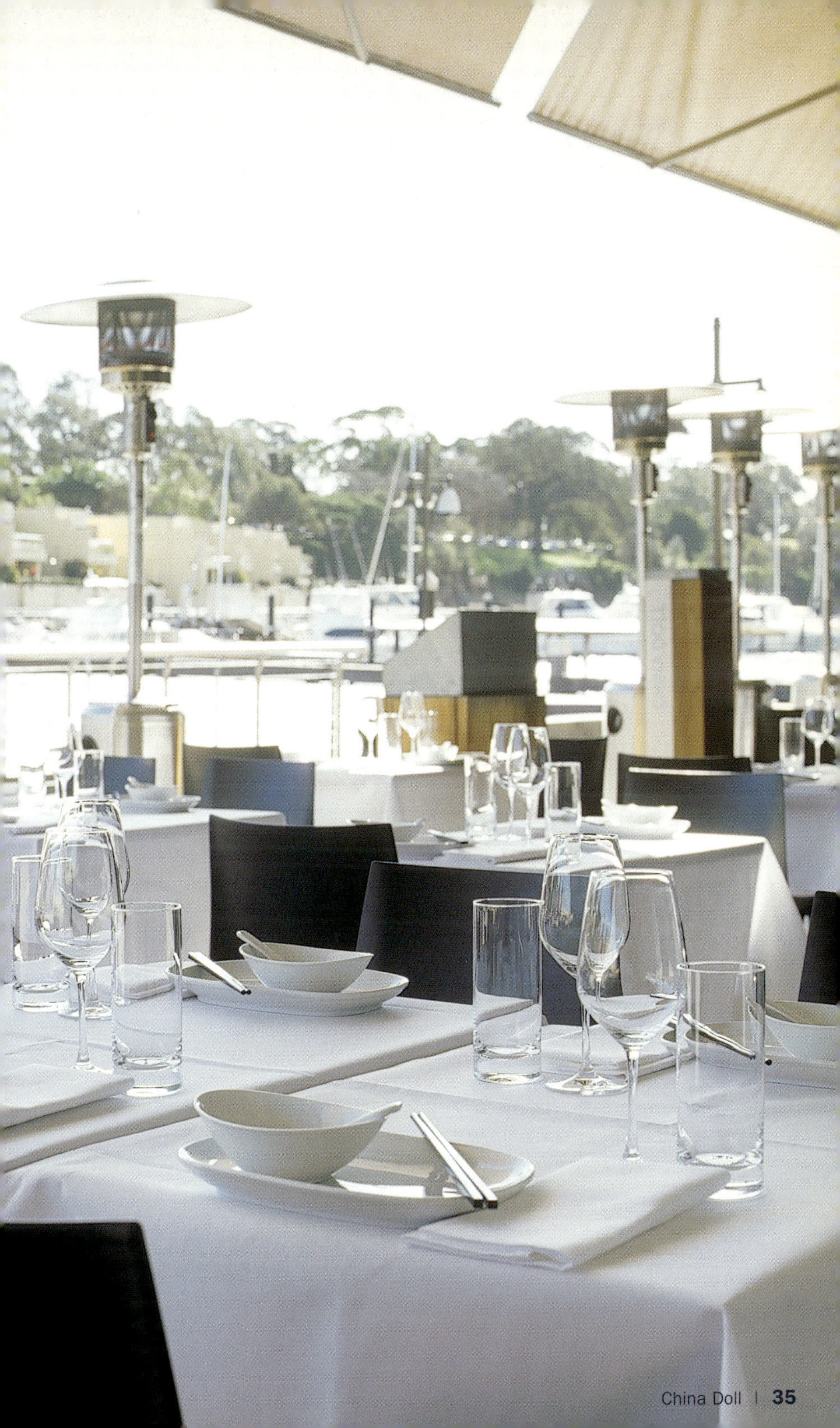

Monkfish
with Curry Paste

Seeteufel mit Currypaste

Lotte à la pâte au curry

Rape con pasta de curry

Rana pescatrice con pasta di curry

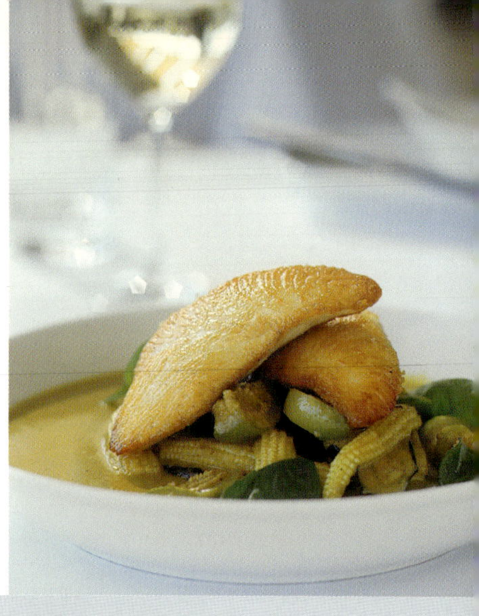

14 oz monkfish
3 medium-size onions
1 garlic clove
7/10 oz fresh coriander
2 ginger roots
4 lemongrass spears
8 long green chilies
4 small green chilies
3 limes
2/5 oz ground turmeric
1/5 oz ground coriander
1/5 oz ground cumin
1/5 oz ground white pepper
1 2/5 oz palm sugar
250 ml coconut milk
Olive oil

For the curry paste, place the finely chopped onions in a bowl and mix with the garlic, coriander (saving a few leaves for a garnish), grated ginger, lemongrass, green chilies cut into strips, 4 ground green chilies, grated lime rind (squeeze and reserve the juice first) and ground turmeric. Mix in a blender. Add the remaining spices and mix again. Heat the oil in a frying pan and cook at a medium heat, stirring repeatedly for 15 minutes. Add the palm sugar and coconut milk and cook for another 3–4 minutes. Add the monkfish, chopped into small pieces. Sear the fish for a few minutes, stirring every now and again.
Make a bed with the pieces of fish, drizzle with limejuice and garnish with some fresh coriander leaves.

400 g Seeteufel
3 mittelgroße Zwiebeln
1 Knoblauchzehe
20 g frischer Koriander
2 Ingwerwurzeln
4 Stängel Zitronengras
8 lange grüne Chilischoten
4 kleine grüne Chilischoten
3 Limetten
10 g gemahlene Kurkuma
5 g gemahlener Koriander
5 g gemahlener Kreuzkümmel
5 g weißer gemahlener Pfeffer
40 g Palmzucker
250 ml Kokosmilch
Olivenöl

Für die Currypaste in einer Schüssel die feingehackten Zwiebeln mit dem Knoblauch, dem Koriander (einige Blätter für die Dekoration aufbewahren), Ingwer geraspelt, Zitronengras, den langen grünen Chilischoten in Streifen geschnitten, den 4 kleinen grünen Chilischoten gemahlen, der geriebenen Limettenschale (vorher den Saft ausdrücken und aufbewahren) und der gemahlenen Kurkuma vermischen. Alles im Mixer zerkleinern. Die restlichen Gewürze zufügen und nochmals mixen. Öl in der Pfanne erhitzen und die Mischung bei mittlerer Hitze unter häufigem Rühren 15 Minuten kochen. Palmzucker und Kokosmilch hinzugeben und weitere 3–4 Minuten kochen. Den Seeteufel, in kleine Stücke geschnitten, zufügen und einige Minuten mitkochen, dabei ab und zu umrühren.
Mit den Fischstücken ein Bett anrichten, mit Limettensaft beträufeln und mit den Korianderblättern garnieren.

400 g de lotte
3 oignons moyens
1 gousse d'ail
20 g de coriandre fraîche
2 racines de gingembre
4 bâtons de citronnelle
8 chilis verts longs
4 petits chilis verts
3 citrons verts
10 g de curcuma en poudre
5 g de coriandre en poudre
5 g de cumin en poudre
5 g de poivre blanc en poudre
40 g de sucre de palme
250 ml de lait de coco
Huile d'olive

Pour la pâte au curry, mélanger dans un récipient les oignons coupés en petits morceaux, l'ail, la coriandre (réserver quelques feuilles pour la décoration), le gingembre râpé, les bâtons de citronnelle, les chilis verts longs coupés en lamelles, les 4 petits chilis verts moulus, les zestes de citrons verts (les presser avant et réserver le jus) et le curcuma en poudre. Mixer au robot. Ajouter le reste des épices et mixer à nouveau. Chauffer l'huile dans une poêle et cuire le mélange à feu moyen en remuant souvent pendant 15 minutes. Ajouter le sucre de palme, le lait de coco et laisse encore cuire pendant 3–4 minutes. Incorporer la lotte coupée en petits morceaux et la cuire quelques minutes, en remuant de temps en temps.
Former un lit avec les morceaux de poisson, arroser de jus de citron vert et décorer avec les feuilles de coriandre.

400 g de rape
3 cebollas medianas
1 diente de ajo
20 g de cilantro fresco
2 raíces de jengibre
4 ramitas de citronela
8 chiles verdes largos
4 chiles verdes pequeños
3 limas
10 g de cúrcuma molida
5 g de cilantro molido
5 g de comino molido
5 g de pimienta blanca molida
40 g de azúcar de palma
250 ml de leche de coco
Aceite de oliva

Para la pasta de curry, mezclar en un recipiente las cebollas cortadas en trozos pequeños, el ajo, el cilantro (reservar unas hojas para la decoración), el jengibre rallado, las ramitas de citronela, los chiles verdes largos cortados en tiras, los 4 chiles verdes pequeños molidos, la piel de las limas rallada (antes exprimirlas y reservar el zumo) y la cúrcuma en polvo. Triturar en la batidora. Añadir el resto de las especias y volver a batir. Calentar aceite en una sartén y cocinar la mezcla a fuego medio removiendo frecuentemente durante 15 minutos. Añadir el azúcar de palma y la leche de coco, y cocer durante 3–4 minutos más. Incorporar el rape cortado en trozos pequeños y cocerlo durante unos pocos minutos, removiendo de vez en cuando.
Formar un lecho con los trozos de pescado, rociar con el zumo de las limas y decorar con las hojas de cilantro.

400 g di rana pescatrice
3 cipolle medie
1 spicchio d'aglio
20 g di coriandolo fresco
2 radici di zenzero
4 rametti di limoncina
8 peperoncini piccanti verdi lunghi
4 peperoncini piccanti verdi piccoli
3 limette
10 g di curcuma tritata
5 g di coriandolo tritato
5 g di cumino tritato
5 g di pepe bianco macinato
40 g di zucchero di palma
250 ml di latte di cocco
Olio d'oliva

Per la pasta di curry, mescolare in un recipiente le cipolle tagliate a pezzettini, l'aglio, il coriandolo (metterne da parte alcune foglie per la decorazione), lo zenzero grattugiato, i rametti di limoncina, i peperoncini verdi lunghi tagliati a listelle, i 4 peperoncini piccoli tritati, la buccia grattugiata delle limette (prima spremerle e mettere da parte il succo) e la curcuma in polvere. Tritare nel tritatutto. Aggiungere il resto delle spezie e tritare nuovamente. In una padella riscaldare un po' d'olio e far cuocere l'impasto ottenuto a fuoco medio rimescolando frequentemente per 15 minuti. Aggiungere lo zucchero di palma e il latte di cocco e far cuocere per altri 3–4 minuti. Unire la rana pescatrice tagliata a pezzetti e cuocere per pochi minuti, rimescolando di tanto in tanto.
Formare un letto con i pezzetti di pesce, cospargere con il succo delle limette e decorare con le foglie di coriandolo.

Cruise

Design: Mandini & Associates | Chef: Ed Halmagyi

West Circular Quay, Overseas Passenger Terminal, Level 3 | Sydney, 2000 | The Rock
Phone: +61 2 9251 1188
www.cruiserestaurant.com.au
Opening hours: Every day from 11 am until late
Average price: Starters A$ 9–15, main courses A$ 18–25, desserts A$ 4–11
Cuisine: European Style
Special features: Spectacular views across Sydney Harbour to the Sydney
Opera House

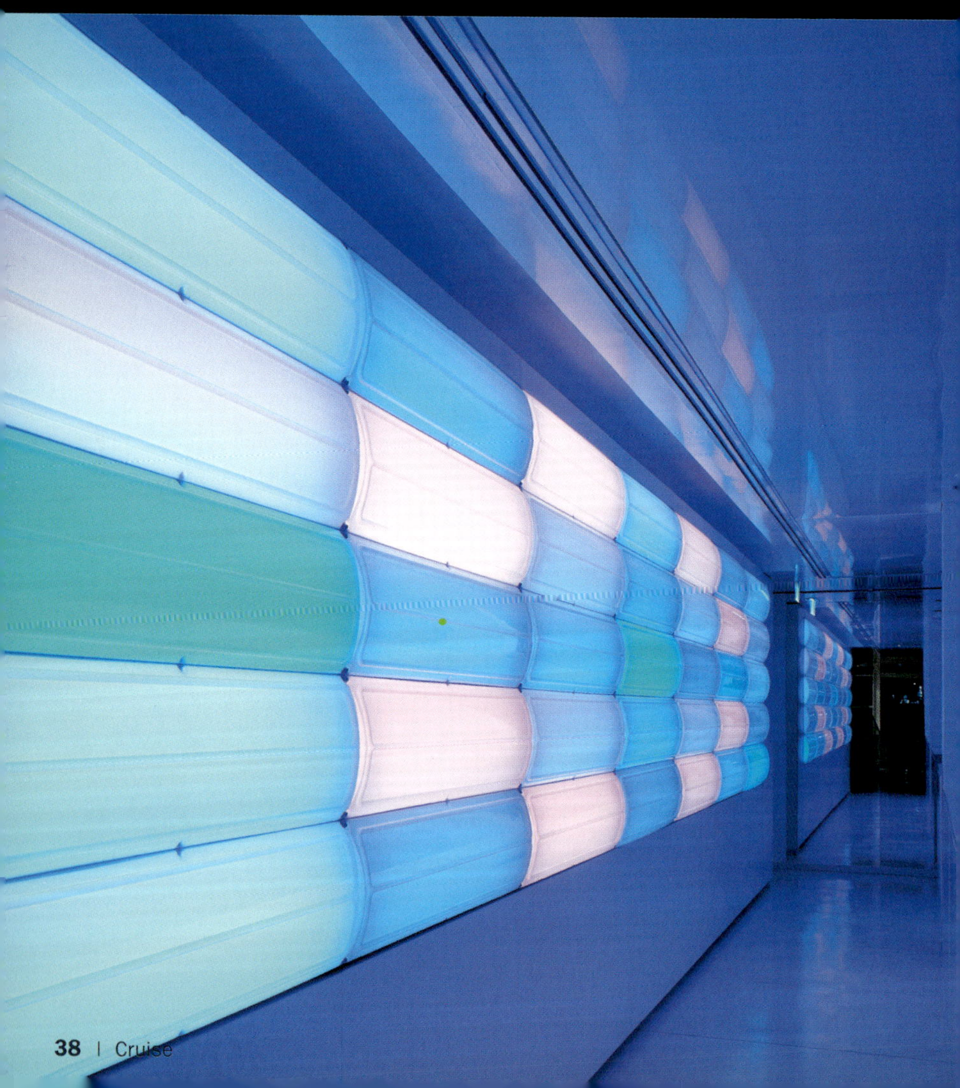

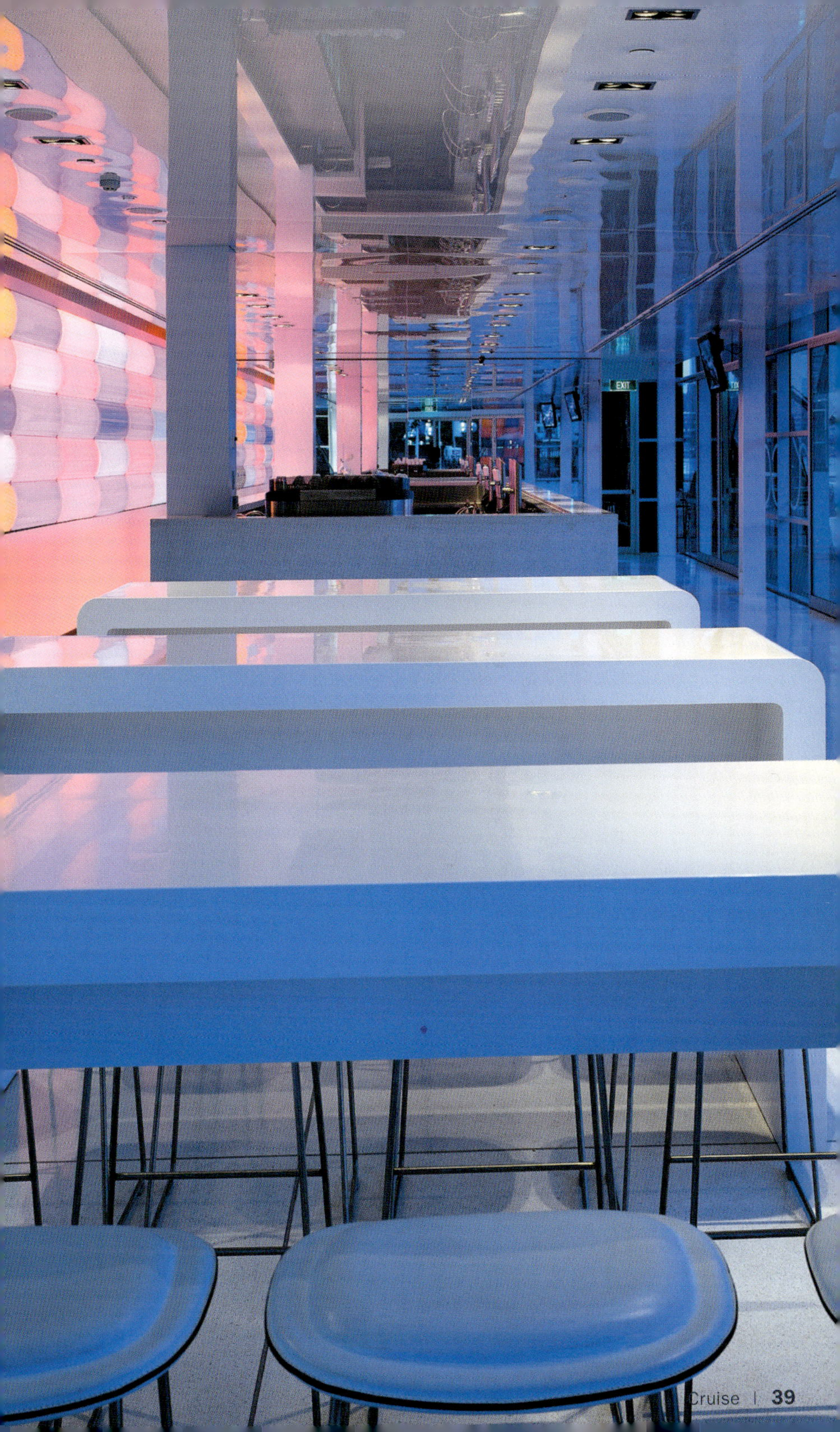

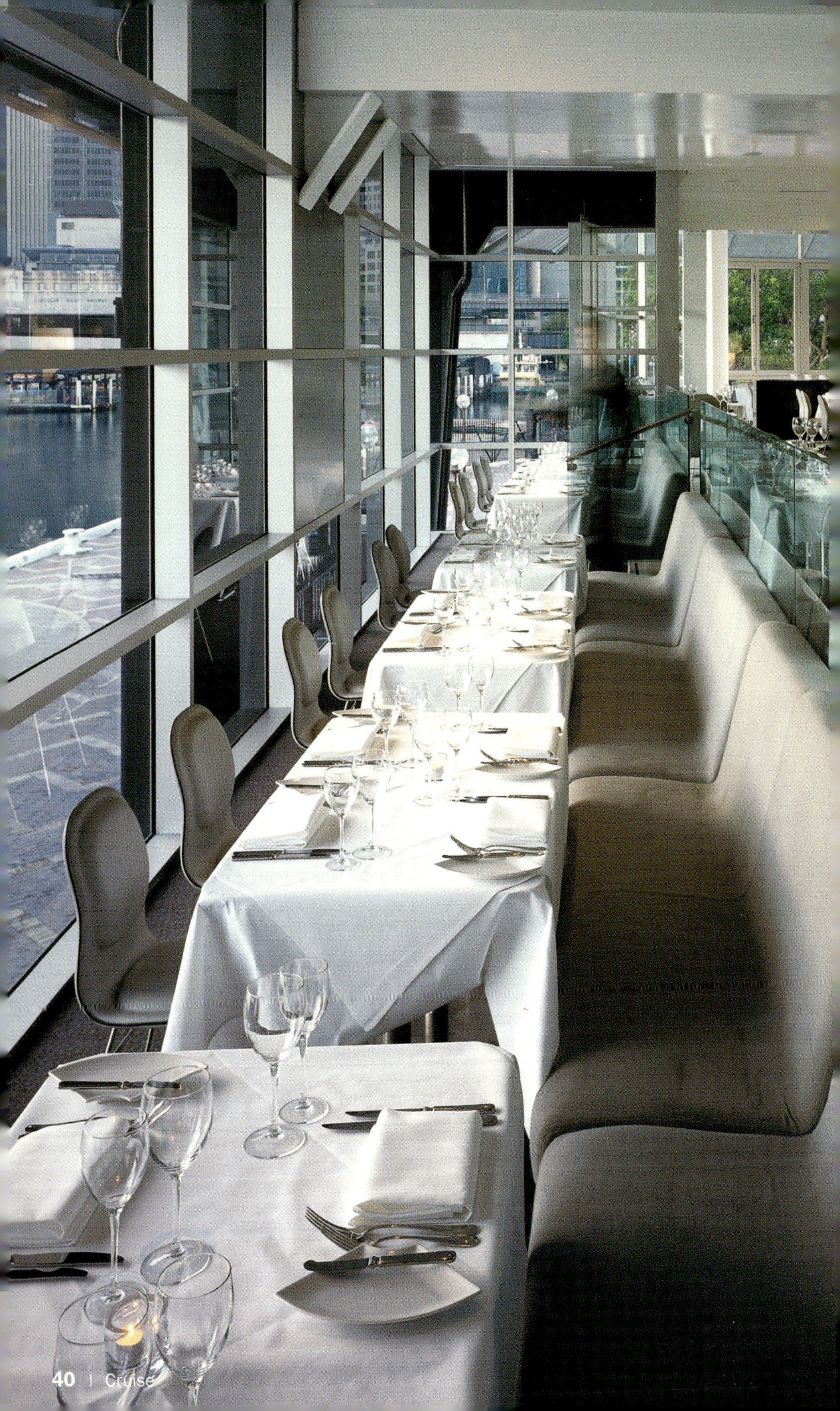

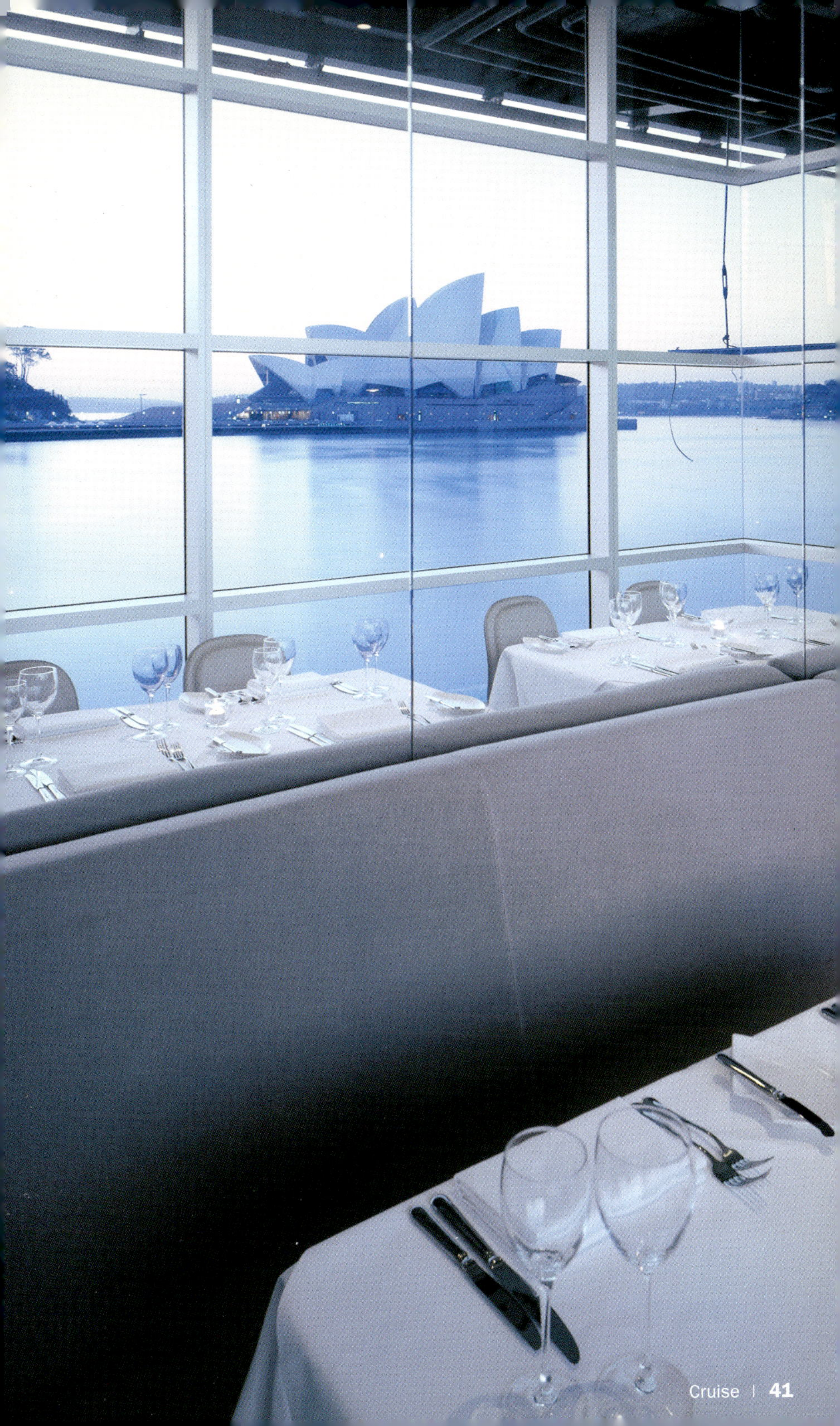

Sea Trout

with Red Beet Gelée and Sour Cream Sorbet

Meeresforelle mit Gelee von roter Beete und Sauerrahmsorbet

Truite de mer à la gélatine de betterave et au sorbet de crème aigre

Trucha de mar con gelatina de remolacha roja y sorbete de nata agria

Trota di mare con gelatina di barbabietola rossa e sorbetto di panna acida

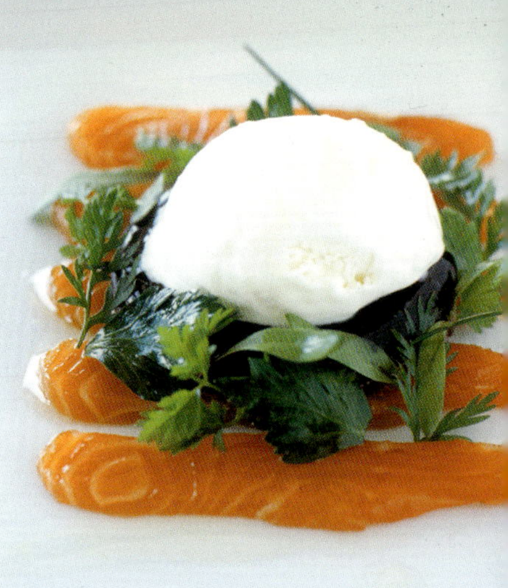

1 3/4 lb sea trout
7 oz course salt
3 1/2 oz sugar
6 star anise
12 coriander seeds
4 limes
1 large red beet
100 ml Cabernet Sauvignon vinegar
200 ml sugar syrup
500 ml water
5 gelatin leaves
200 ml sour cream
100 ml lemon juice
Salt

Mix the course salt, sugar, ground anise, ground coriander seeds, juice of 4 limes and the rind of 2 of them. Cover the fish with this paste, wrap in aluminum foil and refrigerate for 3 hours.

Clean and fillet the fish. Set aside. To make the gelée, peel and chop the beet, place in a bowl and cover with vinegar, 100 ml of sugar syrup and water. Simmer over a low heat for 30 minutes. Soak the gelatin leaves in the warm beet juice. Pour the mixture onto a tray and refrigerate until it solidifies. For the sorbet, mix the sour cream, the remaining 100 ml of sugar syrup and limejuice; add salt to taste and blend until the mixture turns creamy. Then, freeze and allow to solidify.
Arrange the fish fillets on a tray. Add the beet gelée and top with the sorbet.

800 g Meeresforelle
200 g grobes Salz
100 g Zucker
6 Sternanis
12 Korianderkerne
4 Limetten
1 große Rote Beete
100 ml Essig „Cabernet Sauvignon"
200 ml Zuckersirup
500 ml Wasser
5 Blatt Gelatine
200 ml Sauerrahm
100 ml Zitronensaft
Salz

Sternanis und Korianderkerne mahlen und mit grobem Salz, Zucker, dem Saft von 4 Limetten und den geriebenen Schalen von 2 Limetten mischen. Den Fisch mit der Paste bedeckt in Alu-folie einwickeln und 3 Stunden kaltstellen. Den Fisch reinigen und in Filets schneiden. Beiseite stellen. Für das Gelee die Rote Beete schälen und klein schneiden, in ein Gefäß legen und mit Weinessig, 100 ml Zuckersirup und Wasser bedecken. Bei niedriger Hitze 30 Minuten lang köcheln. Die Gelatineblätter im heißen Rote-Beete-Saft einweichen. Die Mischung über ein Blech gießen und erkalten lassen, bis sie fest wird. Für das Sorbet den Sauerrahm, die restlichen 100 ml Zuckersirup und den Limettensaft vermischen; mit Salz nach Geschmack würzen und rühren, bis die Mischung cremig wird, dann im Gefrierfach fest werden lassen.
Die Fischfilets auf einem Blech anrichten, das Rote-Beete-Gelee darübergeben und mit dem Sorbet krönen.

800 g de truite de mer
200 g de gros sel
100 g de sucre
6 étoiles d'anis
12 grains de coriandre
4 citrons verts
1 grosse betterave rouge
100 ml de vinaigre de Cabernet Sauvignon
200 g de sirop de glucose
500 ml d'eau
5 feuilles de gélatine
200 ml de crème aigre
100 ml de jus de citron
Sel

Mélanger le gros sel, le sucre, les étoiles d'anis et les grains de coriandre moulus, le jus des 4 citrons verts et le zeste de 2 d'entre eux. Envelopper le poisson, couvert de la préparation, dans du papier d'aluminium et mettre au réfrigérateur pendant 3 heures. Nettoyer le poisson et lever les filets. Réserver. Pour la gélatine, éplucher et couper la betterave, la disposer dans un récipient et la couvrir de vinaigre, des 100 ml de sirop de glucose et d'eau. Faire bouillir à feu doux pendant 30 minutes. Faire tremper les feuilles de gélatine dans le jus de betterave chaud. Verser le mélange sur une plaque et mettre au réfrigérateur jusqu'à solidification. Pour le sorbet, mélanger la crème aigre, les 100 ml restants de sirop de glucose et le jus de citron ; ajouter du sel à volonté et travailler le mélange jusqu'à obtention d'une consistance crémeuse.
Disposer les filets de poisson sur un plat de service. Ajouter la gélatine de betterave et couronner avec le sorbet.

---

800 g de trucha de mar
200 g de sal gruesa
100 g de azúcar
6 anises estrellados
12 semillas de cilantro
4 limas
1 remolacha roja grande
100 ml de vinagre de Cabernet Sauvignon
200 ml de jarabe de azúcar
500 ml de agua
5 hojas de gelatina
200 ml de nata agria
100 ml de zumo de limón
Sal

Moler los anises y las semillas de cilantro, y mezclarlos con la sal gruesa, el azúcar, el zumo de las 4 limas y la ralladura de la piel de 2 de ellas. Envolver el pescado, recubierto con la mezcla, en papel de aluminio y refrigerar durante 3 horas. Limpiar el pescado y cortarlo en filetes. Reservar. Para la gelatina, pelar y trocear la remolacha, disponerla en un recipiente y cubrirla con el vinagre, 100 ml de jarabe de azúcar y el agua. Hervir a fuego lento durante 30 minutos. Remojar las hojas de gelatina en el jugo de remolacha caliente. Verter la mezcla en una bandeja y refrigerar hasta que se solidifique. Para el sorbete, mezclar la nata agria, los 100 ml restantes de jarabe de azúcar y el zumo de lima; añadir sal al gusto y trabajar la mezcla hasta que tenga una consistencia cremosa. Dejar solidificar en el congelador.
Disponer los filetes de pescado en una bandeja. Añadir la gelatina de remolacha y coronar con el sorbete.

---

800 g di trota di mare
200 g di sale grosso
100 g di zucchero
6 anici stellati
12 semi di coriandolo
4 limette
1 barbabietola rossa grande
100 ml d'aceto di Cabernet Sauvignon
200 ml di sciroppo di zucchero
500 ml d'acqua
5 fogli di gelatina
200 ml di panna acida
100 ml di succo di limone
Sale

Mescolare il sale grosso, lo zucchero, gli anici macinati, i semi di coriandolo tritati, il succo delle 4 limette e la buccia grattugiata di 2 di queste. Ricoprire il pesce con il composto ottenuto, avvolgerlo in della carta di alluminio e mettere in frigo per 3 ore. Pulire il pesce, tagliarlo a filetti, dopodiché metterlo da parte. Per la gelatina, pelare e tagliare a pezzi la barbabietola, riporla in un recipiente e coprirla con l'aceto, 100 ml di sciroppo di zucchero e l'acqua. Cuocere a fuoco lento per 30 minuti. Ammollare i fogli di gelatina nel succo della barbabietola calda. Versare il composto in una teglia e mettere in frigo fino a che non diventi solido. Per preparare il sorbetto, mescolare la panna acida, i 100 ml restanti di sciroppo di zucchero e il succo di limone; correggere di sale secondo i gusti e lavorare l'impasto fino a che non ottenga una consistenza viscosa.
Disporre i filetti di pesce in un vassoio. Aggiungere la gelatina di barbabietola e coronare con il sorbetto.

349 Kent Street, City Hotel, Level 1 I Sydney, 2000 I Central Business District
Phone: +61 2 9262 5900
www.eatcity.com.au
Opening hours: Mon–Fri from noon to 11 pm
Average price: Starters A$ 12, main courses A$ 18, desserts A$ 8
Cuisine: Modern French and Australian
Special features: French Yum Cha

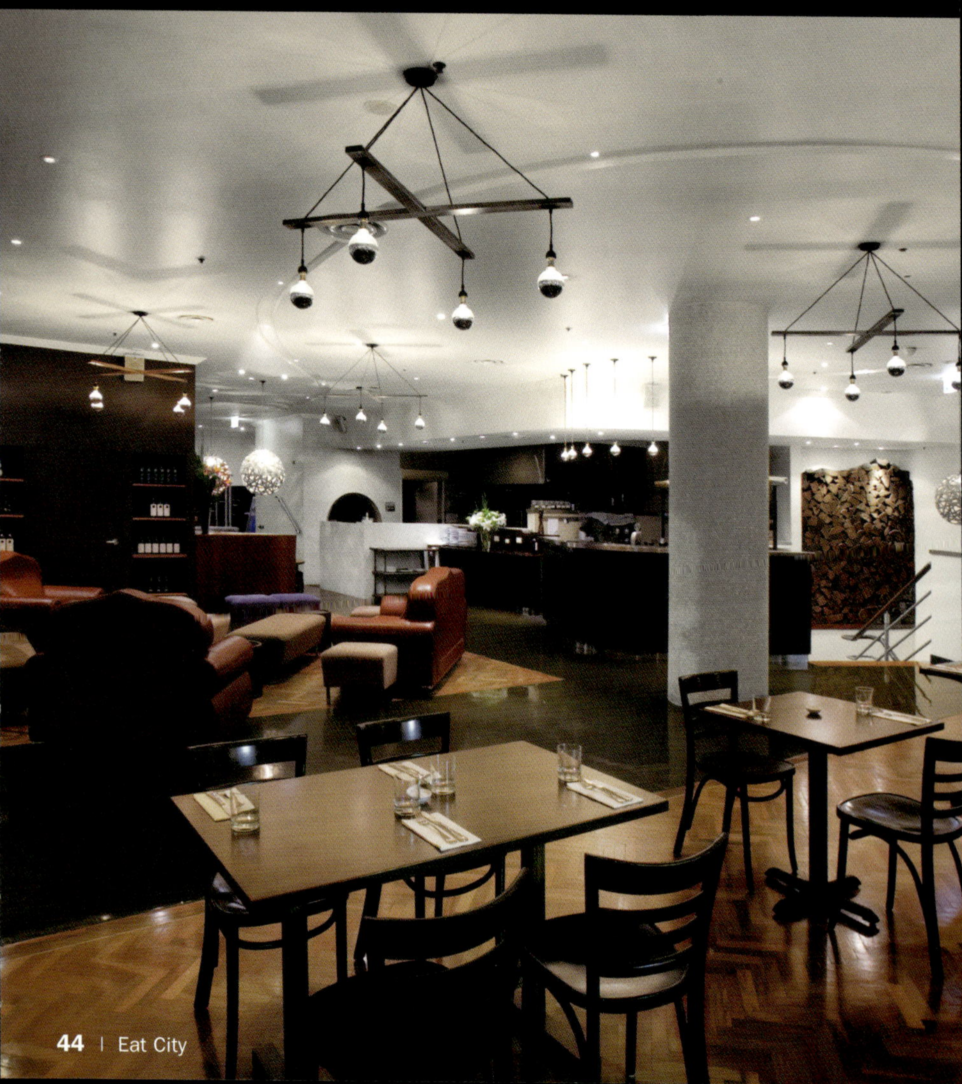

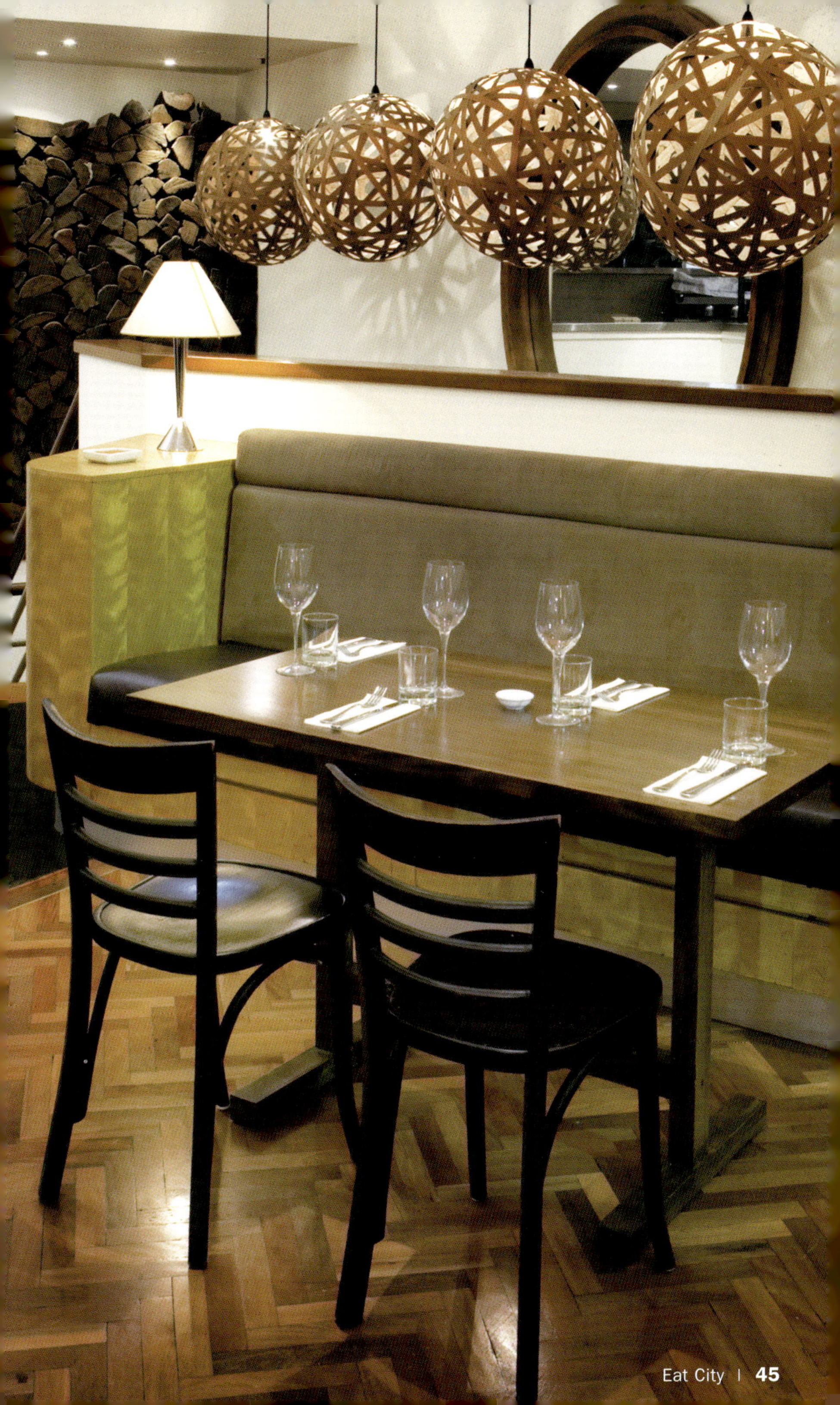

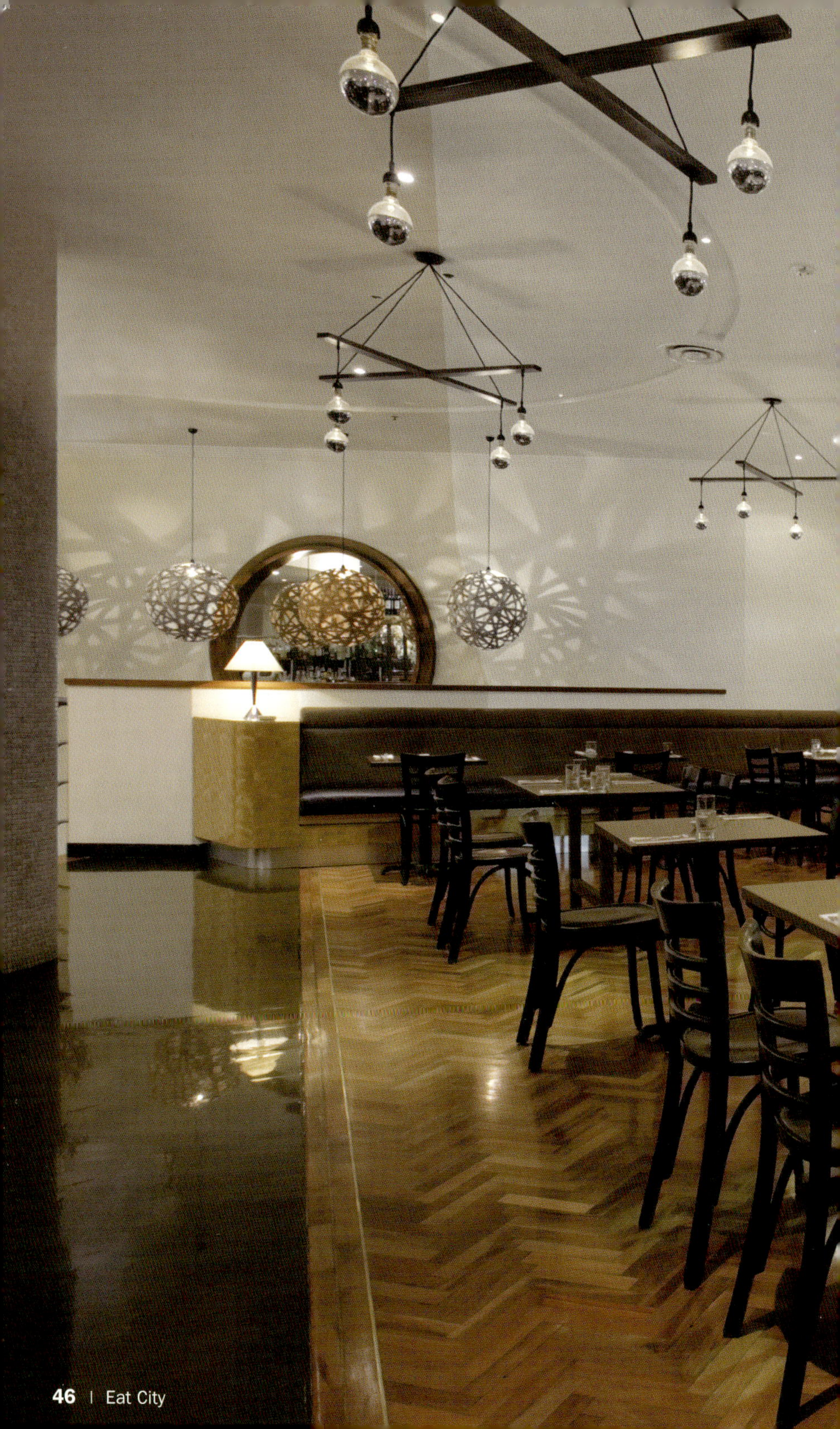

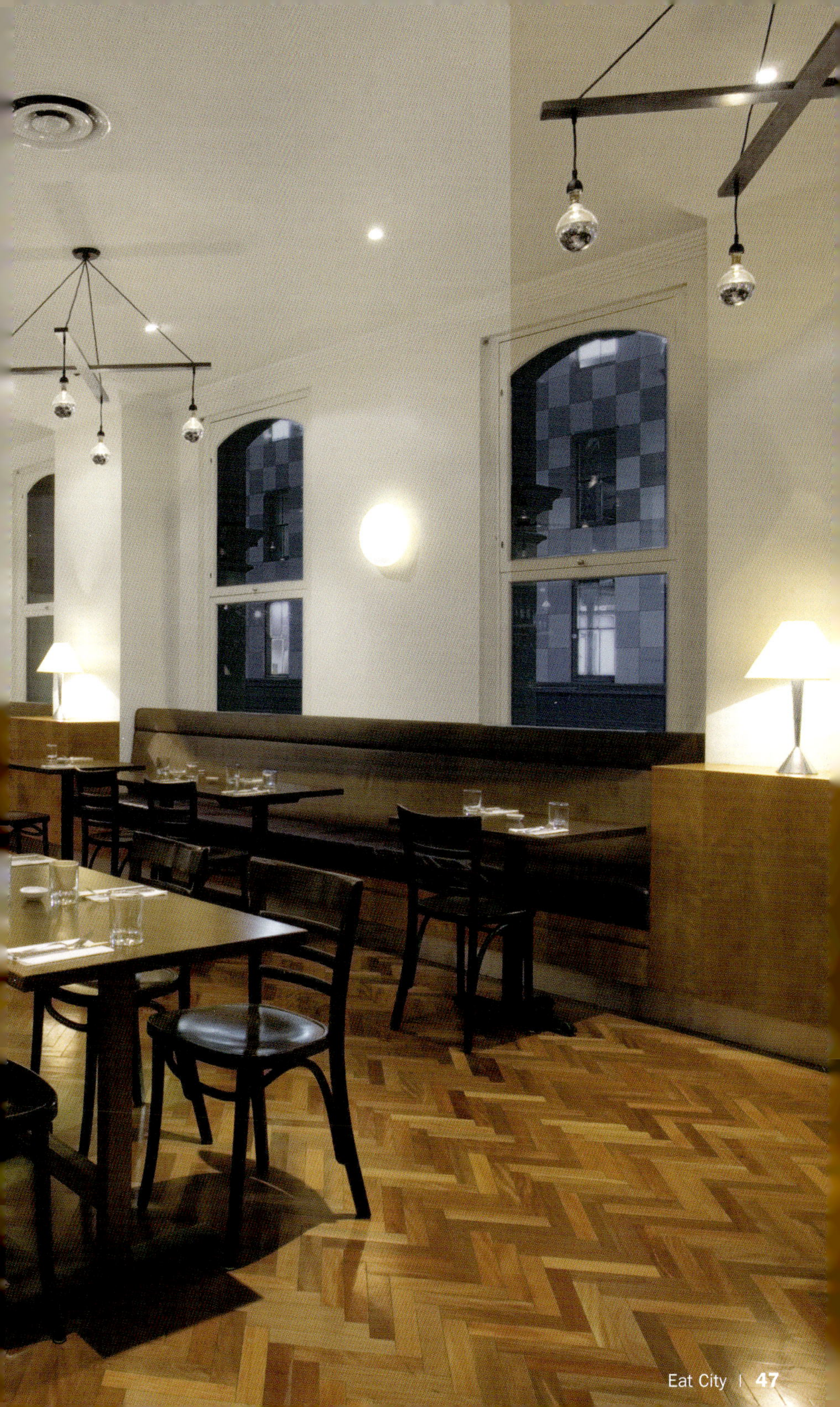

Duck
with Orange Sauce and Spinach

Ente mit Orangensoße und Spinat

Canard à la sauce à l'orange et aux épinards

Pato con salsa de naranja y espinacas

Anatra con salsa all'arancia e spinaci

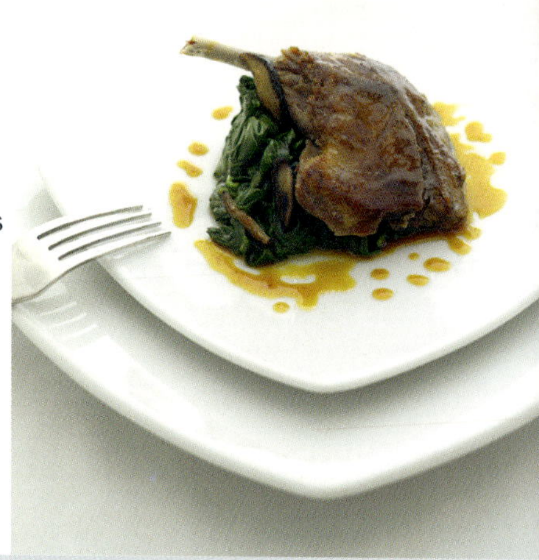

4 duck legs
1 2/5 oz course-ground salt
5 garlic cloves
1 3/4 lbs duck fat
500 ml orange juice
1/5 oz ground juniper
1/5 oz star anise
1/5 oz ground coriander
1/5 oz cardamom
1 1/10 lb spinach
Olive oil
1 2/5 oz butter
Salt

Arrange the duck legs in a bowl and season with the course-ground salt and 4 finely sliced garlic cloves. Refrigerate for 12 hours. Place the duck legs in a saucepan, cover with some fat and simmer over a low heat. When the meat falls off the bones easily, place the legs in a bowl and cover with the remaining duck fat. Store in the refrigerator for 2 days. Heat the orange juice and reduce down with the juniper, star anise, coriander and cardamom. Strain and set aside. Wash the spinach and sauté with one sliced garlic clove and olive oil. Season to taste with salt and set aside. Remove the duck legs from the refrigerator and sauté in a frying pan until golden brown. Bake for 5 minutes at 320 °F. Take out of the oven and pour away the excess fat. Add half of the orange sauce and butter and bake for another 5 minutes.
Place the legs on a dish with a side serving of spinach, pouring over the remaining orange sauce.

4 Entenkeulen
40 g grobes Salz
5 Knoblauchzehen
800 g Entenfett
500 ml Orangensaft
5 g gemahlener Wacholder
5 g Sternanis
5 g gemahlener Koriander
5 g Kardamom
500 g Spinat
Olivenöl
40 g Butter
Salz

Die Entenkeulen in einer Schale anordnen und mit dem groben Salz und 4 in feine Scheiben geschnittenen Knoblauchzehen würzen. Im Kühlschrank 12 Stunden ruhen lassen. Die Entenkeulen in einen Topf geben, mit etwas Fett bedecken und auf schwacher Flamme köcheln, ohne sie aufkochen zu lassen. Wenn das Fleisch sich leicht vom Knochen lösen lässt, die Keulen in eine Schale legen und mit dem restlichen Entenfett bedecken. Im Kühlschrank zwei Tage aufbewahren. Den Orangensaft mit Wacholder, Sternanis, Koriander und Kardamom erhitzen und einkochen lassen. Abseihen und beiseite stellen. Den Spinat putzen und mit einer in Scheiben geschnittenen Knoblauchzehe und Olivenöl anbraten. Mit Salz abschmecken und beiseite stellen. Die Entenkeulen aus dem Kühlschrank nehmen und in einer Pfanne goldbraun braten. Im Ofen 5 Minuten bei 160 °C backen. Aus dem Ofen nehmen und das überschüssige Fett abgießen. Die Hälfte der Orangensoße und die Butter zugeben und weitere 5 Minuten im Ofen backen.
Die Keulen auf einem Teller mit dem Spinat als Beilage anrichten und mit dem Rest der Orangensoße begießen.

4 cuisses de canard
40 g de gros sel
5 gousses d'ail
800 g de graisse de canard
500 ml de jus d'orange
5 g de genièvre en poudre
5 g d'anis étoilé
5 g de coriandre en poudre
5 g de cardamome
500 g d'épinards
Huile d'olive
40 g de beurre
Sel

Disposer les cuisses de canards dans un récipient et assaisonner avec le gros sel et les 4 gousses d'ail coupées en fines rondelles. Laisser reposer 12 heures au réfrigérateur. Mettre le canard dans une casserole, couvrir d'un peu de graisse et cuire à feu doux sans porter à ébullition. Quand la viande se détache facilement de l'os, disposer les cuisses dans un récipient et couvrir de graisse de canard. Conserver au réfrigérateur pendant 2 jours. Faire réduire le jus d'orange avec le genièvre, l'anis, la coriandre et la cardamome. Filtrer et réserver. Nettoyer les épinards et les faire sauter avec de l'ail coupé en fines lamelles et de l'huile d'olive. Saler et réserver. Sortir les cuisses de canard du réfrigérateur et les faire dorer à la poêle. Mettre au four pendant 5 minutes à 160 °C. Retirer du four et ôter l'excédent de graisse. Ajouter la moitié de la sauce à l'orange et le beurre, puis glisser au four pendant 5 minutes.
Disposer les cuisses sur un plat, garnir avec les épinards et arroser avec le reste de sauce à l'orange.

4 muslos de pato
40 g de sal gruesa
5 dientes de ajo
800 g de grasa de pato
500 ml de zumo de naranja
5 g de enebro molido
5 g de anís estrellado
5 g de cilantro molido
5 g de cardamomo
500 g de espinacas
Aceite de oliva
40 g de mantequilla
Sal

Disponer los muslos de pato en un recipiente y aderezar con la sal gruesa y 4 dientes de ajo cortados en láminas finas. Dejar reposar durante 12 horas en la nevera. Colocar el pato en un cazo, cubrir con un poco de grasa y cocer a fuego lento sin llevar a ebullición. Cuando la carne se separe fácilmente del hueso, disponer los muslos en un recipiente y cubrir con el resto de grasa de pato. Guardar en la nevera durante 2 días. Reducir el zumo de naranja con el enebro, el anís, el cilantro y el cardamomo. Colar y reservar. Limpiar las espinacas y freír con un ajo cortado en láminas y aceite de oliva. Rectificar de sal y reservar. Sacar los muslos de pato de la nevera y dorar en una sartén. Hornear a 160 °C durante 5 minutos. Sacar del horno y retirar la grasa sobrante. Añadir la mitad de la salsa de naranja y la mantequilla y hornear durante 5 minutos más.
Disponer los muslos en un plato, acompañar con las espinacas y regar con el resto de la salsa de naranja.

4 cosce d'anatra
40 g di sale grosso
5 spicchi d'aglio
800 g di grasso d'anatra
500 ml di succo d'arancia
5 g di ginepro tritato
5 g di anice stellato
5 g di coriandolo tritato
5 g di cardamomo
500 g di spinaci
Olio d'oliva
40 g di burro
Sale

Collocare le cosce d'anatra in un recipiente e condire con il sale grosso e 4 spicchi d'aglio tagliati a lamelle sottili. Far riposare per 12 ore in frigo. Sistemare le cosce d'anatra in una pentola, coprire con un po' di grasso e cuocere a fuoco lento senza portare ad ebollizione. Quando la carne si può separare facilmente dall'osso, disporre le cosce in un recipiente e coprire con il grasso d'anatra. Conservare in frigo per 2 giorni. Ridurre il succo d'arancia assieme al ginepro, l'anice, il coriandolo e il cardamomo. Colare e mettere da parte. Pulire gli spinaci e friggere con un aglio tagliato a lamelle e olio d'oliva. Correggere di sale e mettere da parte. Estrarre le cosce d'anatra dal frigo e farle dorare in una padella. Infornare per 5 minuti a 160 °C. Toglierle dal forno e rimuovere il grasso in eccesso. Aggiungere la metà della salsa d'arancia e il burro e cuocere in forno per altri 5 minuti.
Disporre le cosce in un piatto, accompagnare con gli spinaci e cospargere con il resto della salsa d'arancia.

est.

Design: SJB Design | Chef: Peter Doyle

252 George Street, Level 1 | Sydney, 2000 | Australia Square
Phone: +61 2 9240 3010
www.merivale.com/establishment/est
Opening hours: Mon–Fri lunch from noon to 3 pm, dinner from 6 pm until late, Sat dinner from 6 pm until late
Average price: Starters A$ 28–36, main courses A$ 38–45, desserts A$ 16–24
Cuisine: Modern Australian
Special features: Sophisticated dining with elegant furnishings and fittings. More than 10 different champagnes

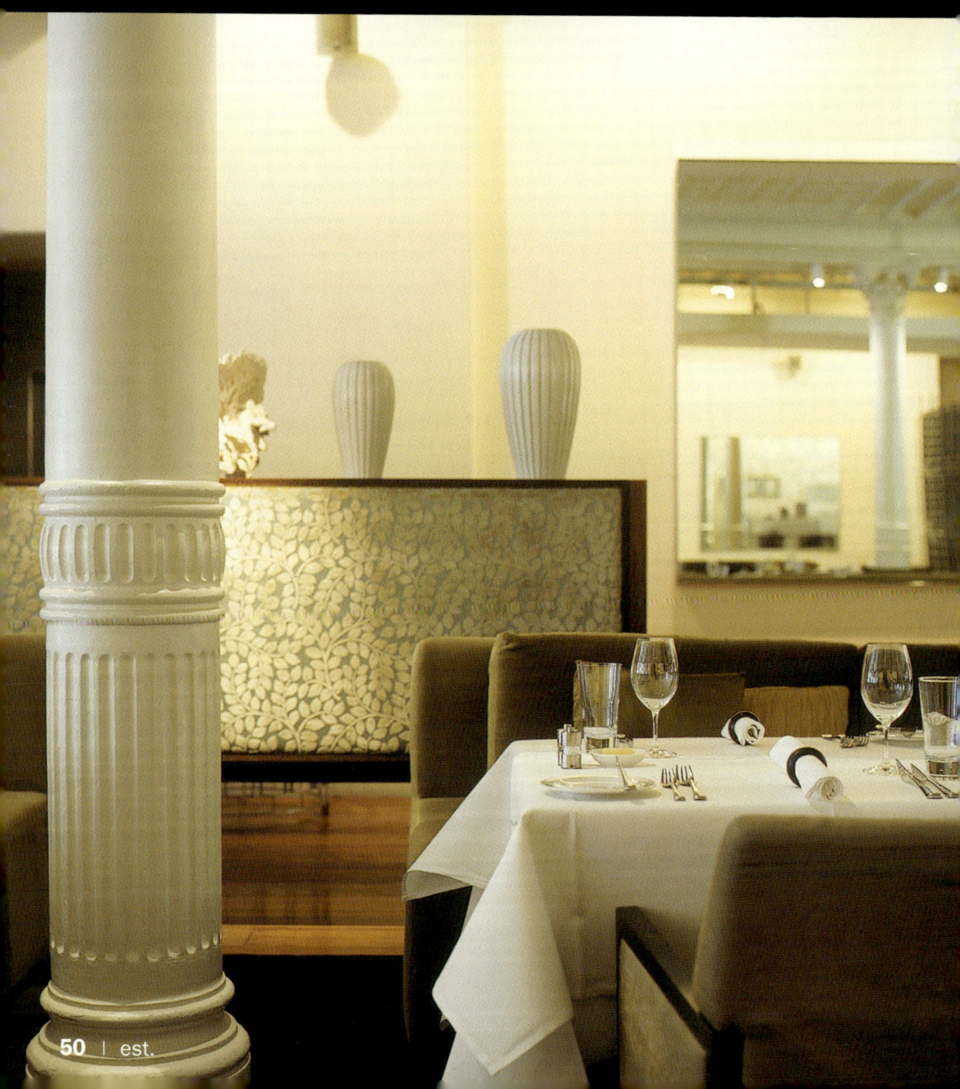

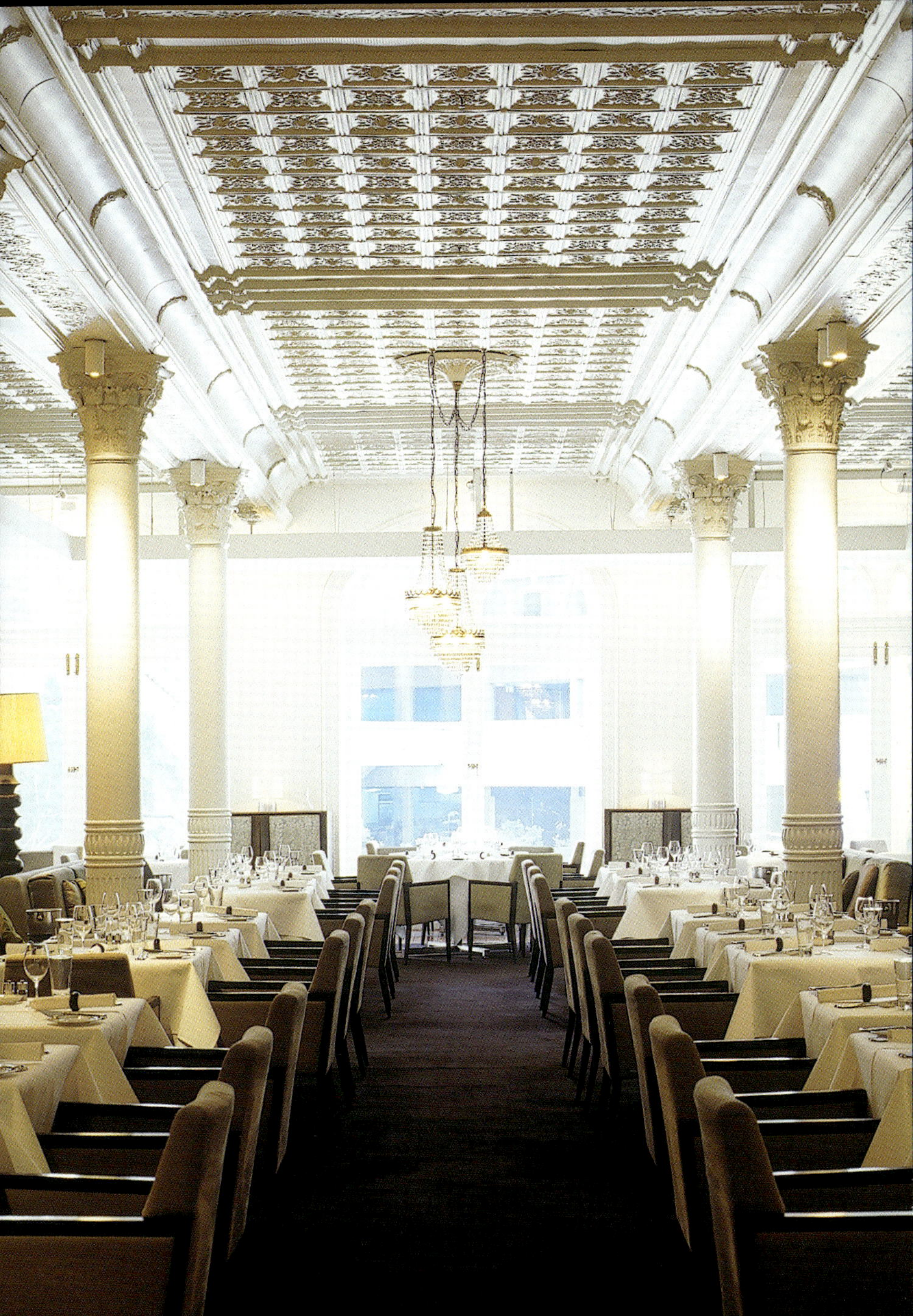

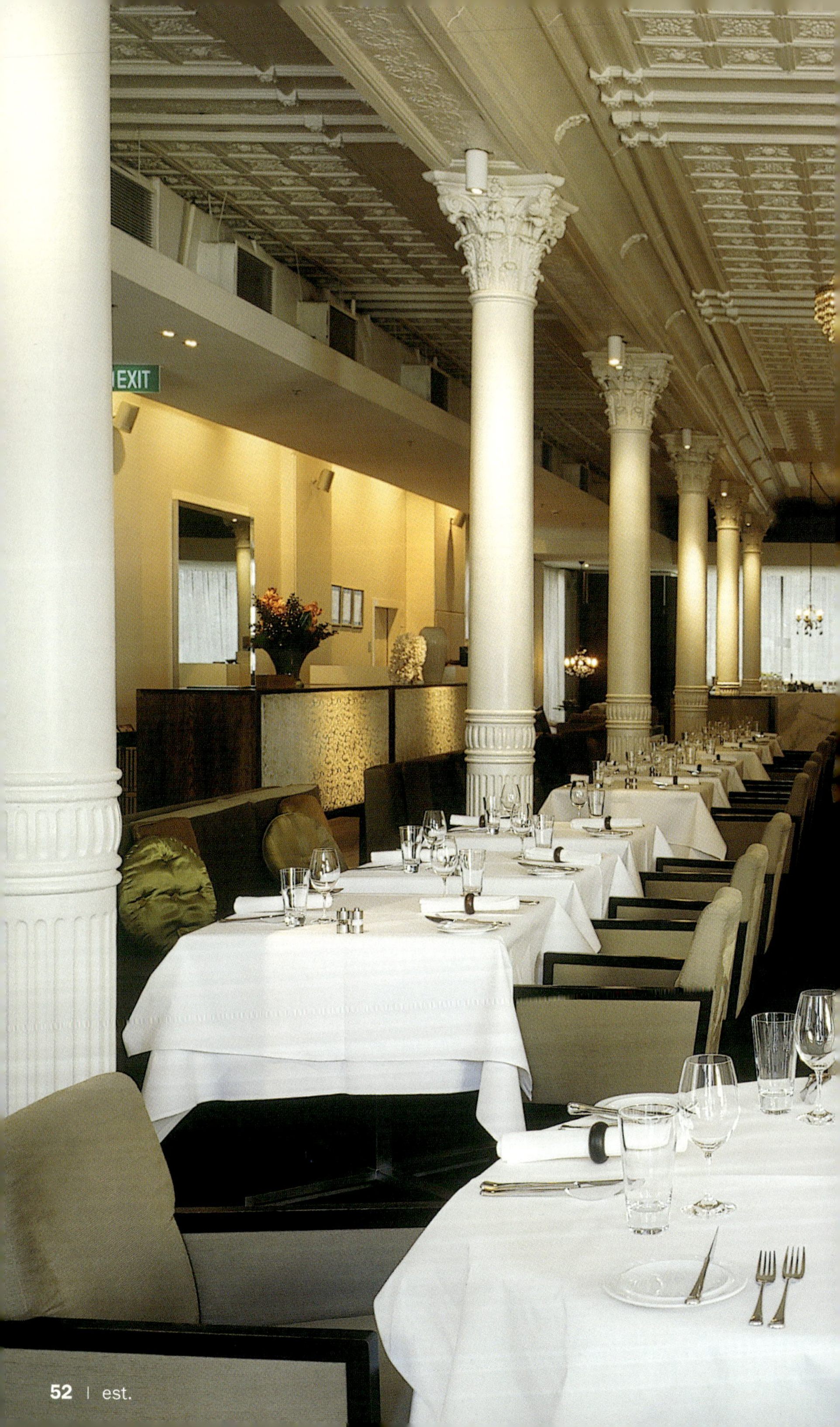
EXIT

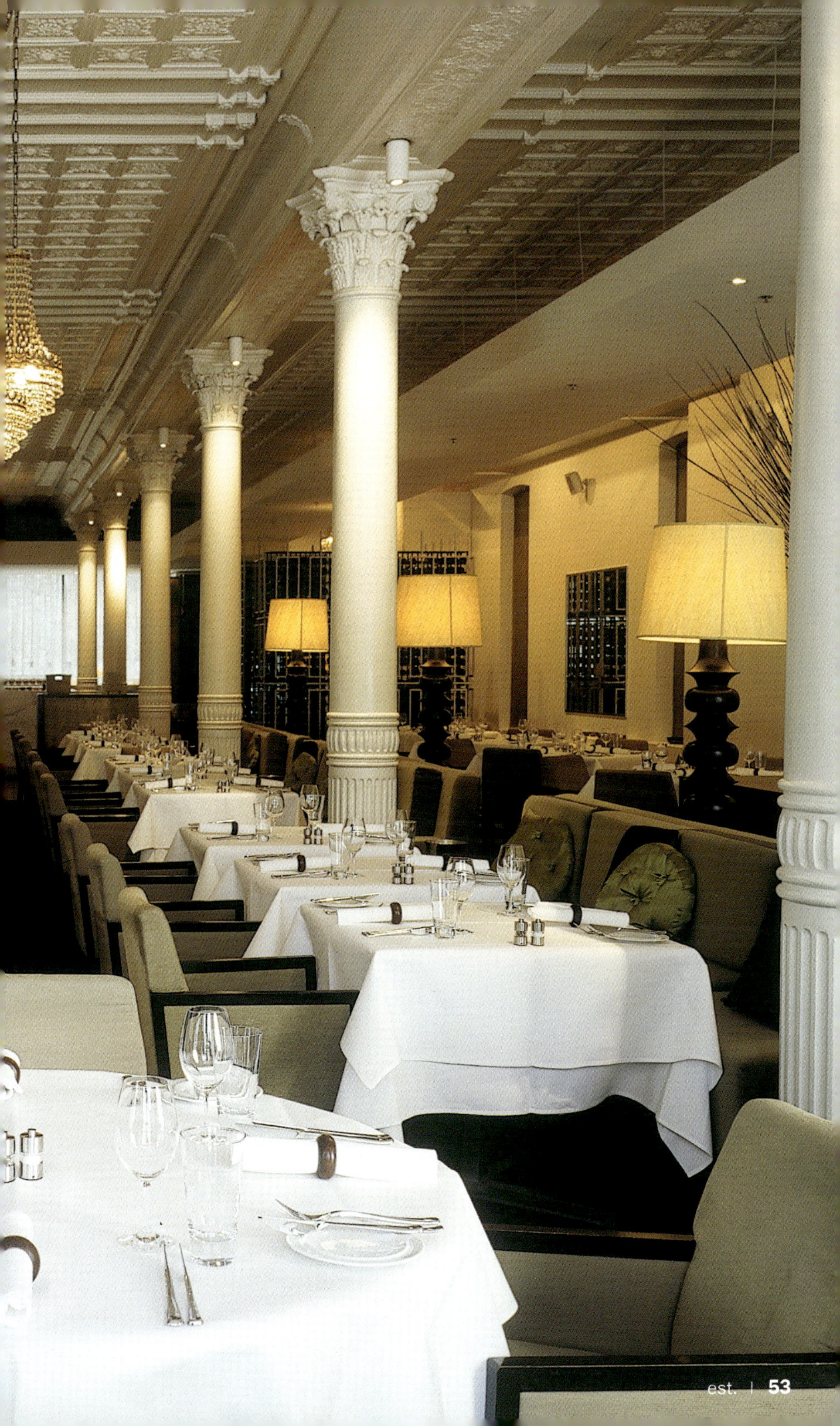

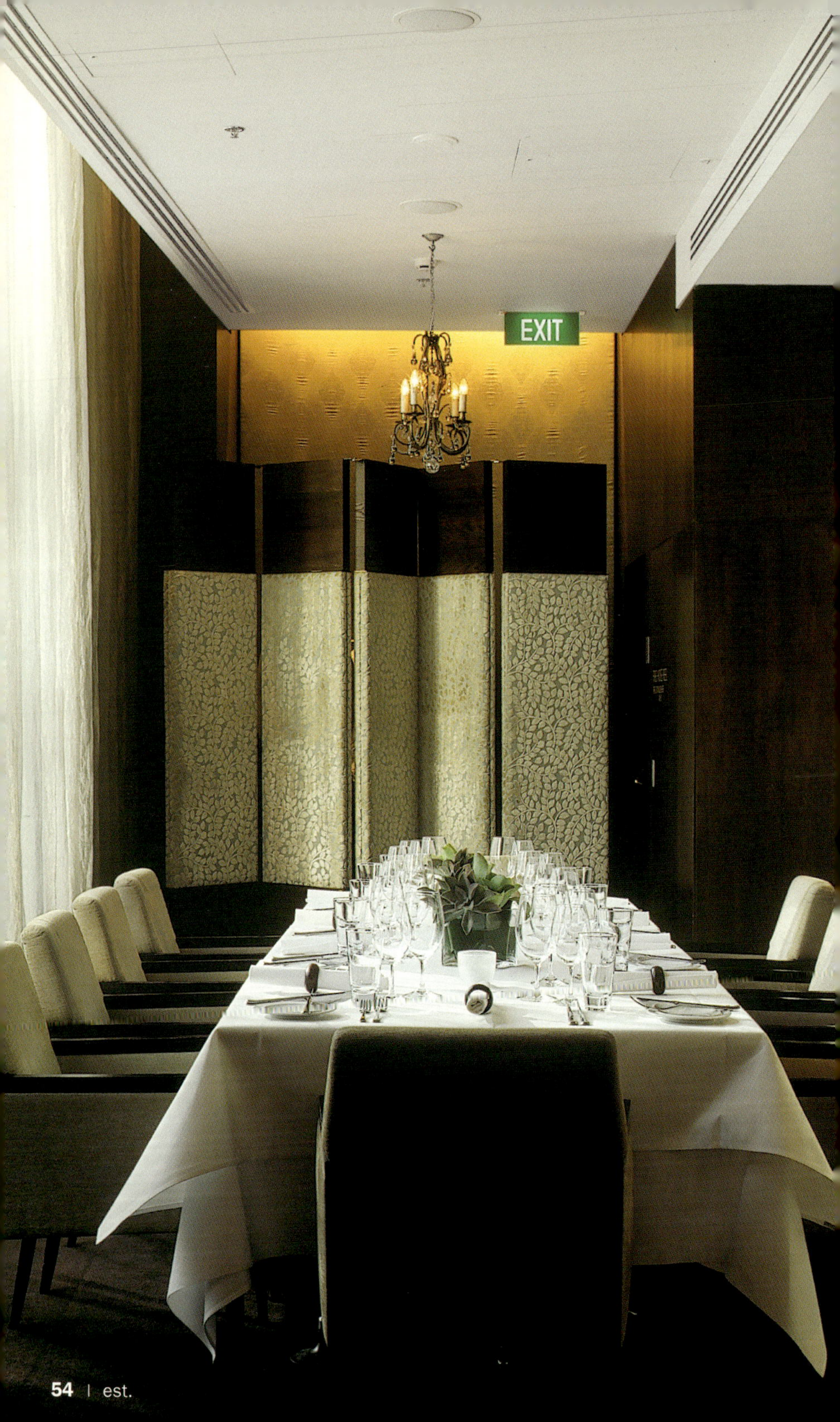
EXIT

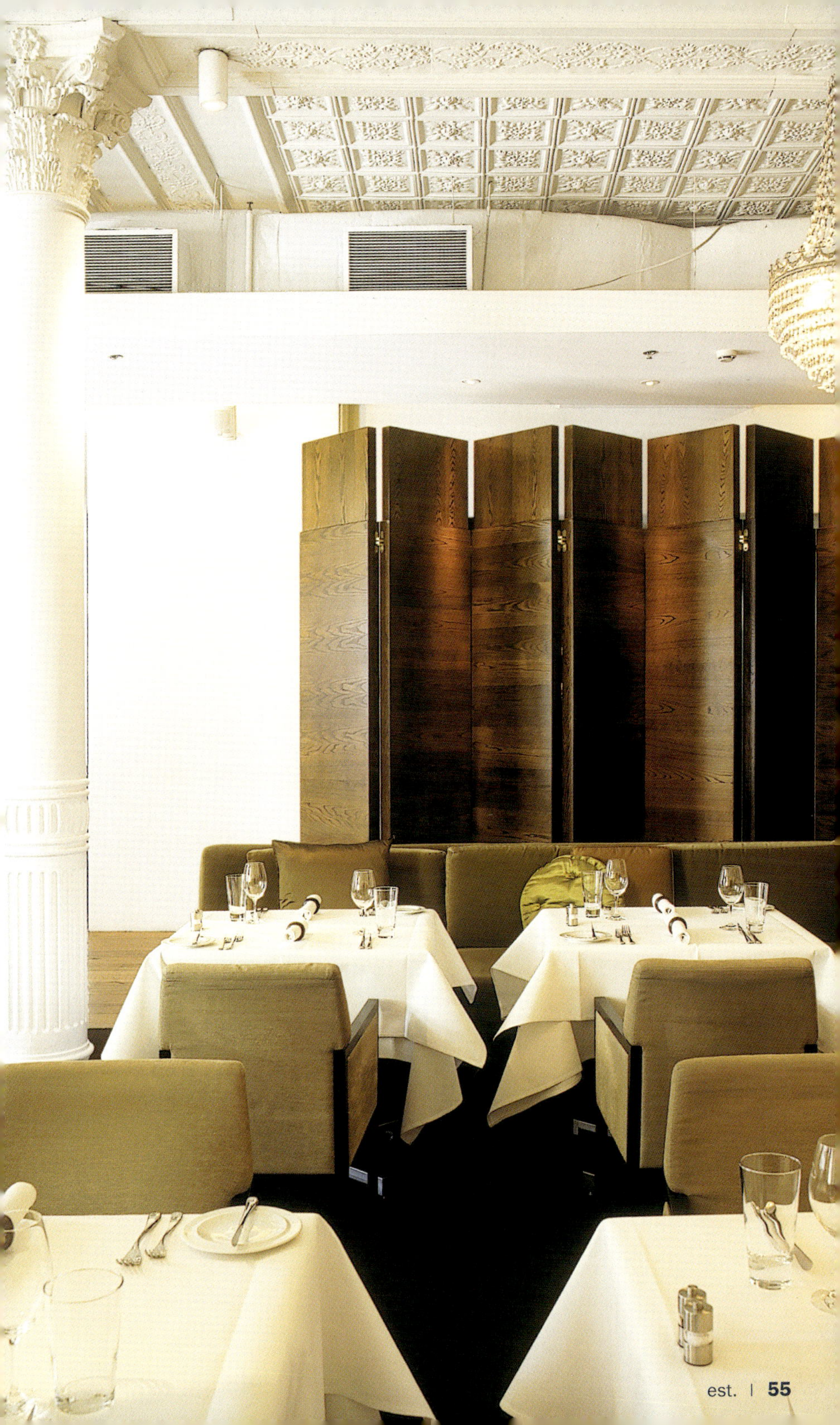

Icebergs

Design: Lazzarini Pickering Architects | Chef: Robert Machetti

1 Notts Avenue | Sydney, 2026 | Bondi Beach
Phone: +61 2 9365 9000
www.idrb.com
Opening hours: Tue–Sat from noon to midnight, Sun from noon to 10 pm
Average price: Starters A$ 19–31, main courses A$ 34–43, desserts A$ 9–18
Cuisine: Mediterranean, emphasis on seafood
Special features: Awe-inspiring location with panoramic view of Bondi Beach

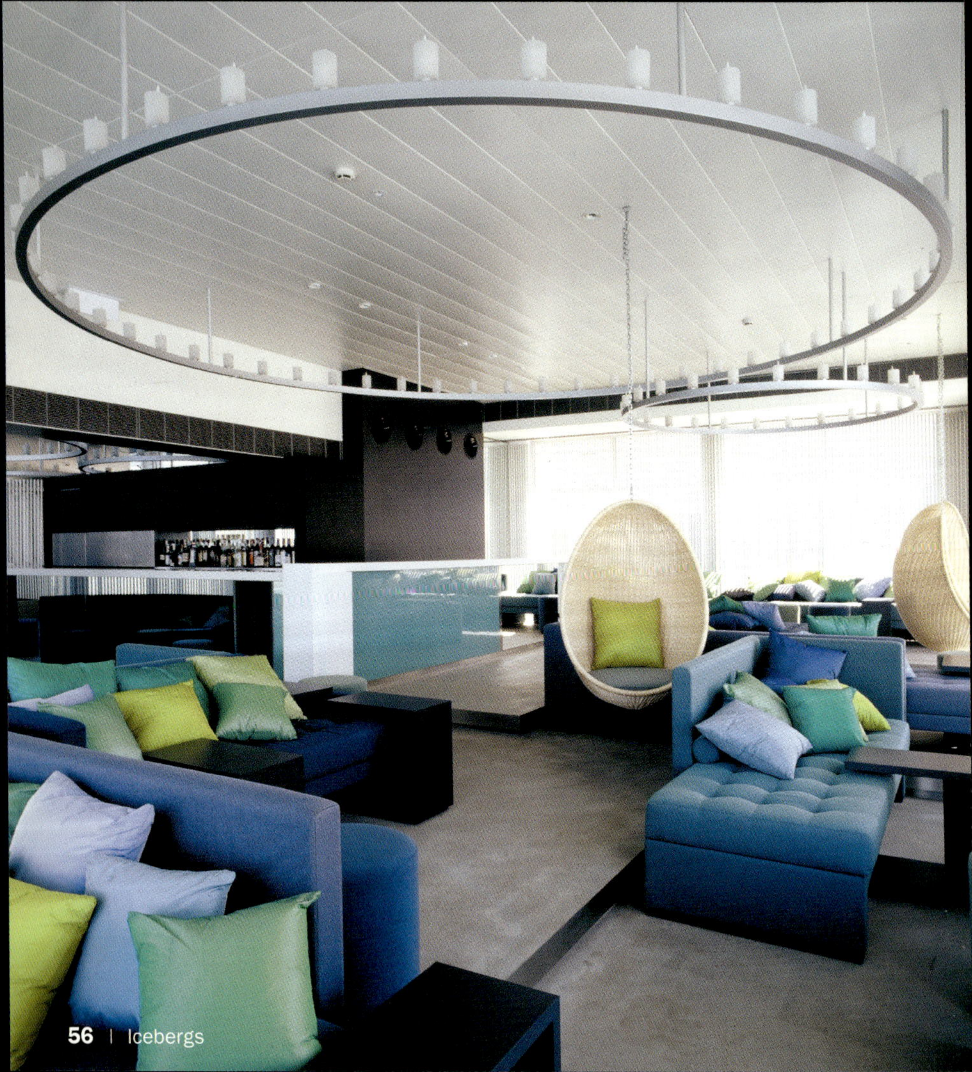

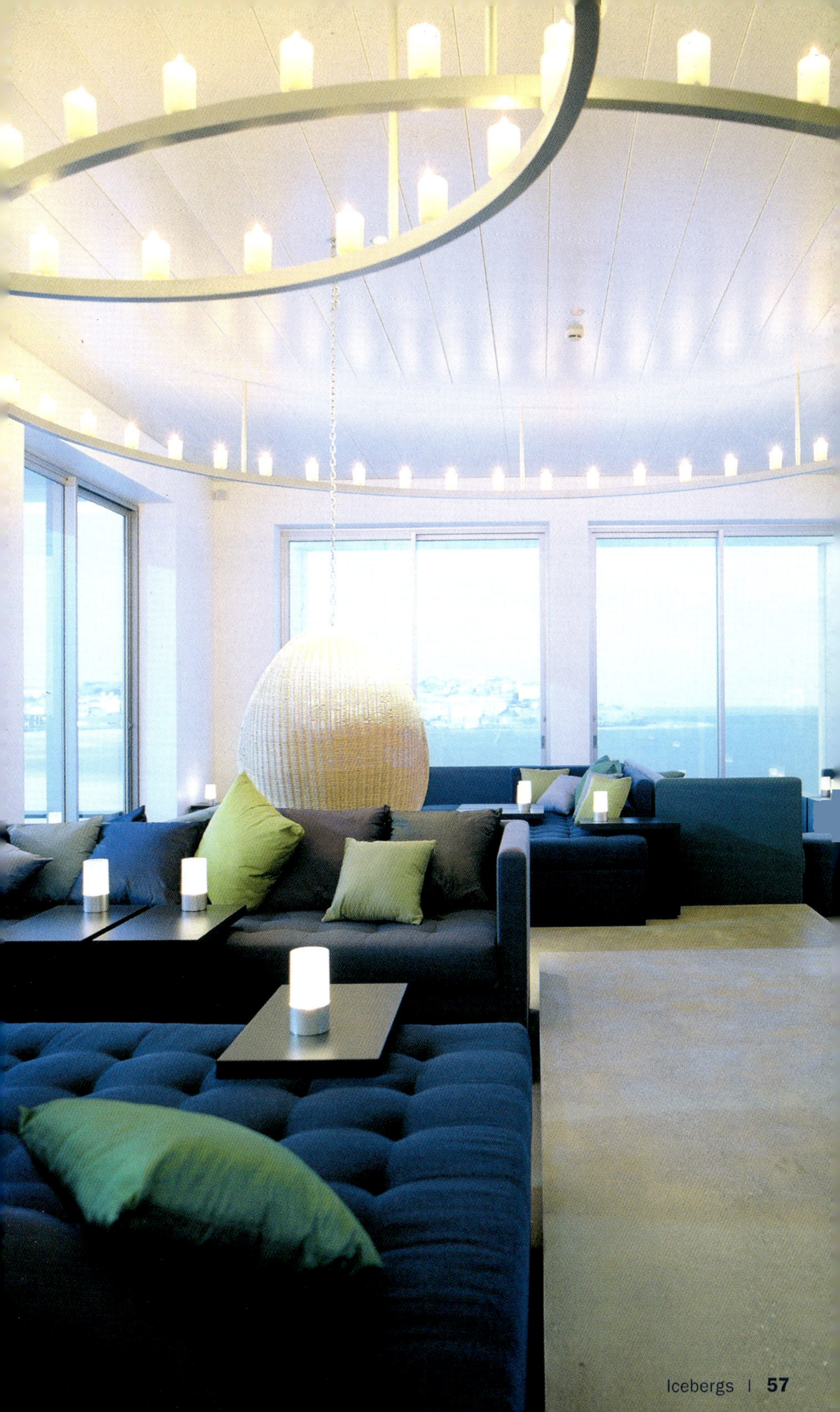

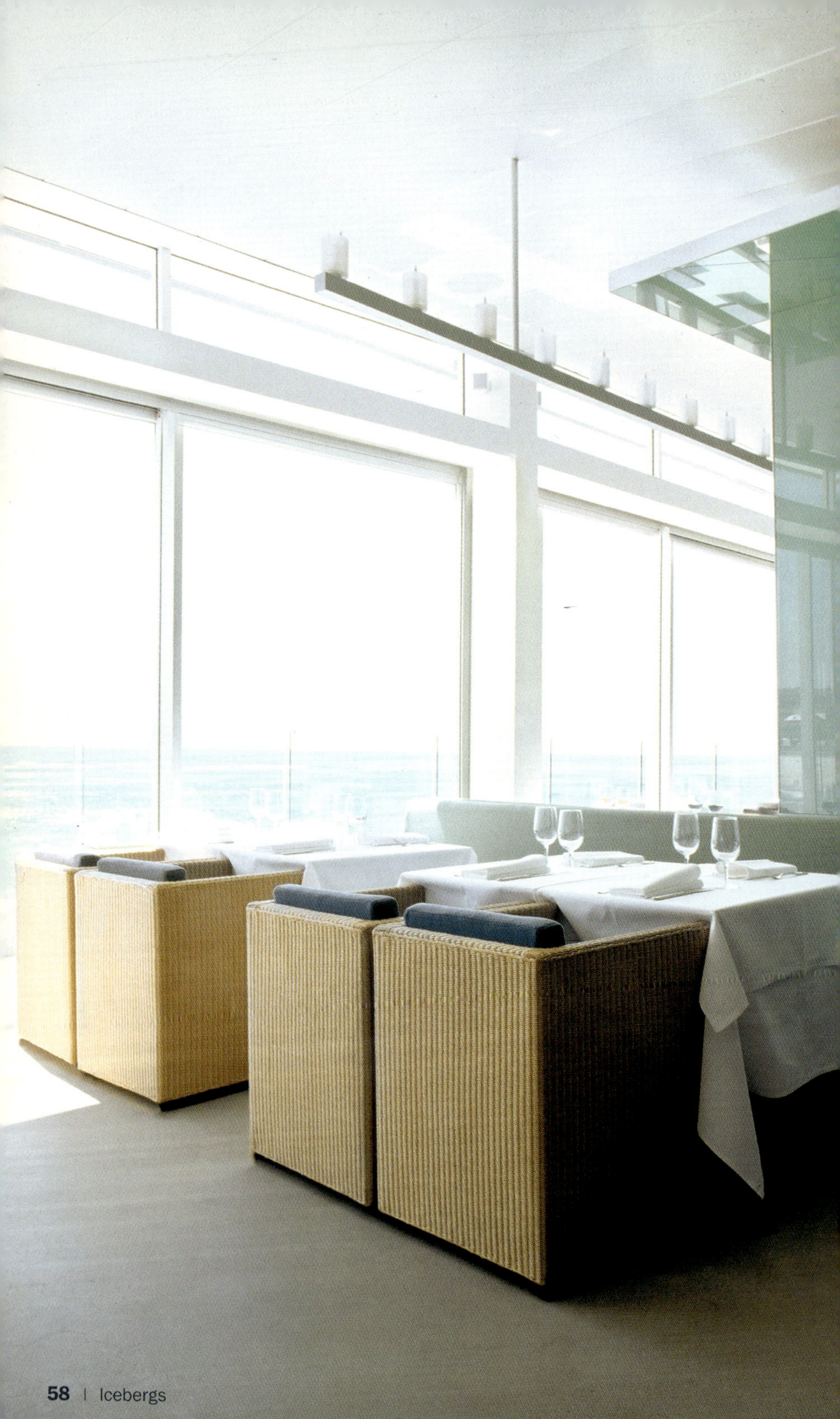

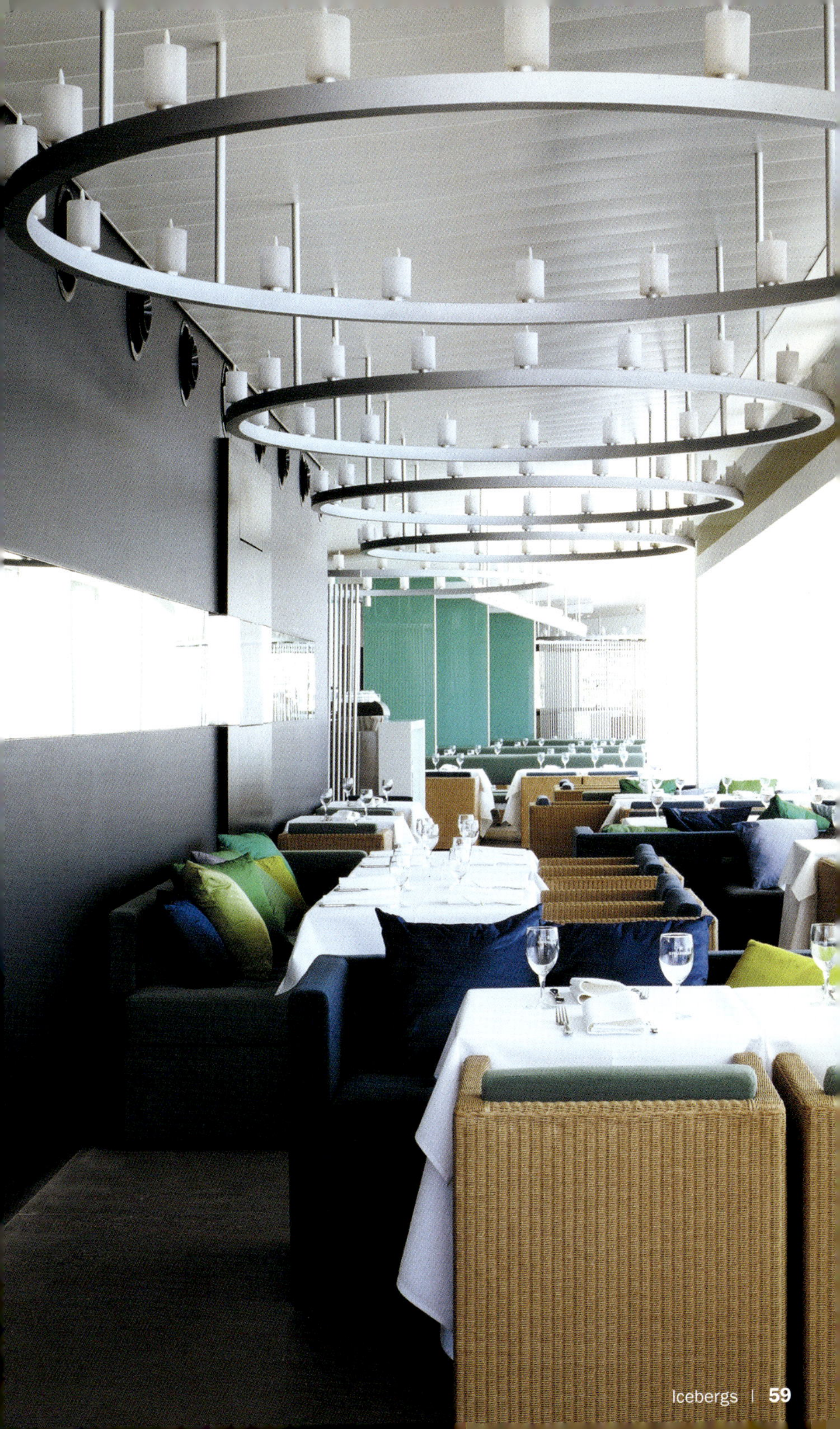

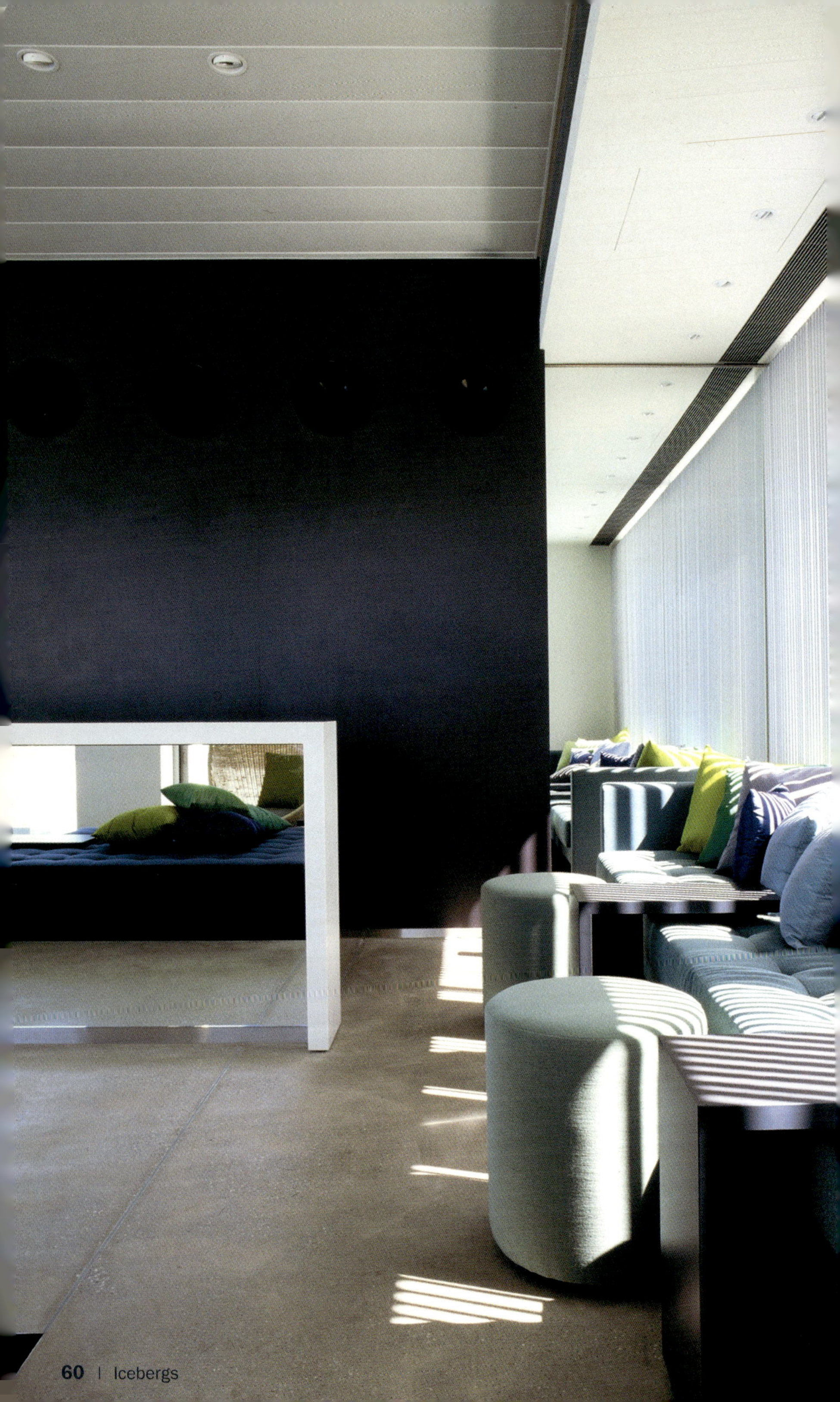

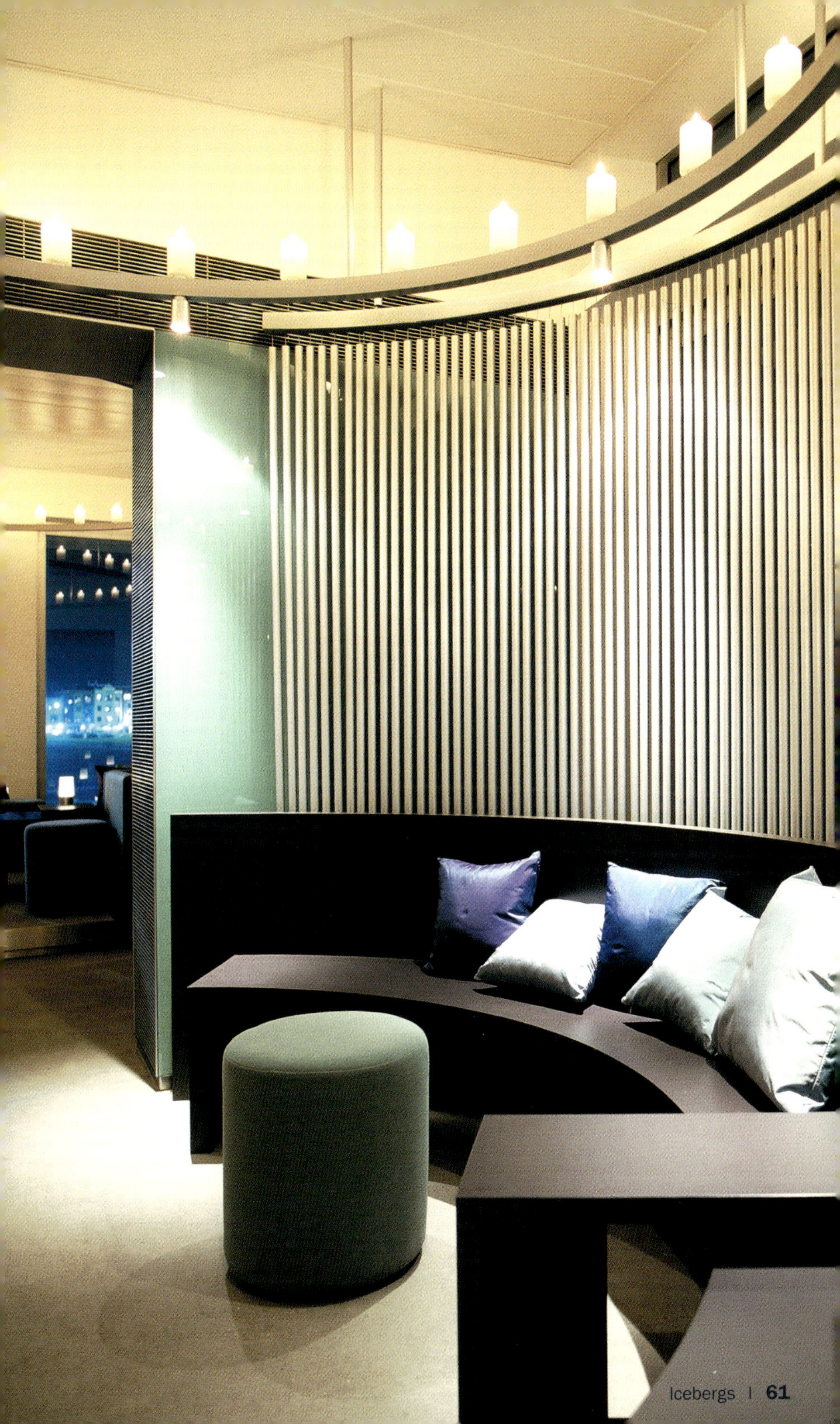

La Cita

Design: Arc Linea Interior Design | Chef: Salvador Hernández

9 Lime Street | Sydney, 2000 | King Street Wharf
Phone: +61 2 9299 9100
www.lacita.com.au
Opening hours: Sun–Wed from 9 am to midnight, Thu–Sat from 9 am to 3 am
Average price: Starters A$ 8–30, main courses A$ 22–65, desserts A$ 10–12
Cuisine: Modern Latin American
Special features: Cuban salsa classes

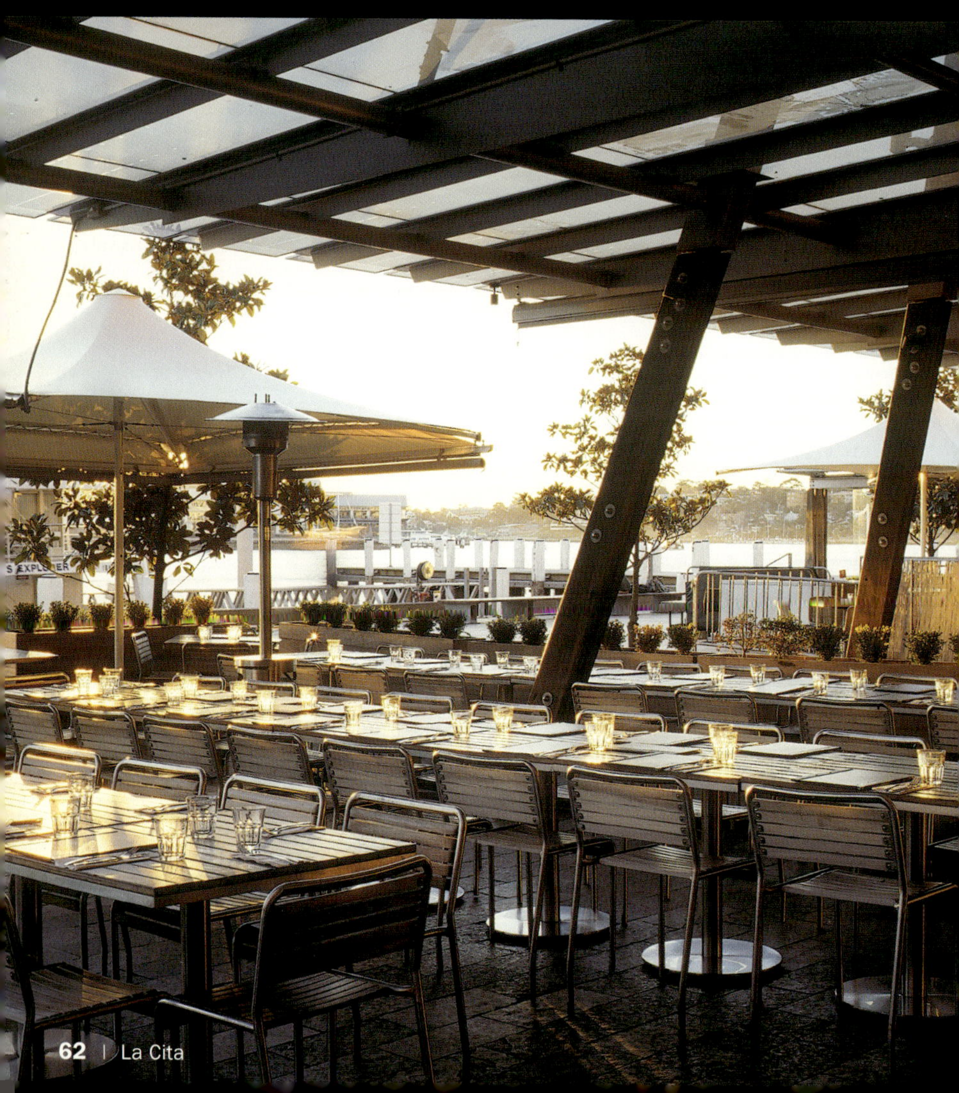

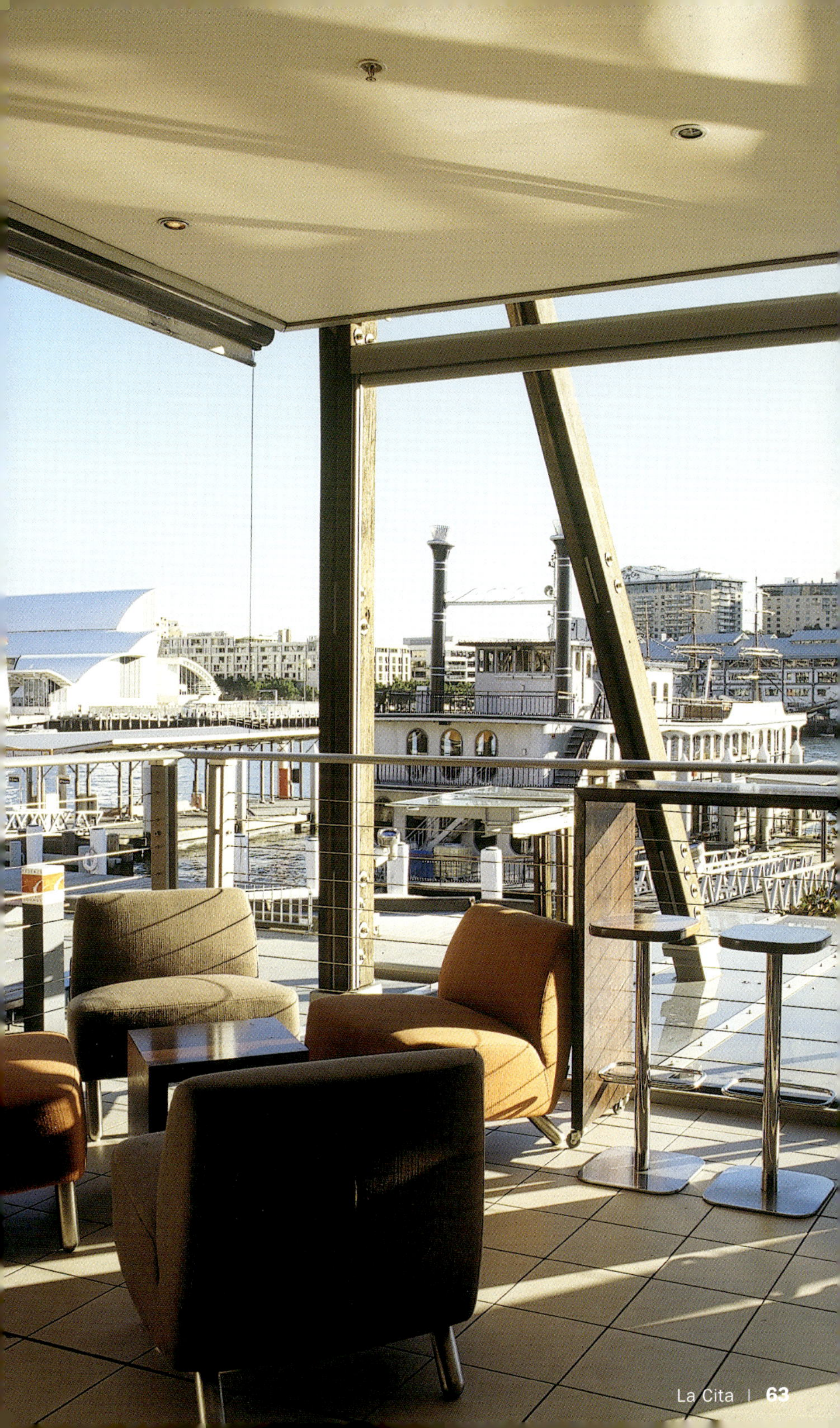

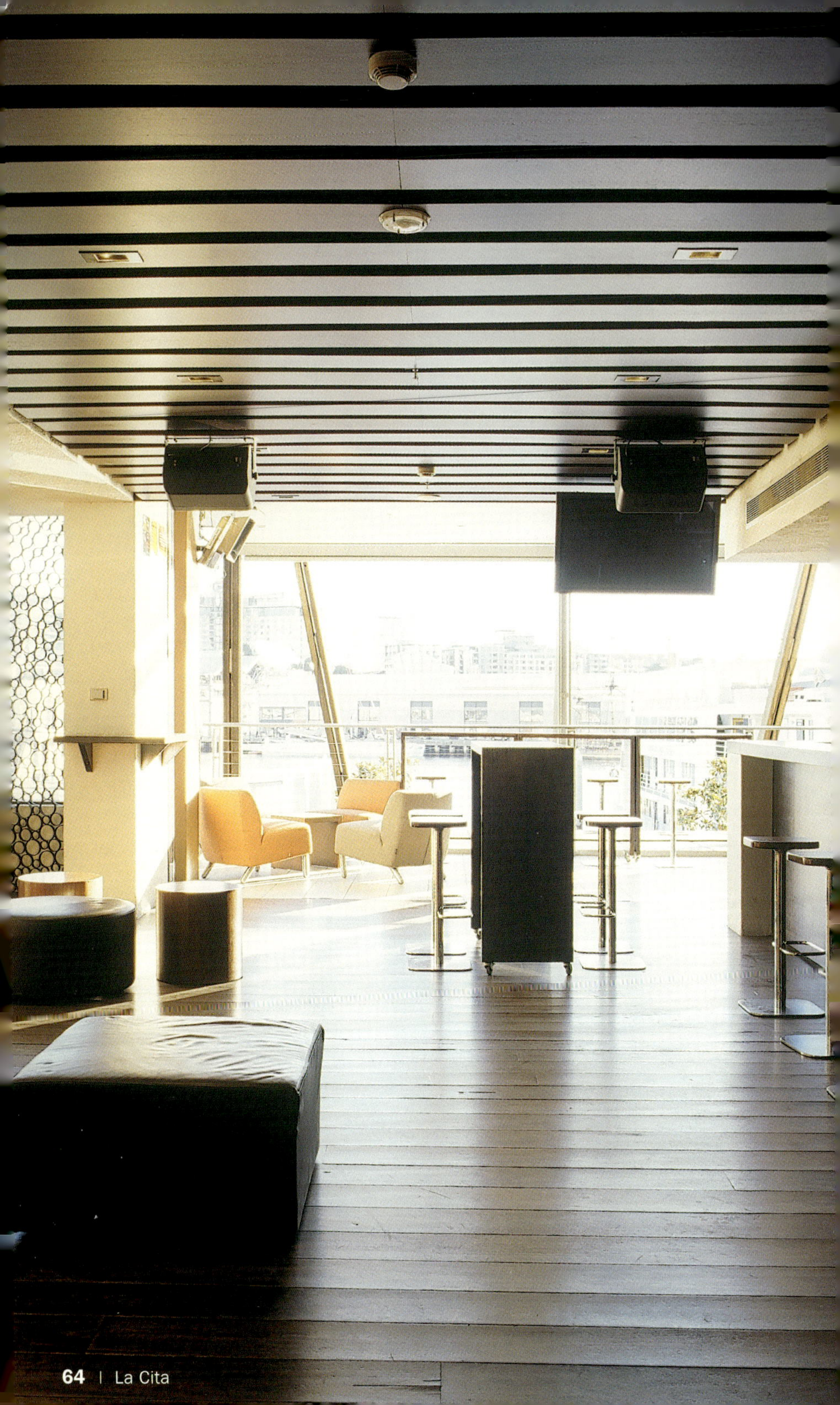

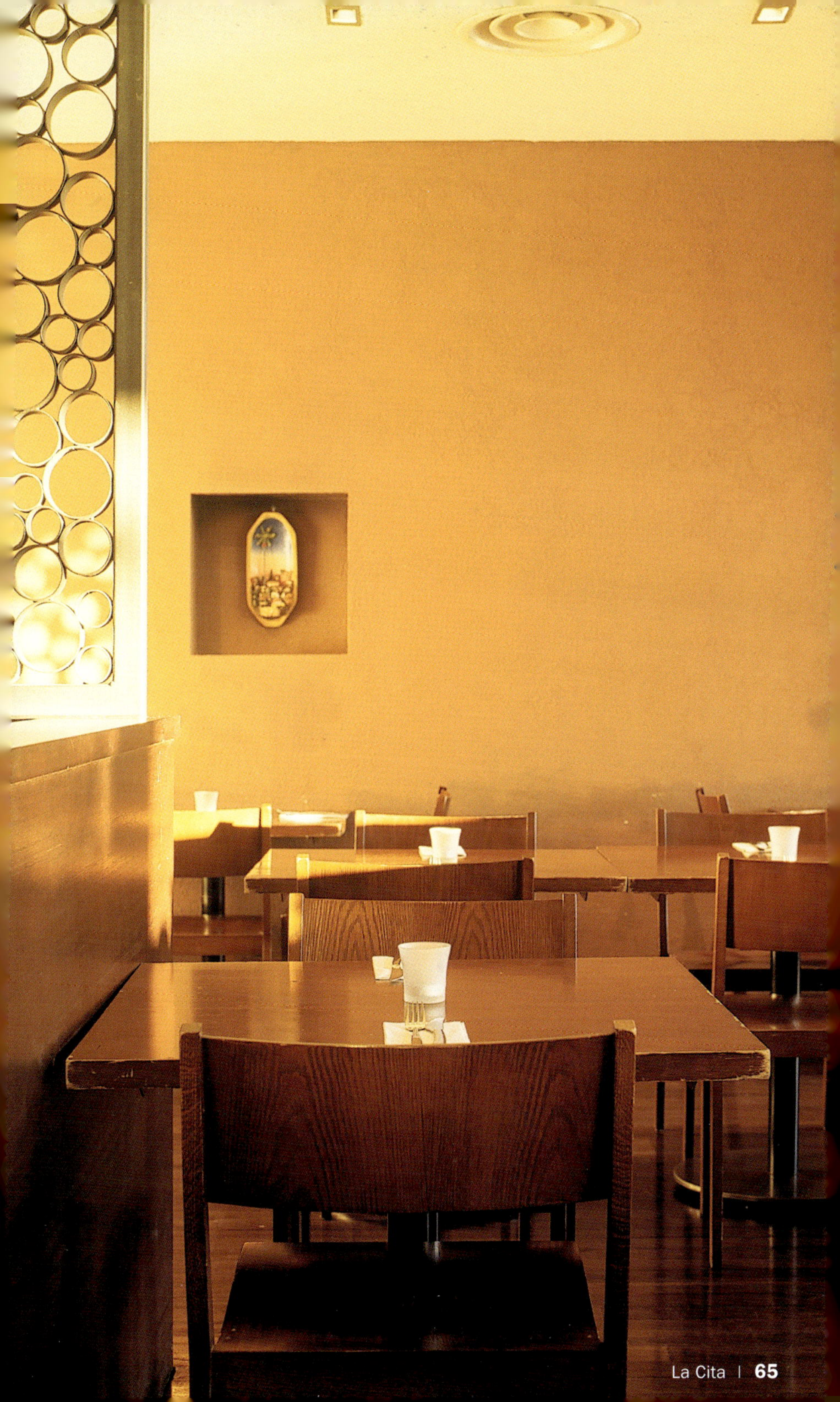

Lamb Roast

Gebratenes Lamm

Agneau rôti

Cordero asado

Agnello al forno

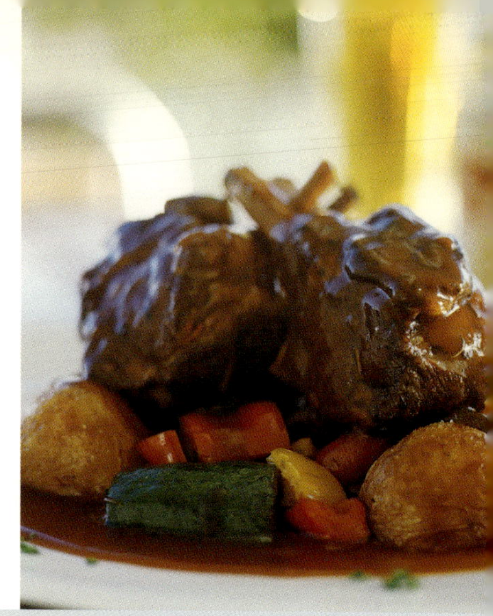

4 lamb ribs
2 garlic cloves
1/2 oz ground pepper
2/5 oz cumin
2/5 oz ground coriander
20 ml olive oil
2/5 oz fresh oregano
2 sage leaves
1 potato
1/2 red pepper
1/2 yellow pepper
1 zucchini
Salt
Pepper

Peel and crush the garlic cloves, then mix in a bowl with the ground pepper, cumin, coriander and olive oil. Season to taste with salt and mix to form a smooth paste. Allow to stand for 10 minutes, so that the aromas blend. Coat the lamb ribs with the paste and sprinkle with the oregano and sage. Marinate overnight. Peel the potato, wash the peppers and zucchini, chop them into pieces and place in an ovenproof dish. Arrange the ribs on a bed of vegetables and bake for 30 minutes.

4 Lammkarree
2 Knoblauchzehen
15 g gemahlener Pfeffer
10 g Kreuzkümmel
10 g gemahlener Koriander
20 ml Olivenöl
10 g frischer Oregano
2 Salbeiblätter
1 Kartoffel
1/2 rote Paprika
1/2 gelbe Paprika
1 Zucchini
Salz
Pfeffer

Die Knoblauchzehen schälen, zerdrücken und in einer Schüssel mit dem gemahlenen Pfeffer, Kümmel, Koriander und Olivenöl vermischen. Mit Salz abschmecken und verrühren, bis eine homogene Paste entsteht. 10 Minuten ruhen lassen, damit sich die Aromen mischen. Die Lammkarrees mit der Masse bestreichen und darüber Oregano und Salbeiblätter geben. So über Nacht marinieren. Die Kartoffel schälen, Paprika und Zucchini putzen, alles in Stücke schneiden und in eine Backform legen. Die Lammkarrees auf dem Gemüsebett verteilen und 30 Minuten backen.

4 carrés d'agneau
2 gousses d'ail
15 g de poivre en poudre
10 g de cumin
10 g de coriandre en poudre
20 ml d'huile d'olive
10 g d'origan frais
2 feuilles de sauge
1 pomme de terre
1/2 poivron rouge
1/2 poivron jaune
1 courgette
Sel
Poivre

Nettoyer et écraser les gousses d'ail et les mélanger dans une terrine avec le poivre en poudre, le cumin, la coriandre et l'huile d'olive. Saler et remuer jusqu'à obtenir une masse homogène. Laisser reposer 10 minutes afin que les arômes se mêlent. Napper les carrés d'agneau avec la préparation et ajouter l'origan et la sauge. Laisser mariner toute une nuit. Éplucher, laver et couper en morceaux la pomme de terre, les poivrons et la courgette et disposer le tout dans un plat à four ; placer les carrés sur le lit de légumes et glisser au four pendant 30 minutes.

4 costillas de cordero
2 dientes de ajo
15 g de pimienta molida
10 g de comino
10 g de cilantro molido
20 ml de aceite de oliva
10 g de orégano fresco
2 hojas de salvia
1 patata
1/2 pimiento rojo
1/2 pimiento amarillo
1 calabacín
Sal
Pimienta

Limpiar y machacar el ajo y mezclarlo en un recipiente con la pimienta molida, el comino, el cilantro y el aceite de oliva. Rectificar de sal y remover hasta conseguir una pasta homogénea. Dejar reposar durante 10 minutos para que los aromas se mezclen. Untar las costillas de cordero con el preparado y añadir el orégano y la salvia. Marinar durante toda una noche. Pelar la patata y limpiar y trocear esta, los pimientos y el calabacín, y disponerlos en una fuente de horno. Colocar las costillas sobre el lecho de verduras y hornear durante 30 minutos.

4 costine di agnello
2 spicchi d'aglio
15 g di pepe macinato
10 g di cumino
10 g di coriandolo tritato
20 ml di olio d'oliva
10 g di origano fresco
2 foglie di salvia
1 patata
1/2 peperone rosso
1/2 peperone giallo
1 zucchina
Sale
Pepe

Pulire e schiacciare gli spicchi d'aglio e in un recipiente mescolarli assieme al pepe macinato, il cumino, il coriandolo e l'olio d'oliva. Correggere di sale e mescolare fino ad ottenere una pasta omogenea. Lasciare riposare per 10 minuti in modo tale che gli aromi si mescolino tra loro. Ungere le costine d'agnello con l'impasto preparato, aggiungendo l'origano e la salvia. Far marinare per una notte intera. Pelare, pulire e tagliare a pezzi la patata, i peperoni e la zucchina e disporre il tutto in una teglia da forno; su questo letto di verdure sistemarvi le costine e cuocere in forno per 30 minuti.

Lotus Bistro

Design: Hecker Phelan Guthrie | Chef: Genevieve Copeland

22 Challis Avenue | Sydney, 2011 | Potts Point
Phone: +61 2 9326 9000
www.merivale.com/lotus/bistro
Opening hours: Tue–Sat dinner only
Average price: Starters A$ 18, main courses A$ 29
Cuisine: Home-style influences with fresh Mediterranean flavors
Special features: Funky bar hidden in the back of the bistro

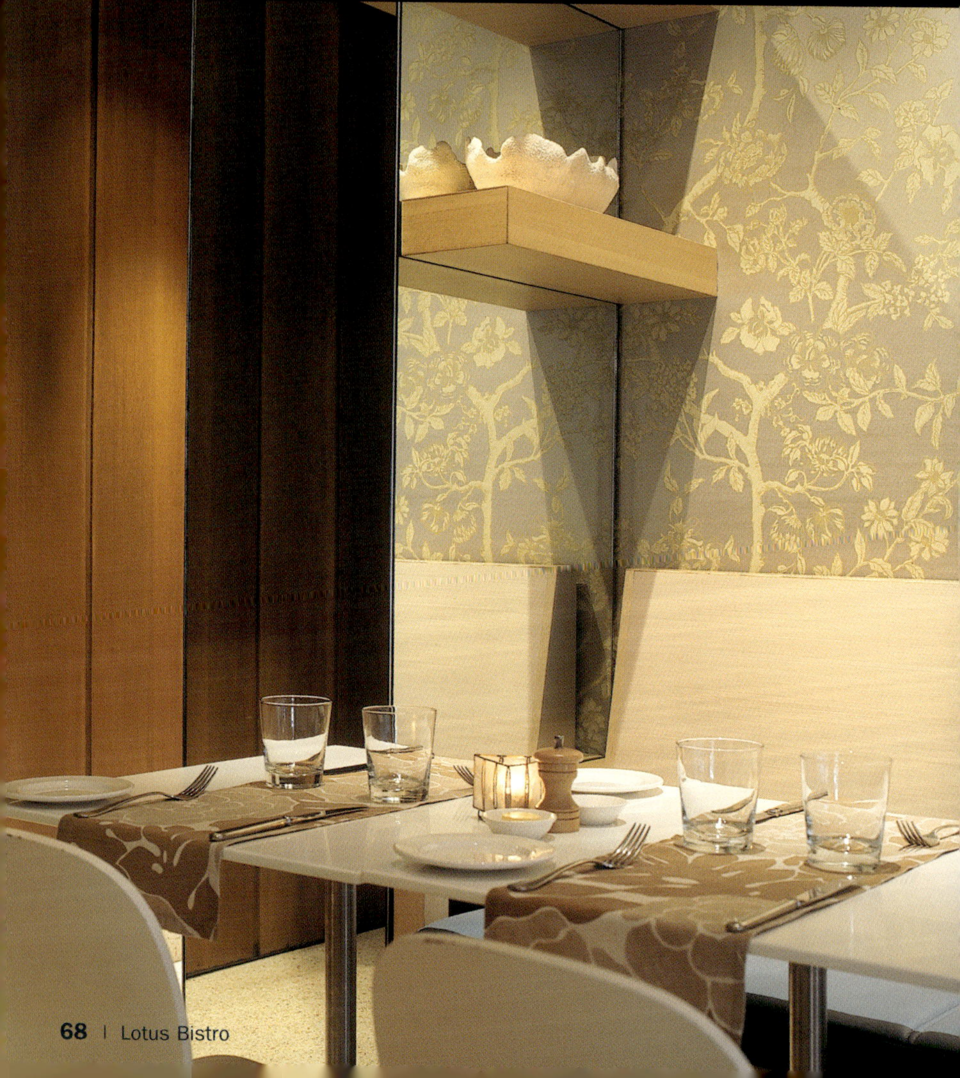

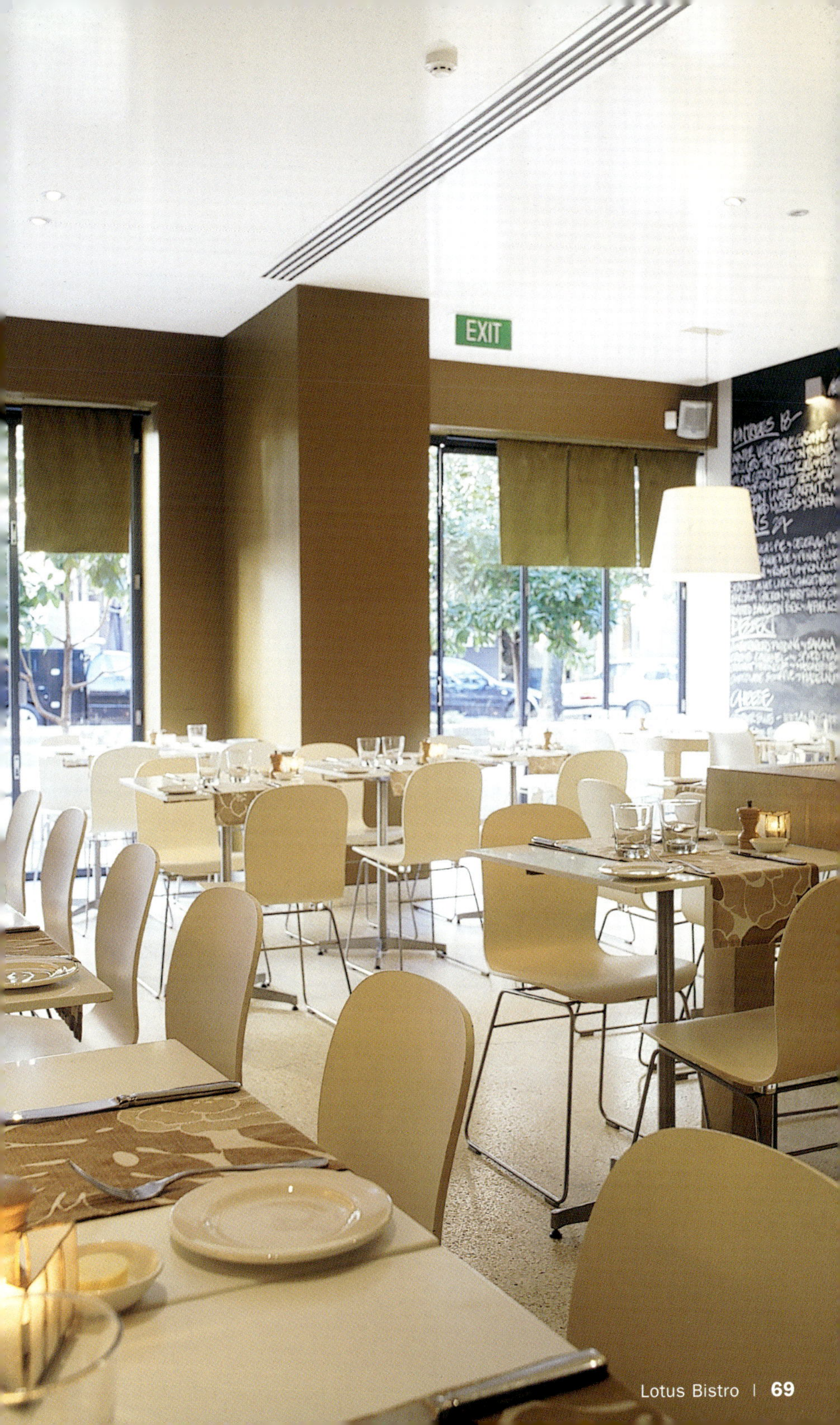

EXIT

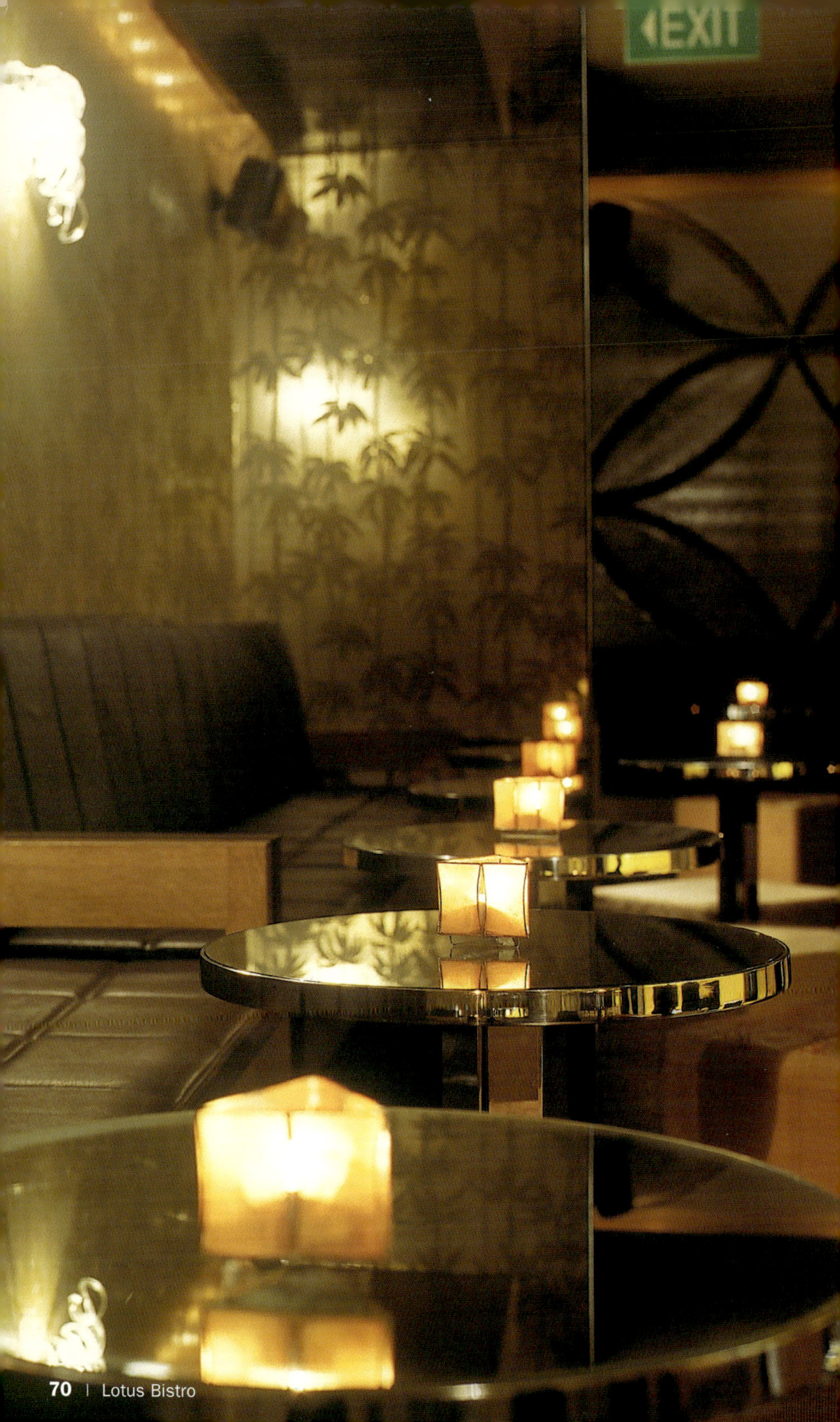
EXIT

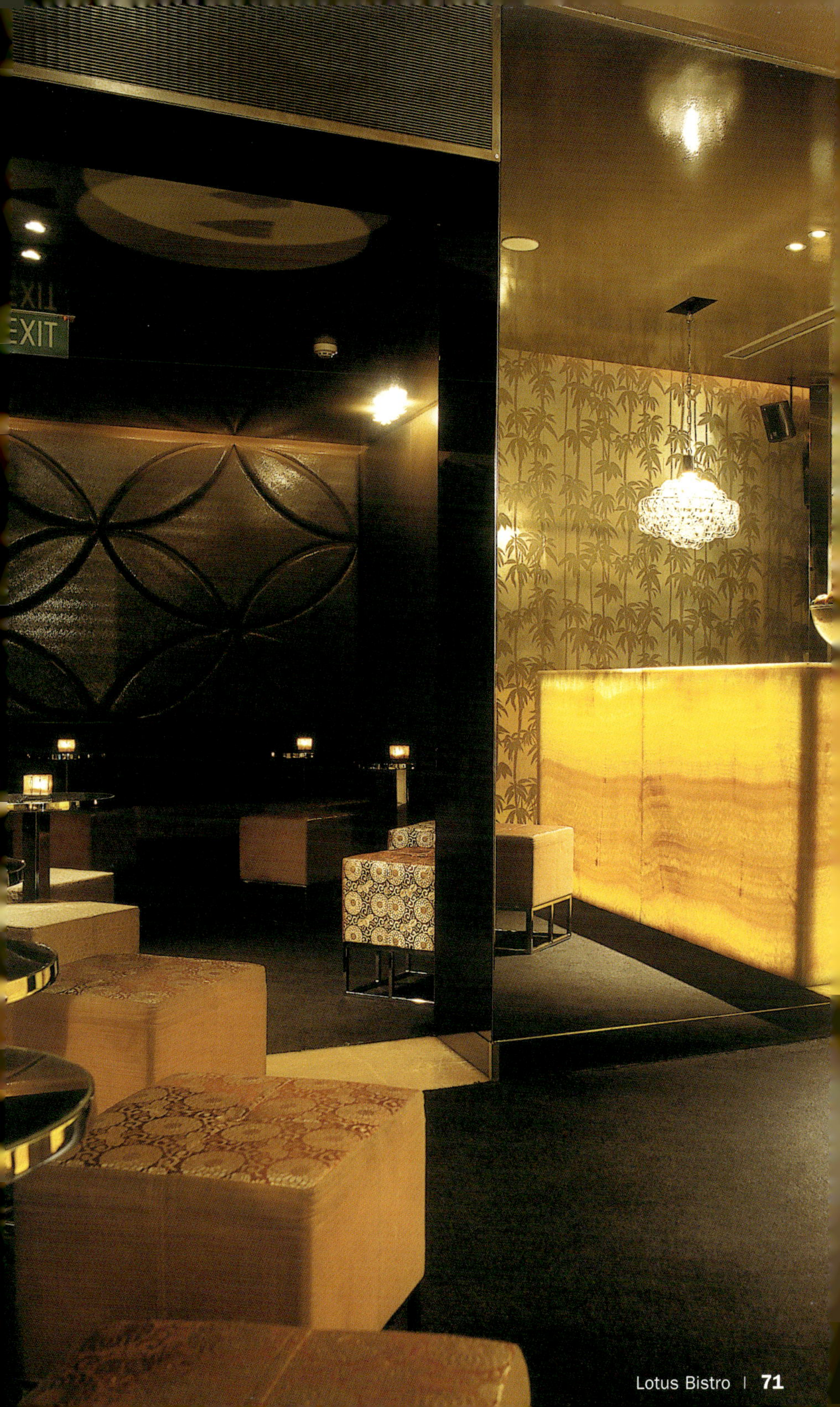

Manly Phoenix

Design: 3R Design | Chef: Bill Su and Sum Tang

Manly Wharf, Shops 22–23, East Esplanade | Sydney, 2095 | Manly
Phone: +61 2 9977 2988
www.skyphoenix.com.au
Opening hours: Every day from 9 am to 11 pm
Average price: Starters A$ 10–15, main courses A$ 10–16
Cuisine: Chinese
Special features: Yum Cha Menu with beautiful harbor view

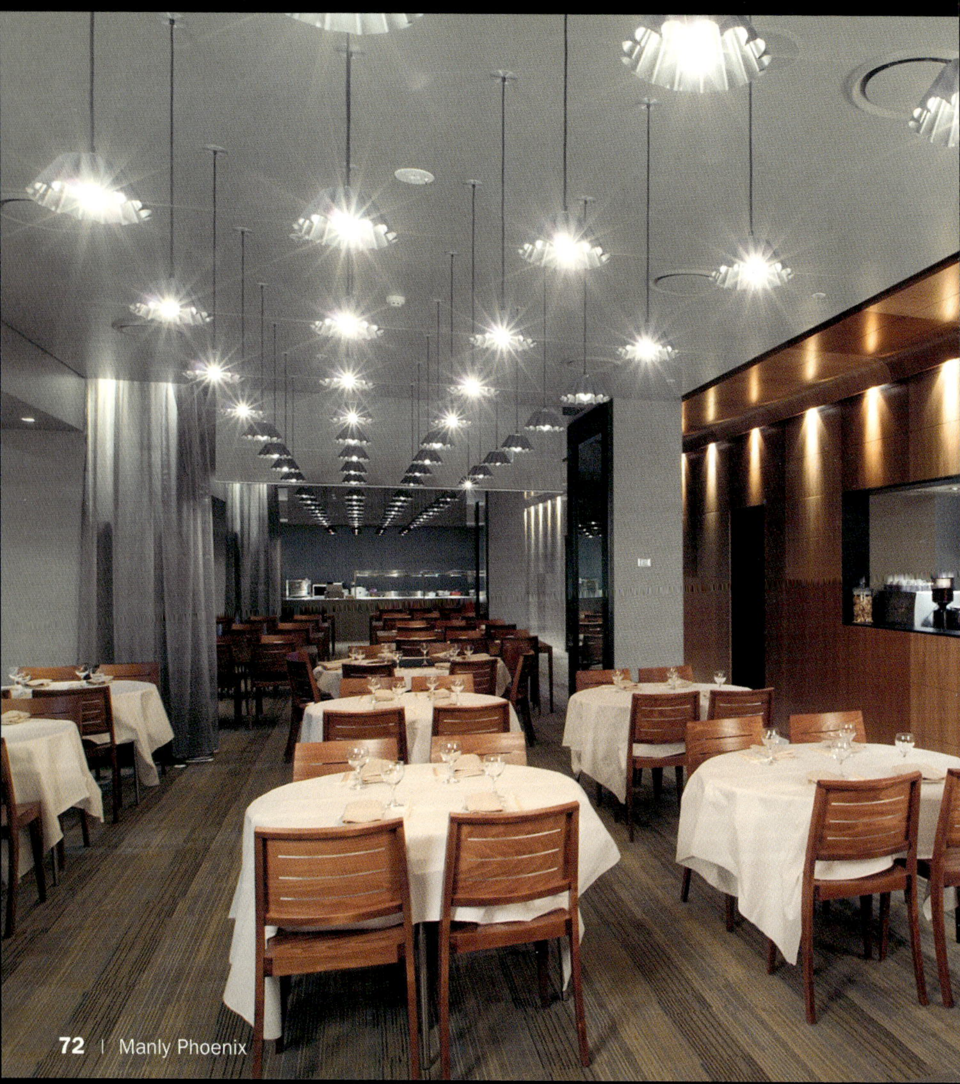

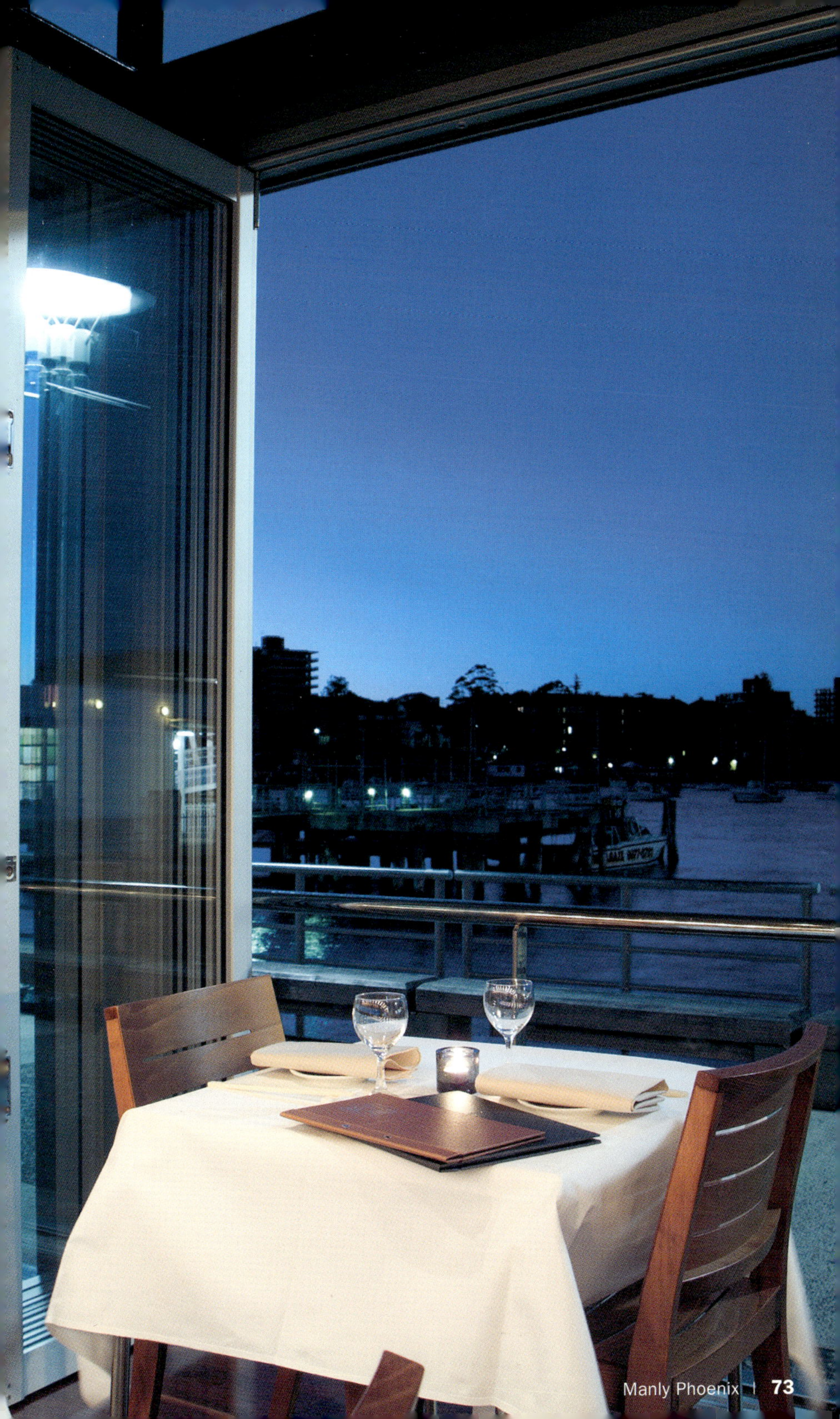

Vegetables
with Abalone Sauce

Gemüse mit Soße von Abalone-Muscheln

Légumes à la sauce aux abalones

Verduras con salsa de abulón

Verdure con salsa di aliotide

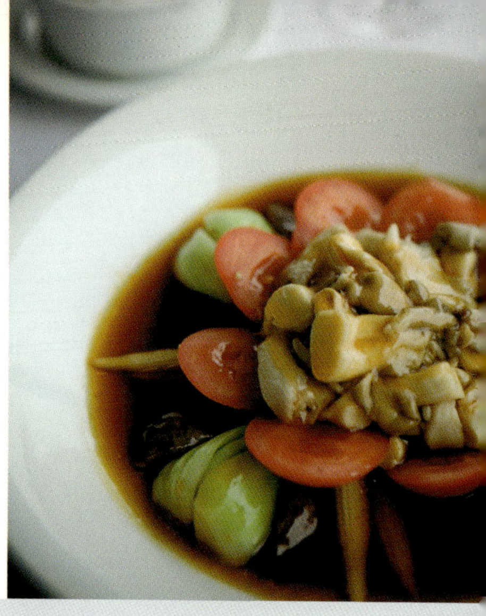

4 bok choy (a kind of Chinese cabbage)
8 corn cobs
500 ml chicken stock
3 1/2 oz shiitake mushrooms
3 1/2 oz oyster mushrooms
Olive oil
2 tomatoes
100 ml abalone juice
20 ml oyster sauce
20 ml soy sauce
7/10 oz potato starch
1/5 oz sugar
1/5 oz salt

Chop the bok choy in 4 parts lengthways. Boil for 2 minutes with the corn cobs in 450 ml chicken stock. Drain and set aside. Sauté the shiitake and oyster mushrooms. Add 50 ml chicken stock and reduce for 1 minute. Set aside. Blanch the tomatoes for 2 minutes and slice, discarding the very top and bottom. For the abalone sauce, put the abalone juice, oyster sauce, soy sauce, potato starch, sugar and salt in a frying pan and bring to a boil.
Arrange the vegetables on a dish and drench with the abalone sauce.

4 Buk Choy (chinesischer Kohl)
8 Maiskolben
500 ml Hühnerbrühe
100 g Shiitake-Pilze
100 g Austernpilze
Olivenöl
2 Tomaten
100 ml Saft von Abalone-Muscheln
20 ml Austernsoße
20 ml Sojasoße
20 g Kartoffelstärke
5 g Zucker
5 g Salz

Den Buk Choy längs in 4 Stücke schneiden. Zusammen mit den Maiskolben in 450 ml Hühnerbrühe 2 Minuten kochen. Abtropfen lassen und beiseite stellen. Shiitake- und Austernpilze andünsten. 50 ml Hühnerbrühe angießen und 1 Minute lang reduzieren. Beiseite stellen. Die Tomaten 2 Minuten lang abbrühen und in Scheiben schneiden, wobei die oberste und unterste Scheibe weggelassen werden. Für die Abalone-Soße in einer Pfanne den Abalone-Saft, die Austernsoße, die Sojasoße, die Kartoffelstärke, den Zucker und das Salz aufkochen.
Das Gemüse auf einem Teller anrichten und mit der Abalone-Soße begießen.

4 buk choy (chou chinois)
8 épis de maïs
500 ml de bouillon de poulet
100 g de champignons shiitake
100 g de pleurotes (en forme d'huître)
Huile d'olive
2 tomates
100 ml de jus d'abalones
20 ml de sauce aux huîtres
20 ml de sauce soja
20 g de fécule de pomme de terre
5 g de sucre
5 g de sel

Couper le buk choy en 4 dans la longueur. Faire cuire avec les épis de maïs dans 450 ml de bouillon de poulet pendant 2 minutes. Égoutter et réserver. Faire revenir les champignons shiitaké et les pleurotes (en forme d'huître). Ajouter 50 ml de bouillon de poulet et faire réduire 1 minute. Réserver. Ébouillanter les tomates pendant 2 minutes et les couper en rondelles en ôtant la partie supérieure et la partie inférieure. Pour la sauce aux abalones, mélanger dans une poêle le jus d'abalones, la sauce aux huîtres, la sauce soja, la fécule de pomme de terre, le sucre et le sel, porter à ébullition.
Disposer les légumes sur un plat et arroser avec la sauce aux abalones.

4 buk choy (tipo de col china)
8 mazorcas de maíz
500 ml de caldo de pollo
100 g de setas shiitake
100 g de setas ostra
Aceite de oliva
2 tomates
100 ml de jugo de abulón
20 ml de salsa de ostras
20 ml de salsa de soja
20 g de fécula de patata
5 g de azúcar
5 g de sal

Cortar el buk choy en 4 partes a lo largo. Cocer junto con las mazorcas en 450 ml de caldo de pollo durante 2 minutos. Escurrir y reservar. Rehogar las setas shiitake y las setas ostra. Añadir 50 ml de caldo de pollo y reducir durante 1 minuto. Reservar. Escaldar los tomates durante 2 minutos y cortar en rodajas descartando las rodajas superior e inferior. Para la salsa de abulón, mezclar en una sartén el jugo de abulón, la salsa de ostras, la salsa de soja, la fécula de patata, el azúcar y la sal, y llevar a ebullición.
Disponer las verduras en un plato y regar con la salsa de abulón.

4 buk choy (tipo di cavolo cinese)
8 pannocchie di mais
500 ml di brodo di pollo
100 g di funghi shiitake
100 g di geloni
Olio d'oliva
2 pomodori
100 ml di succo di aliotide
20 ml di salsa di ostriche
20 ml di salsa di soia
20 g di fecola di patate
5 g di zucchero
5 g di sale

Tagliare il buk choy in 4 parti per lungo. Far cuocere assieme alle pannocchie in 450 ml di brodo di pollo per 2 minuti. Colare e mettere da parte. Rosolare i funghi shiitake e i geloni. Aggiungere 50 ml di brodo di pollo e ridurre per 1 minuto. Mettere da parte. Scottare i pomodori per 2 minuti e tagliarli a rondelle scartando quella superiore ed inferiore. Per preparare la salsa di aliotide, in una padella mescolare il succo di aliotide, la salsa di ostriche, la salsa di soia, la fecola di patate, lo zucchero, il sale e portare ad ebollizione.
Disporre le verdure in un piatto e cospargere con la salsa di aliotide.

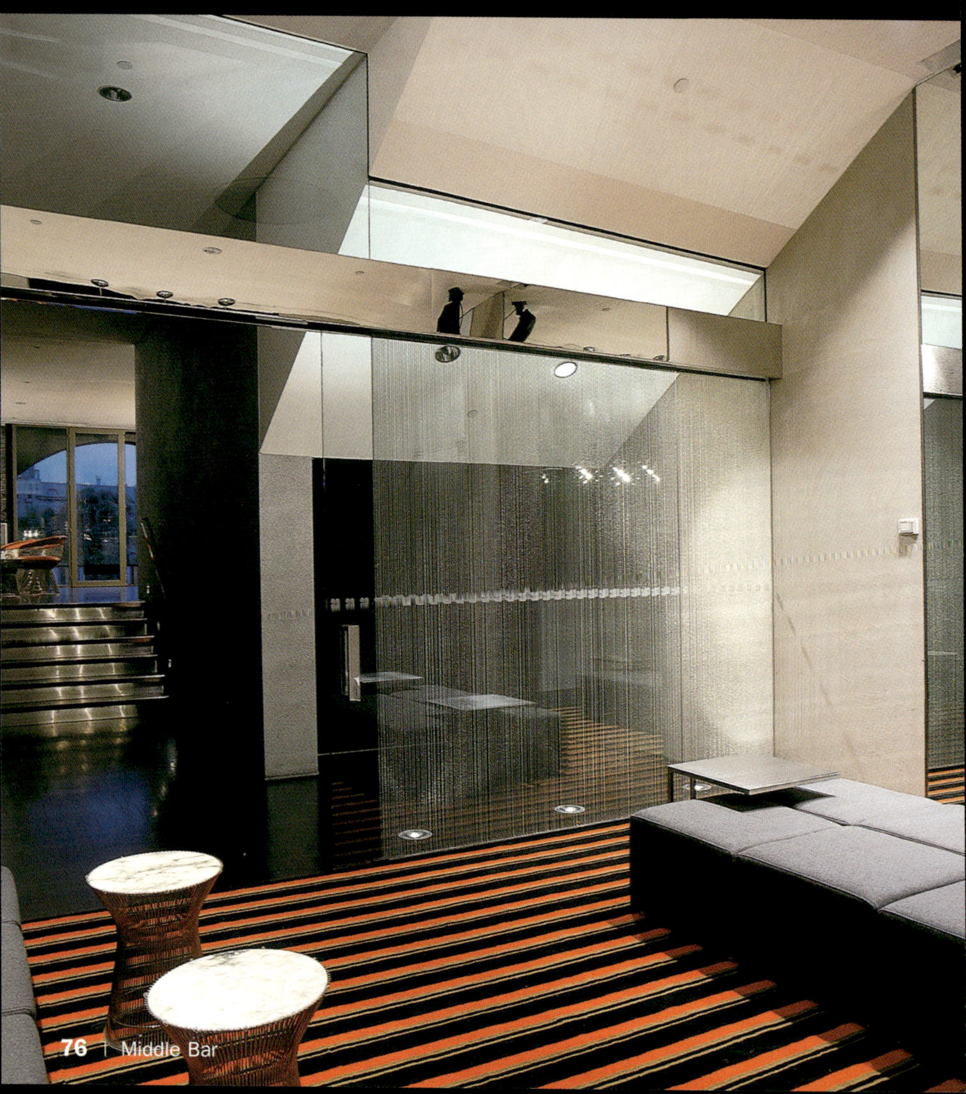

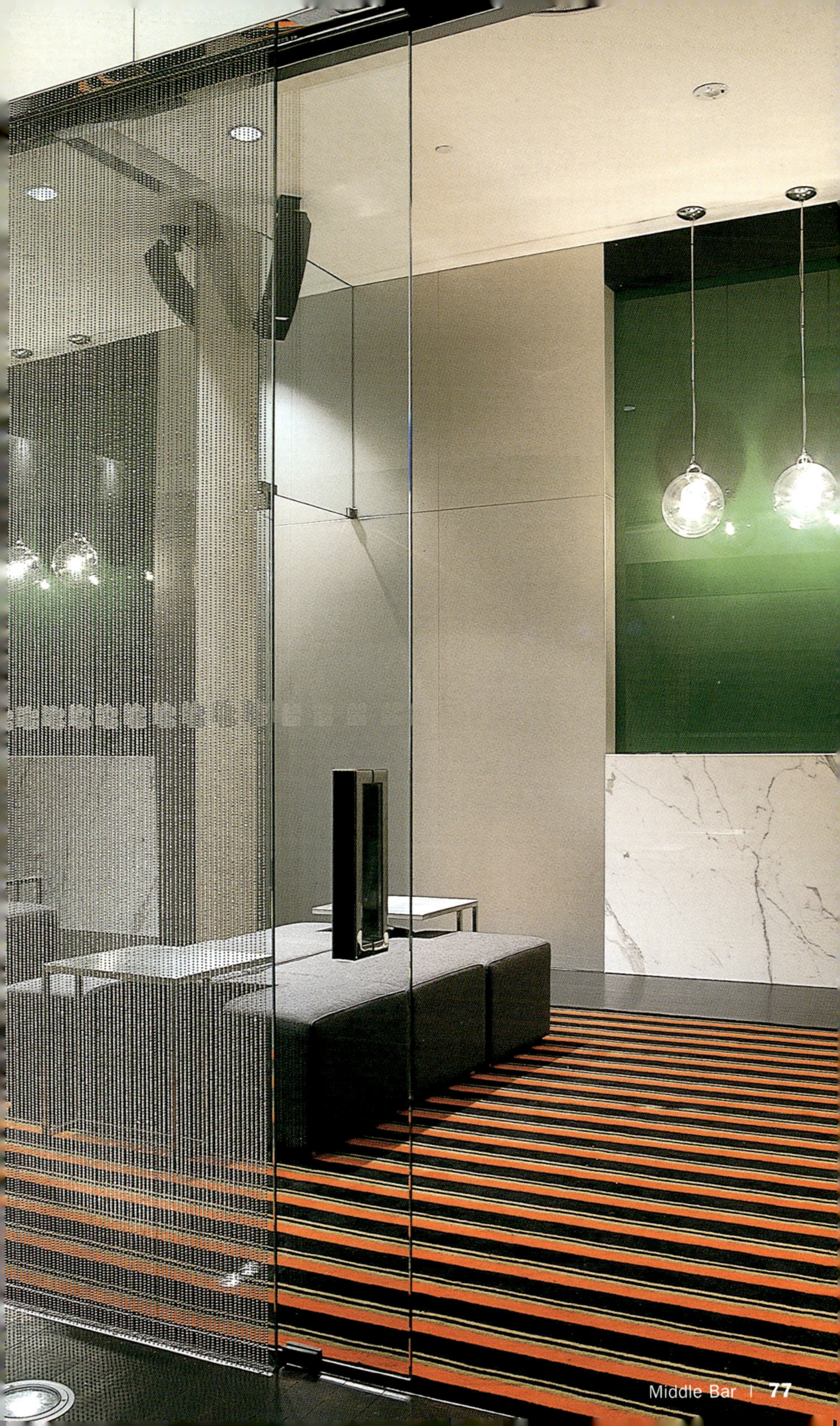

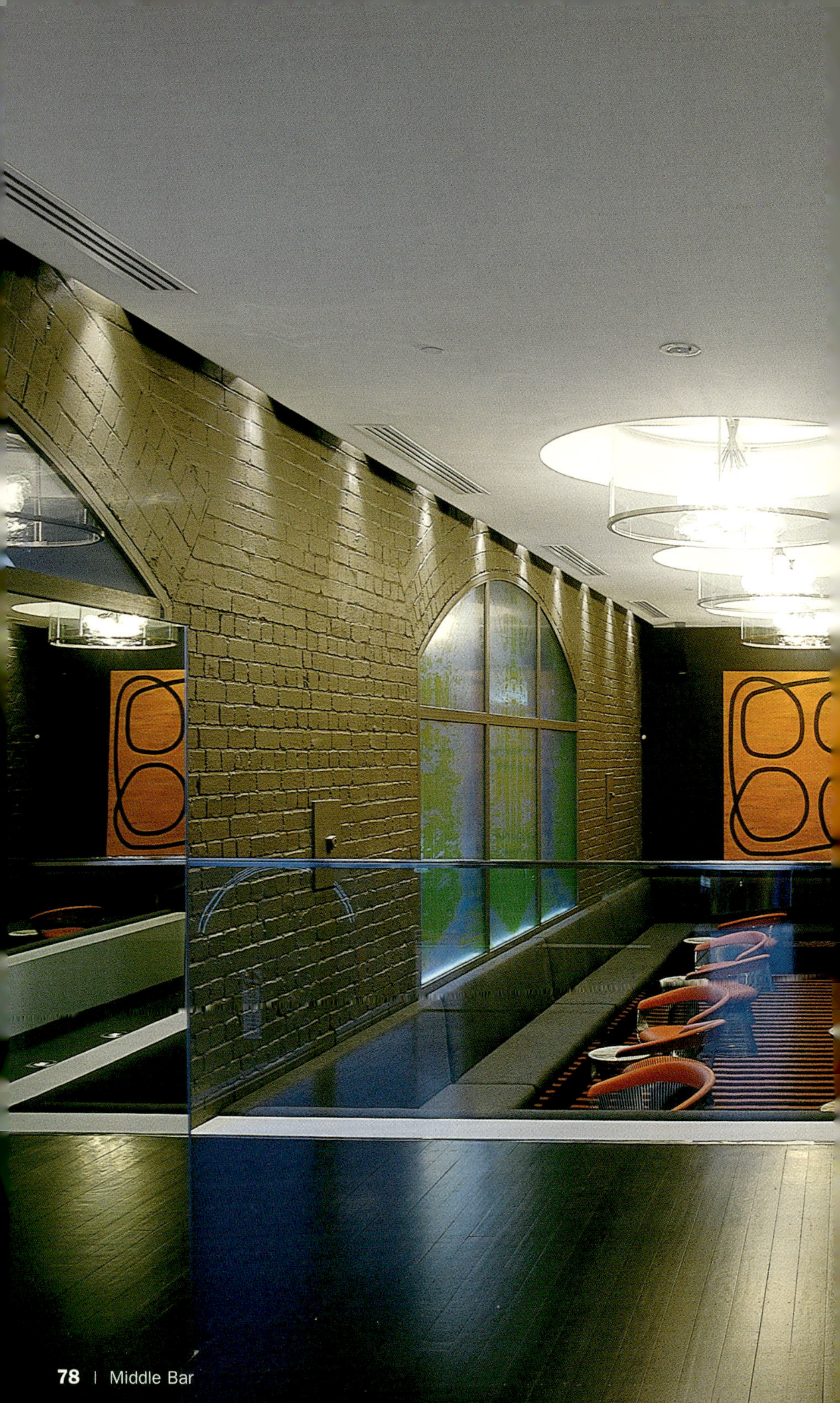

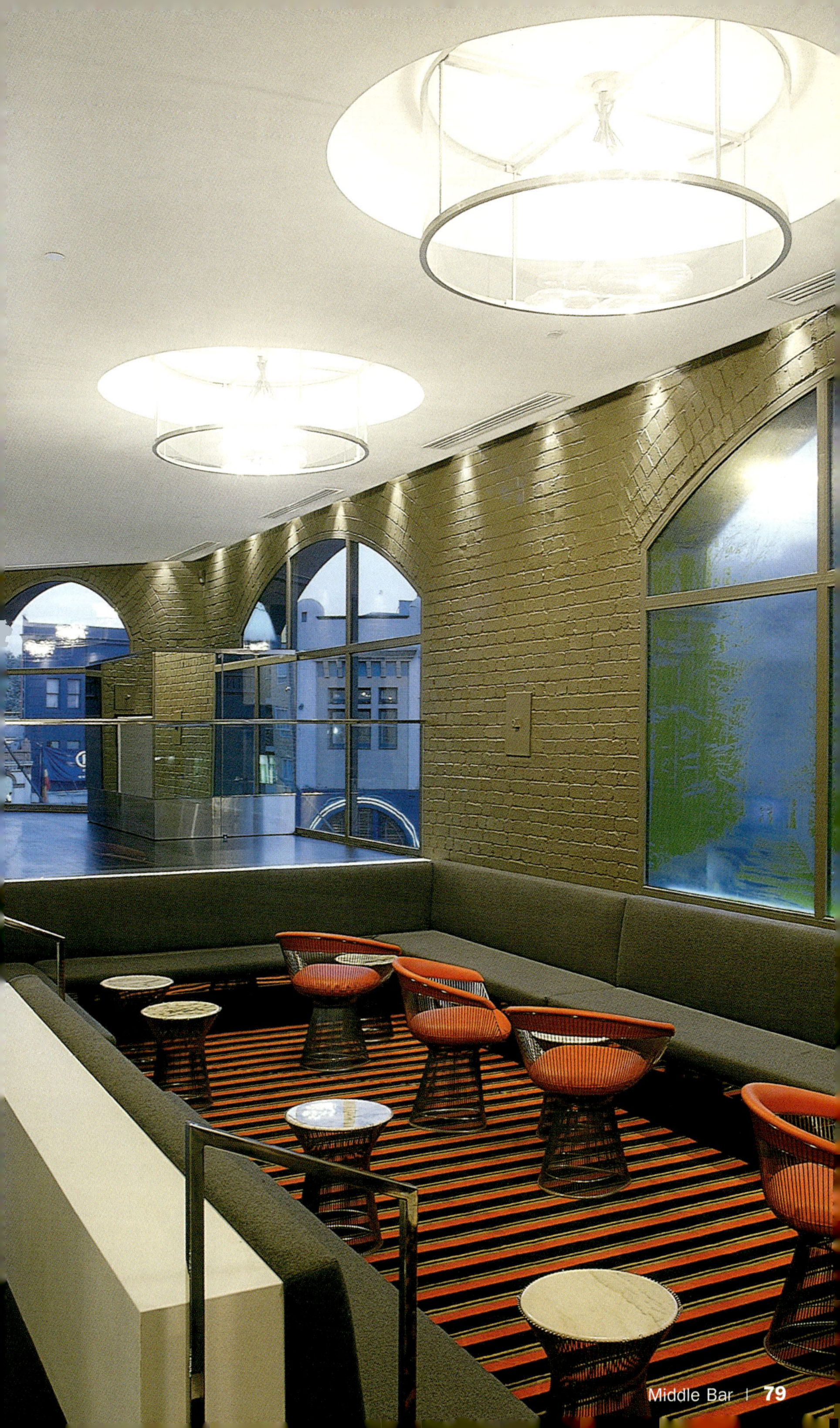

MINC Level Three

Design: John Harrs | Chef: Andrew Caroll

The Blacket Hotel, 70 King Street | Sydney, 2000
Phone : +61 2 9279 3030
www.theblacket.com/mincrest.htm
Opening hours: Tue–Fri lunch from noon to 3 pm; Tue–Sat dinner from 6 pm
to 10:30 pm
Average price: Starters A$ 12–20, main courses A$ 18–25, desserts A$ 10
Cuisine: Creative, modern cuisine of the finest quality
Special features: Extensive wine list and an emphasis on service

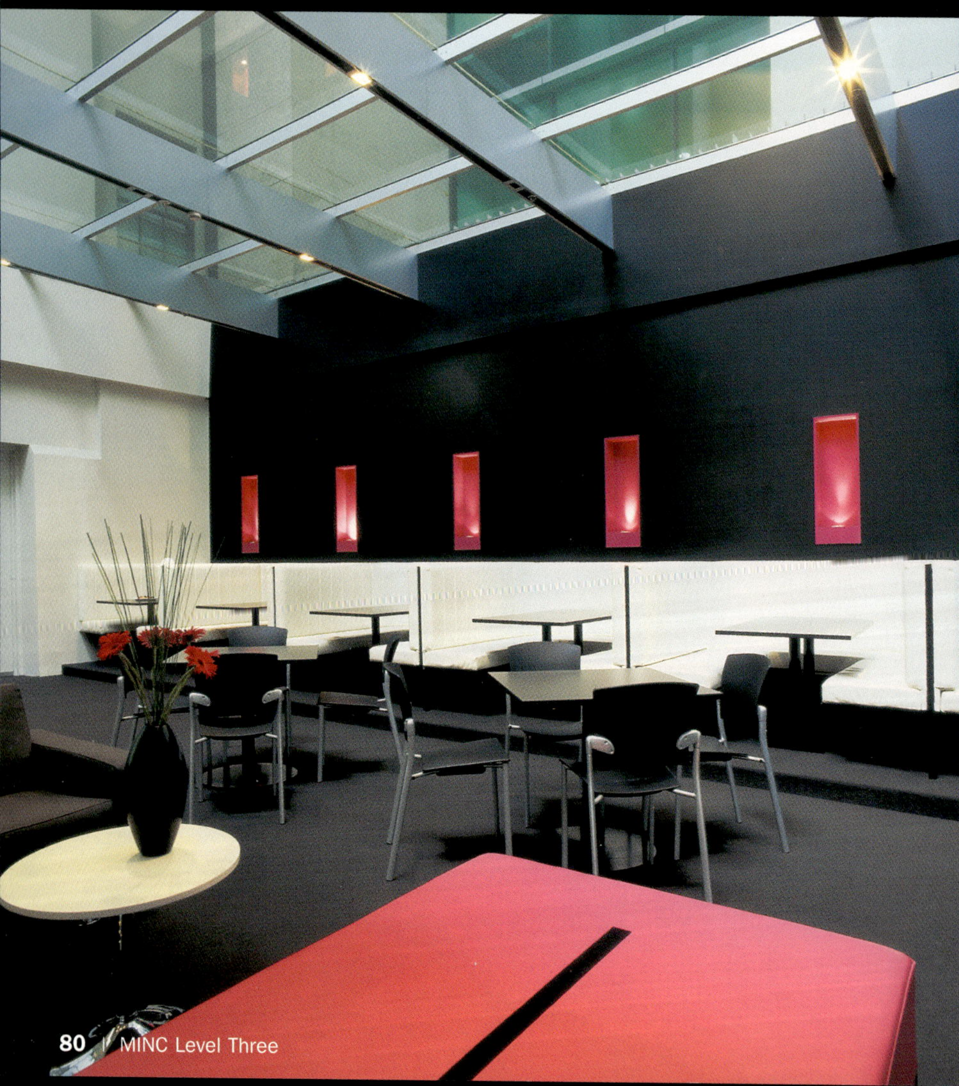

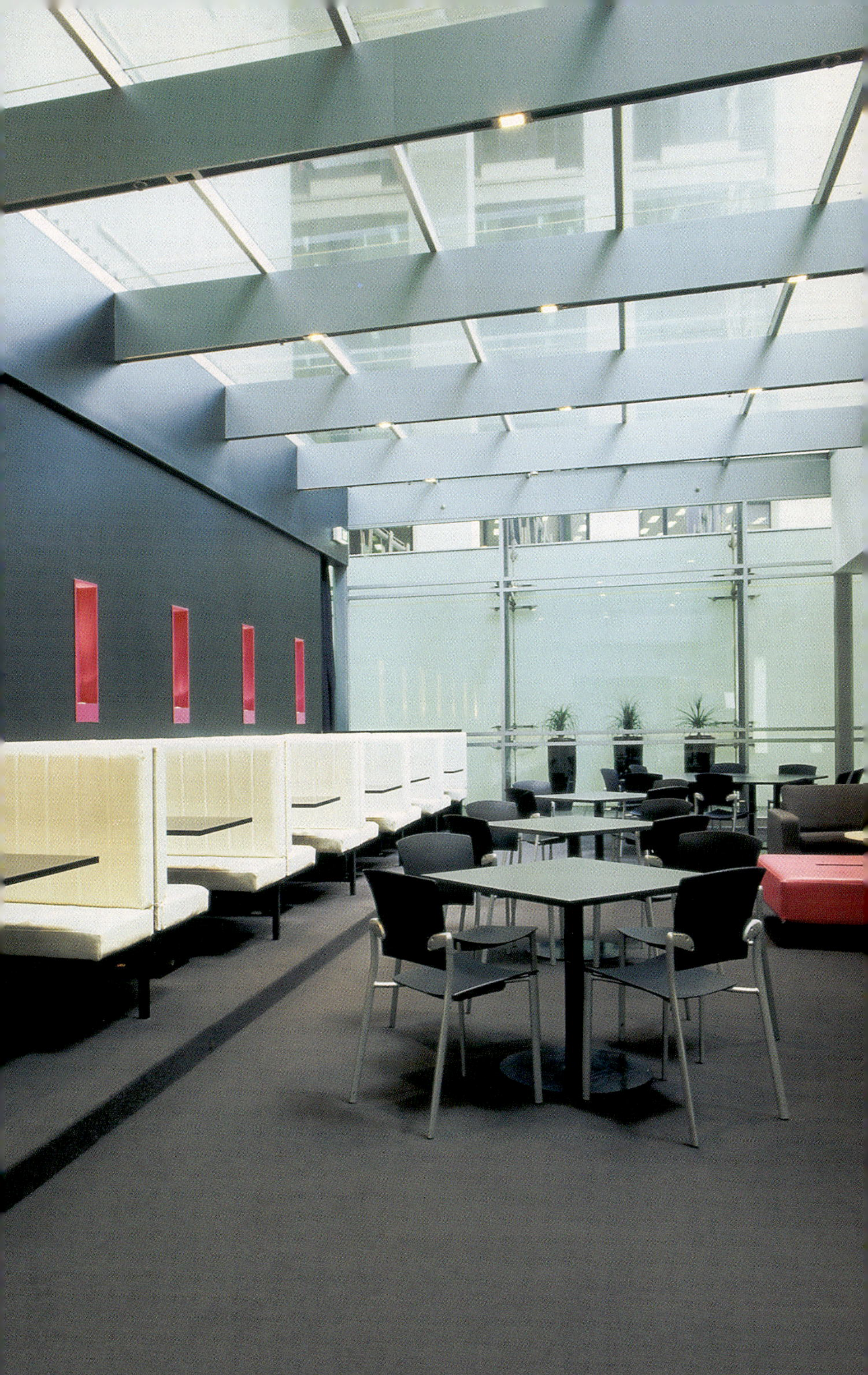

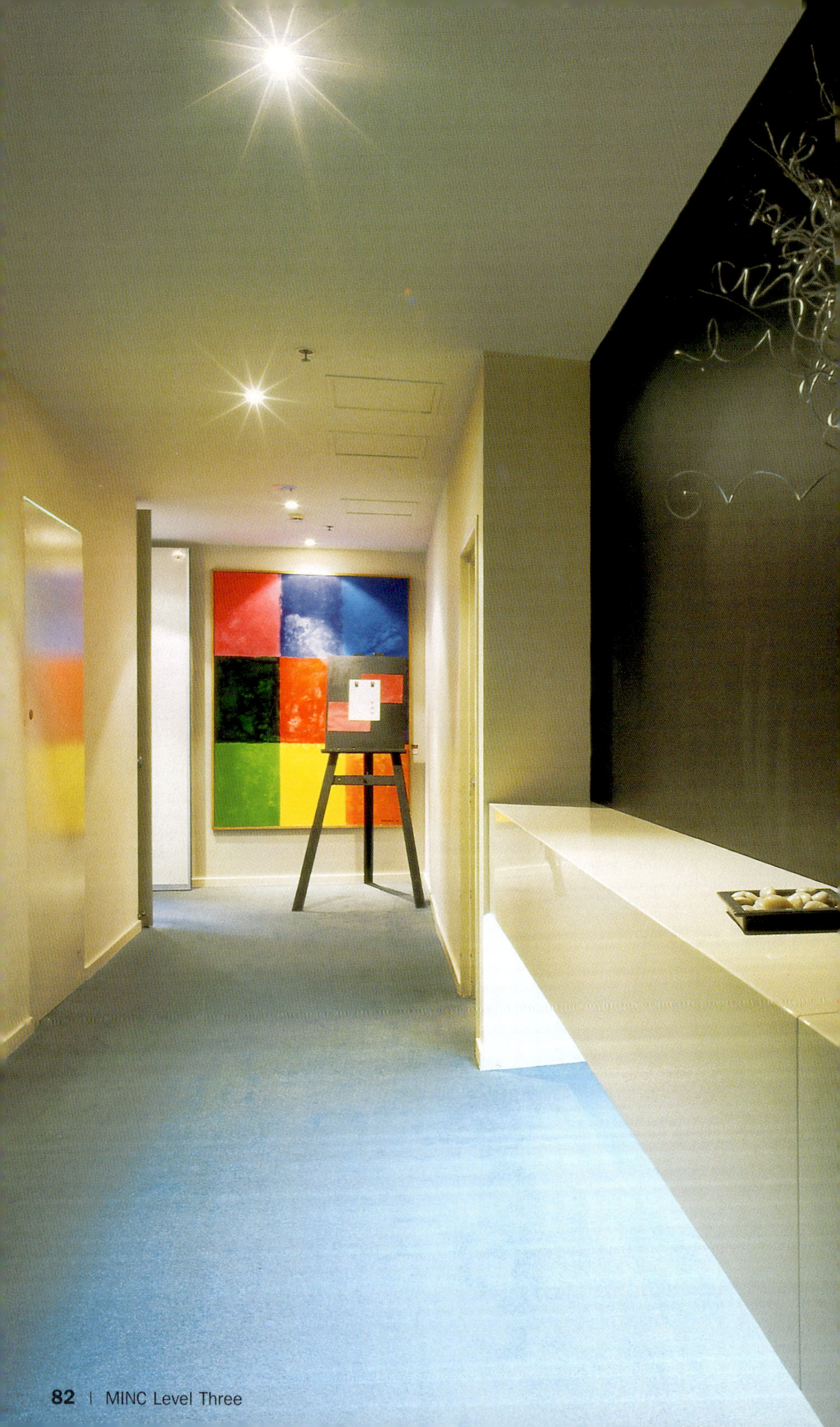

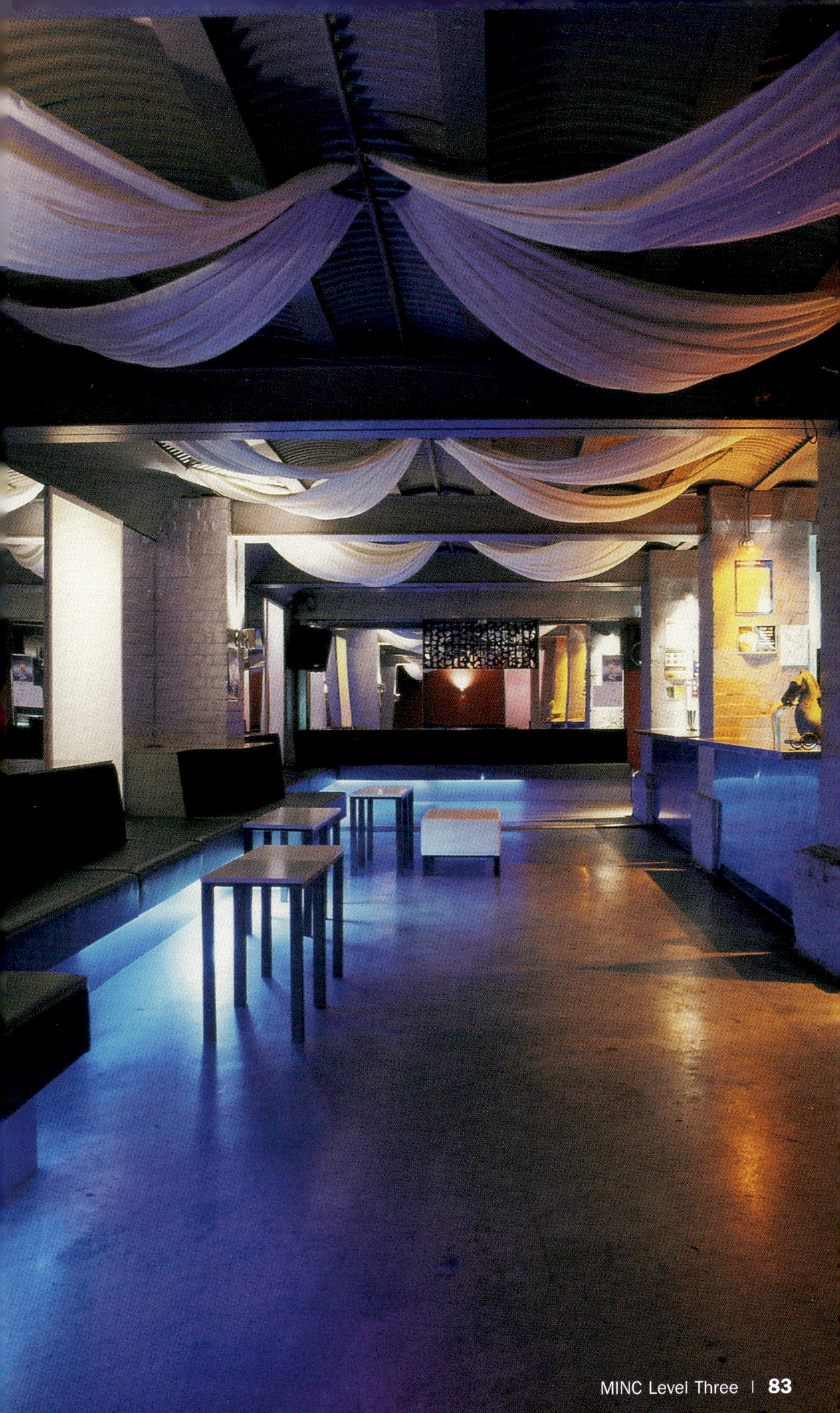

oh! Calcutta

Design: Burley Katon Halliday | Chef: Basil Daniell

251 Victoria Street | Sydney, 2010 | Darlinghurst
Phone: +61 2 9360 3650
www.ohcalcutta.com.au
Opening hours: Mon–Sat dinner from 6 pm to midnight
Average price: Starters A$ 9–14, main courses A$ 17–28, desserts A$ 9–13
Cuisine: Modern Indian
Special features: Balcony seating. Awarded "Best Indian Restaurant" 1995–2005

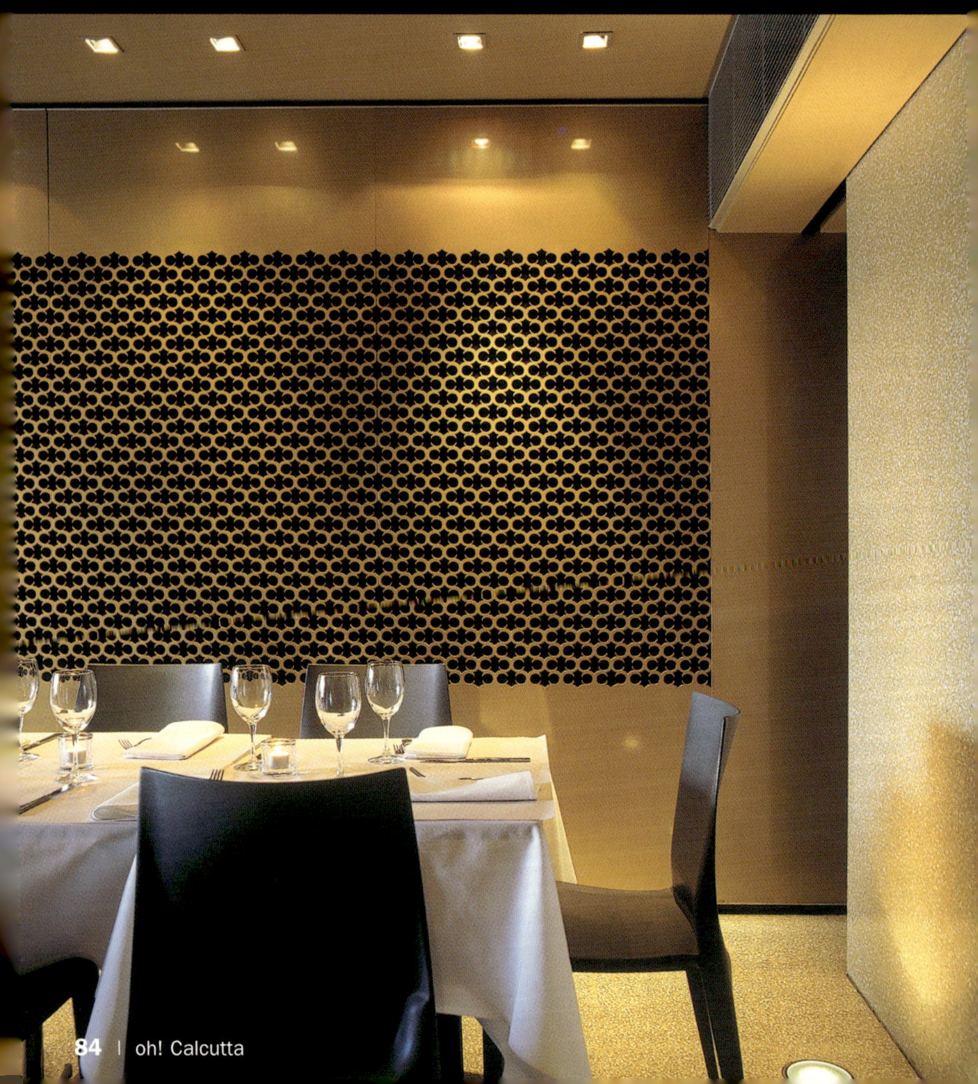

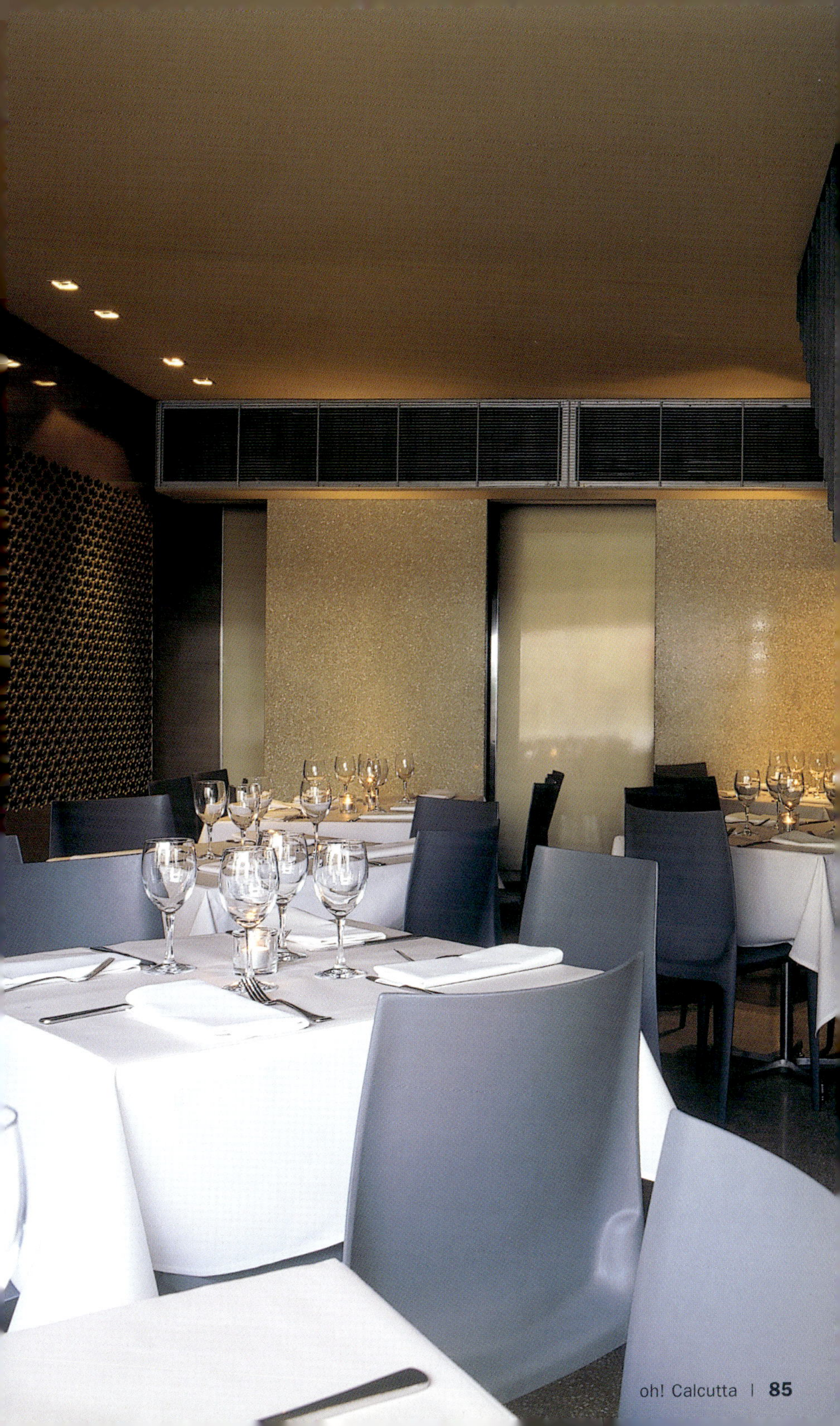

Quail Breast

with Pomegranate, Chicory, Red Pepper and Bulgur Salad

Wachtelbrüstchen mit Granatapfel, Chicorée,
Salat von roter Paprika und Bulgur

Blancs de caille avec grenade, endive,
salade de poivrons rouges et boulgour

Pechugas de codorniz con granada, endibia
y ensalada dc pimienta roja y bulgur

Petti di quaglia con granata, indivia e
insalata al pepe rosso e bulgur

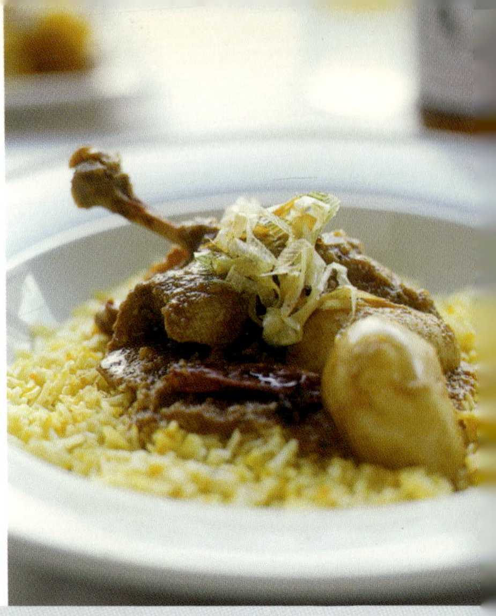

4 quail breasts
7 oz bulgur
7/10 oz pomegranate concentrate
1 2/5 oz yogurt
2/5 oz butter
1 chicory
30 ml grape juice
2/5 oz red peppercorns
Olive oil
Salt
Pepper

Braise the bulgur for 2 hours. Strain and set aside. In a bowl, mix the pomegranate concentrate and yogurt, and marinate the quail in it for 2 hours. Strain the quail and add salt and pepper. Heat a drizzle of oil and butter in a non-stick frying pan and sauté the quail for 6 minutes. Set aside. For the salad, dress the chicory with olive oil, grape juice, red peppercorns and salt.
On a platter, arrange a bed of bulgur and place the quail breasts on top. Sprinkle with cracked peppercorns and serve with the salad.

1 Wachtelbrüstchen
200 g Bulgur
20 g Granatapfelkonzentrat
40 g Joghurt
10 g Butter
1 Chicorée
30 ml Traubensaft
10 g rote Pfefferkörner
Olivenöl
Salz
Pfeffer

Den Bulgur 2 Stunden lang garen. Abseihen und beiseite stellen. In einem Gefäß das Granatapfelkonzentrat mit Joghurt mischen, die Wachteln darin 2 Stunden marinieren. Die Wachteln abtropfen lassen, salzen und pfeffern. Einen Schuss Öl und die Butter in einer beschichteten Pfanne erhitzen und darin die Wachteln 6 Minuten anbraten. Beiseite stellen. Für den Salat den Chicorée mit Olivenöl, Traubensaft und einigen roten Pfefferkörnern und Salz anmachen.
In einer Schale ein Bett aus dem Bulgur vorbereiten und die Wachteln daraufsetzen. Mit den zerdrückten Pfefferkörnern bestreuen und mit dem Salat reichen.

4 blancs de caille
200 g de boulgour
20 g de concentré de grenade
40 g de yaourt
10 g de beurre
1 endive
30 ml de jus de raisin
10 g de poivre rouge en grains
Huile d'olive
Sel
Poivre

Faire bouillir le boulgour pendant 2 heures. Égoutter et réserver. Dans un bol, mélanger le concentré de grenade et le yaourt et mettre les cailles à mariner dans le mélange pendant 2 heures. Égoutter les cailles, saler, poivrer. Chauffer un peu d'huile et le beurre dans une poêle antiadhésive et faire frire les cailles pendant 6 minutes. Réserver. Pour la salade, assaisonner les endives avec l'huile d'olive, le jus de raisin et quelques grains de poivre rouge. Saler.
Dans un plat, préparer un lit de boulgour et dresser les blancs de caille. Saupoudrer de poivre en grains et accompagner avec la salade.

4 pechugas de codorniz
200 g de bulgur
20 g de concentrado de granada
40 g de yogur
10 g de mantequilla
1 endibia
30 ml de zumo de uva
10 g de pimienta roja en grano
Aceite de oliva
Sal
Pimienta

Hervir el bulgur durante 2 horas. Colar y reservar. En un recipiente, mezclar el concentrado de granada y el yogur y marinar las codornices en la mezcla durante 2 horas. Escurrir las codornices y salpimentar. Calentar un chorro de aceite y la mantequilla en una sartén antiadherente y freír las codornices durante 6 minutos. Reservar. Para la ensalada, aliñar las endibias con aceite de oliva, el zumo de uva y unos granos de pimienta roja. Salar.
En una fuente, preparar un lecho de bulgur y colocar encima las pechugas de codorniz. Espolvorear con la pimienta en grano machacada y acompañar con la ensalada.

4 petti di quaglia
200 g di bulgur
20 g di concentrato di granata
40 g di yogurt
10 g di burro
1 indivia
30 ml di succo d'uva
10 g di pepe rosso in grani
Olio d'oliva
Sale
Pepe

Far cuocere il bulgur per 2 ore. Colare e mettere da parte. In un recipiente, mescolare il concentrato di granata e lo yogurt e lasciare marinare le quaglie nel composto ottenuto per 2 ore. Colare le quaglie e condire con sale e pepe. In una padella antiaderente riscaldare un filo d'olio e il burro e friggere le quaglie per 6 minuti. Mettere da parte. Per l'insalata, condire le indivie con olio d'oliva, il succo d'uva e dei grani di pepe rosso. Salare.
In un piatto di portata preparare un letto di bulgur e sopra sistemarvi i petti di quaglie. Spolverizzare con alcuni grani schiacciati di pepe rosso e accompagnare con l'insalata.

Olio

Design: 3R Design | Chef: Nicholas Aspros

201–205 Pacific Highway, Shop 1 | Sydney, 2065 | St. Leonards Station
Phone: +61 2 9439 8988
www.olio.com.au
Opening hours: Mon from 7 am to 6 pm, Tue–Fri from 7 am to 9 pm
Average price: Starters A\$ 6–20, main courses A\$ 15–25
Cuisine: Modern Mediterranean
Special features: Breakfast menu specialties of bruschettas and muffins

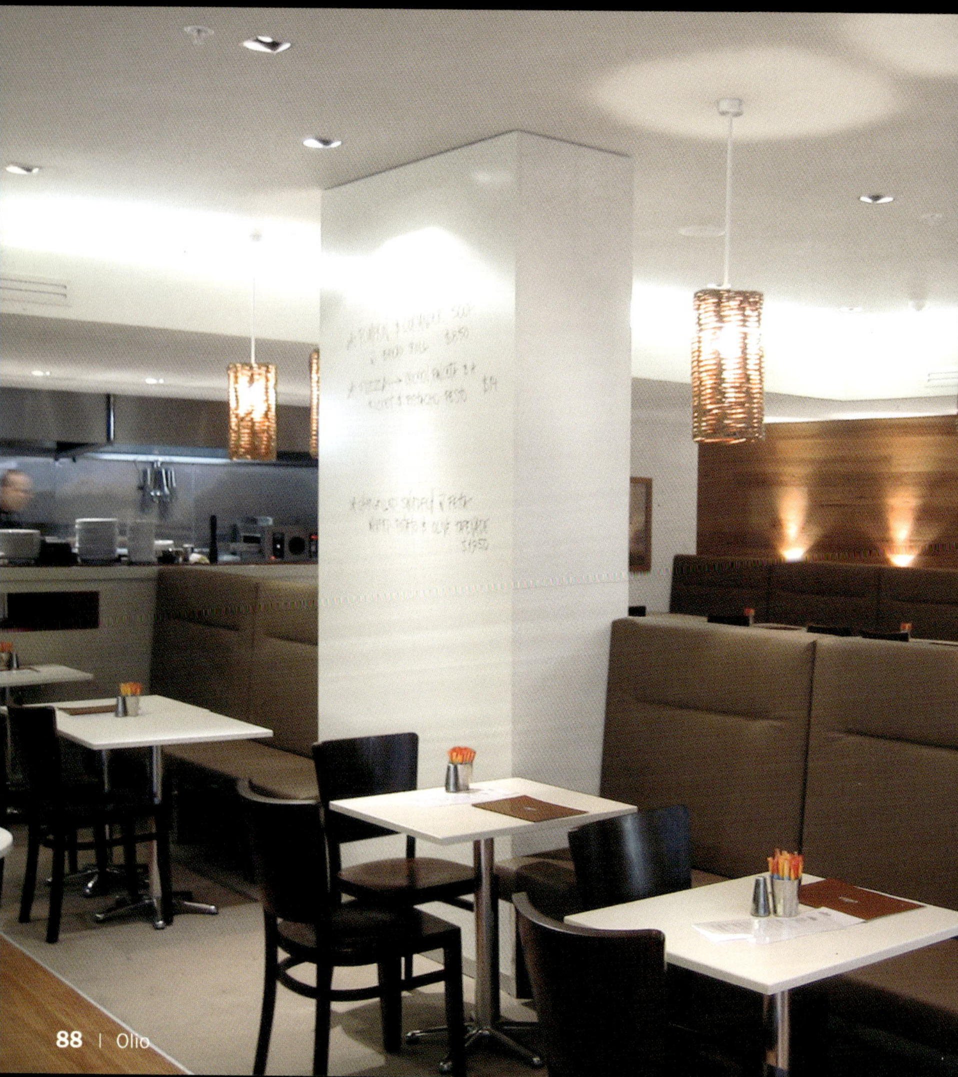

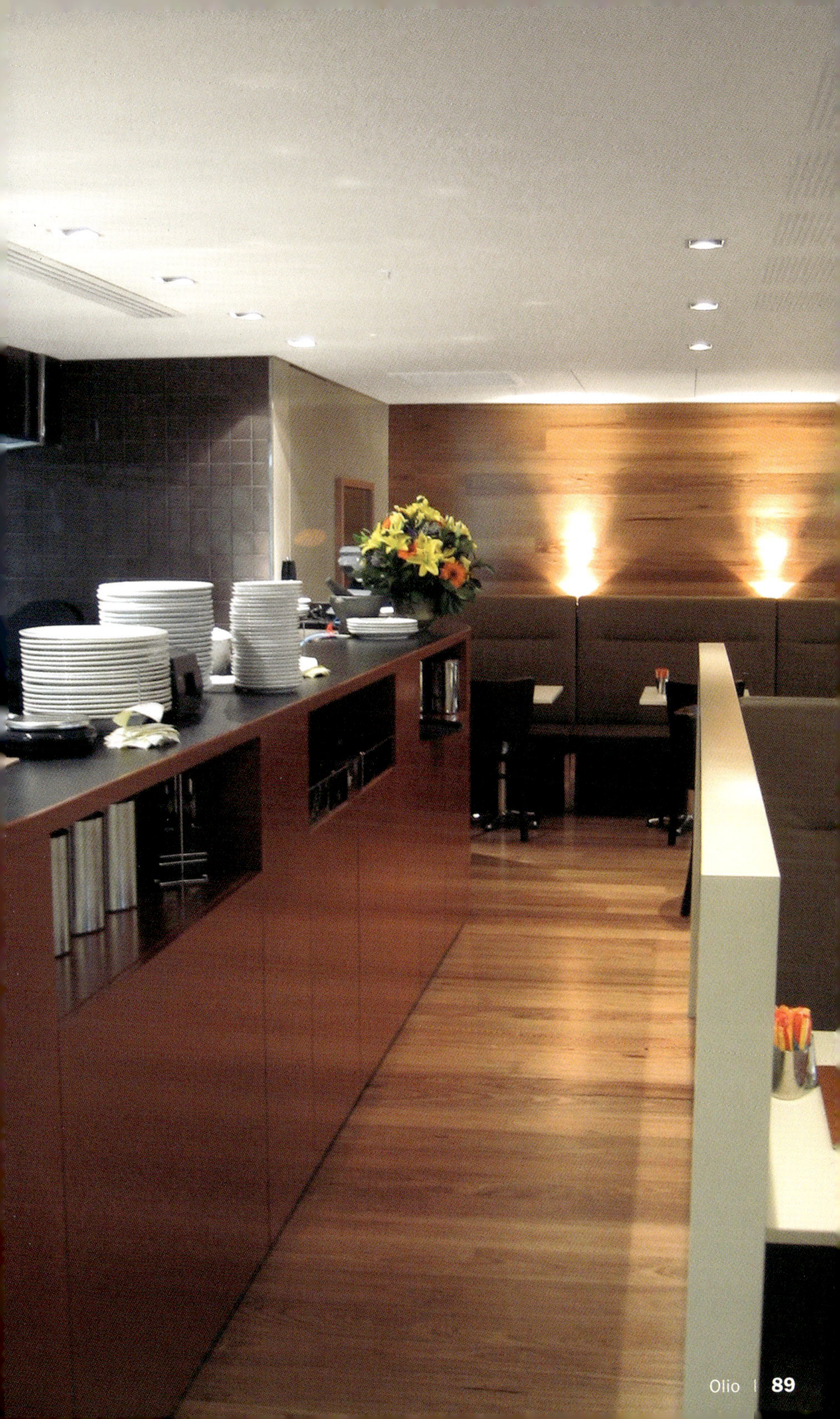

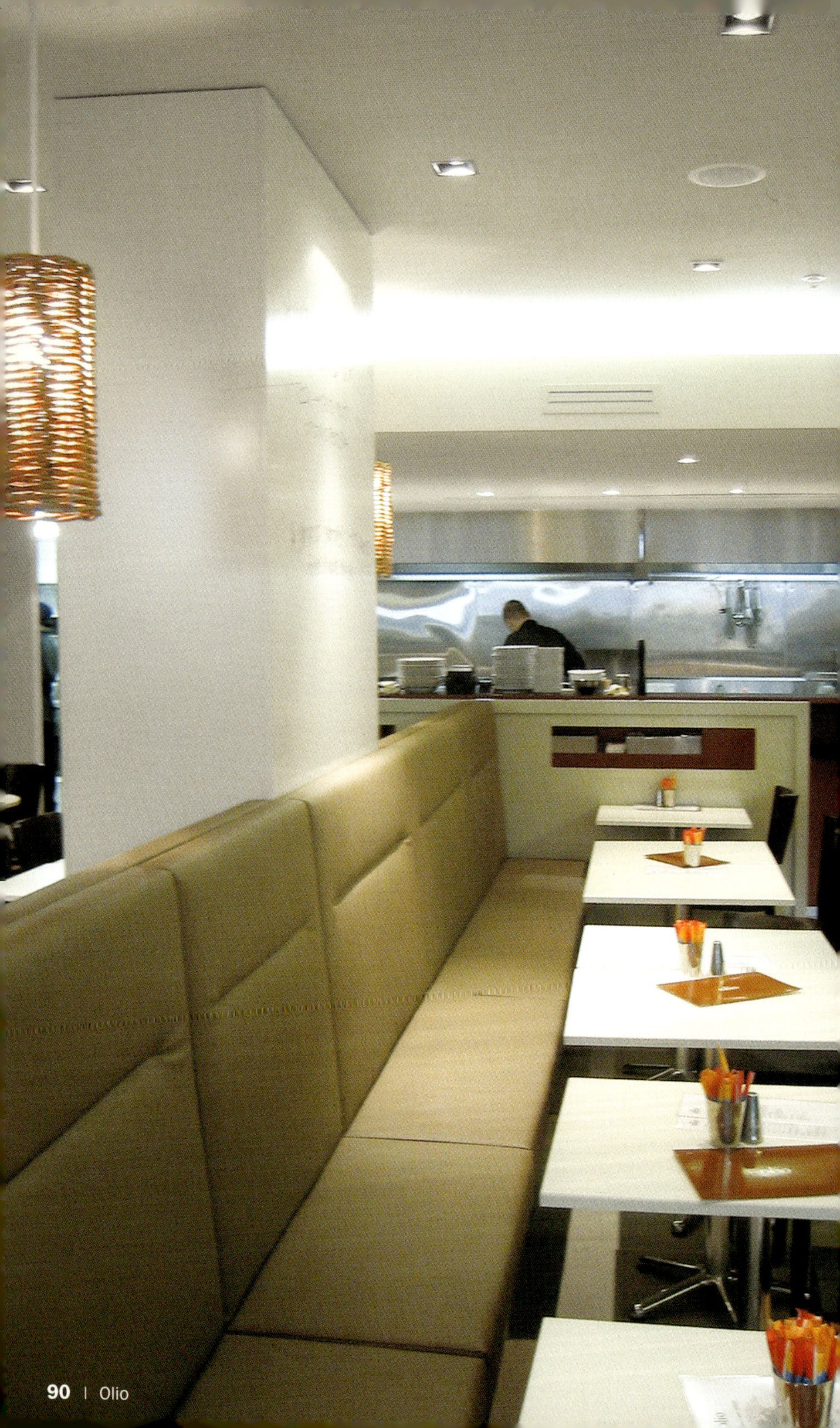

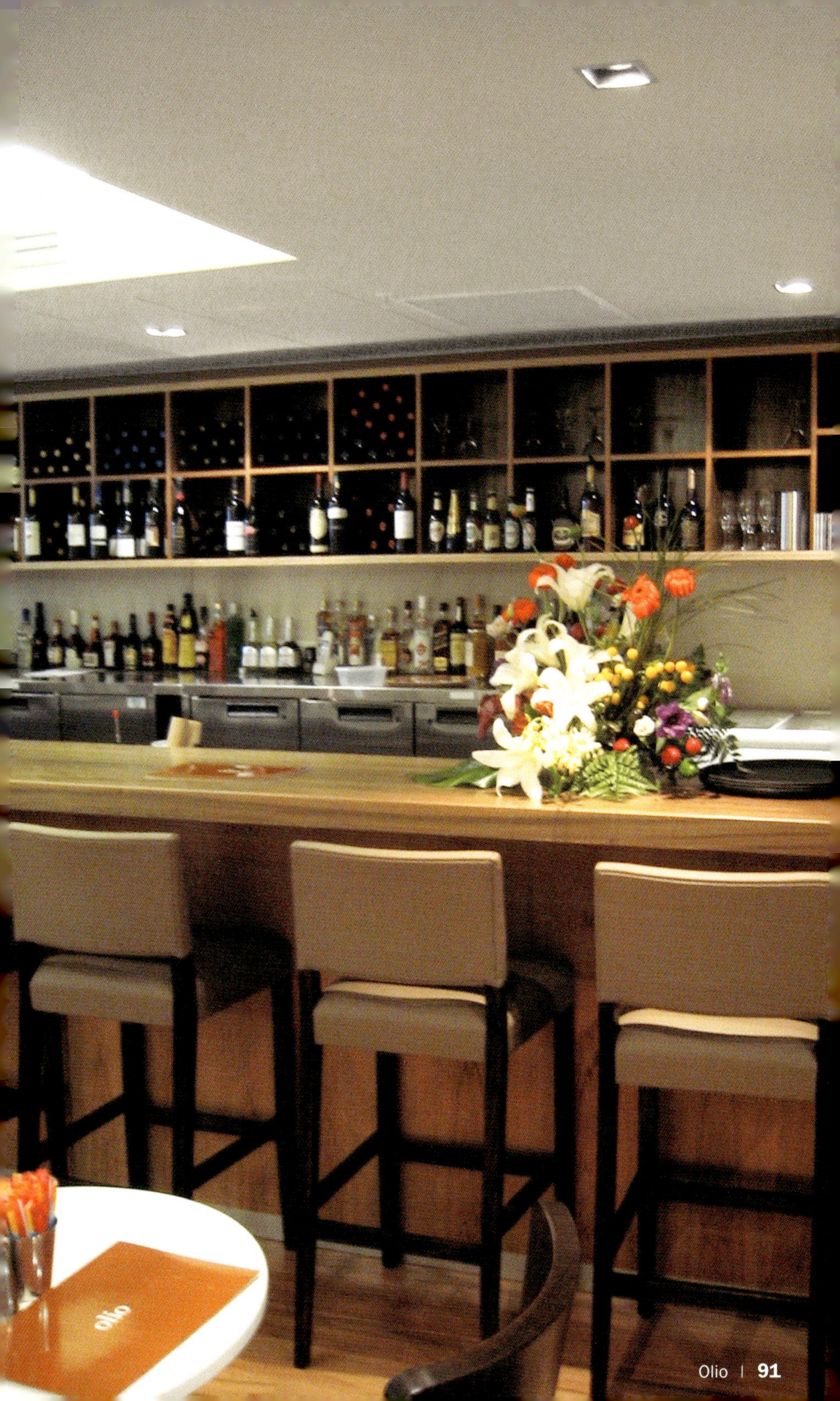

Fettuccini

with Rocket and Pistachio Pesto

Fettuccini mit Rucola und Pistazienpesto

Fettuccini à la roquette et au pesto
de pistaches

Fettuccini con rúcula y pesto de pistacho

Fettuccine con rucola e pesto al pistacchio

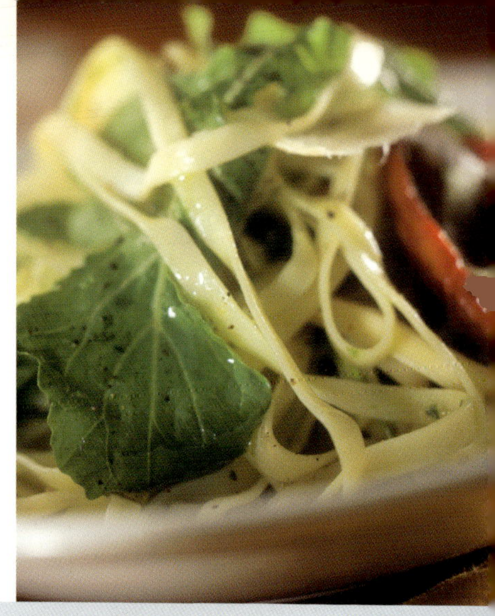

4 1/5 oz fresh rocket
7/10 oz basil
2 garlic cloves
Olive oil
50 ml lemon juice
1 3/4 oz pistachios
5 1/4 grated parmesan
6 pear tomatoes
Modena balsamic vinegar
1 lb 1/10 oz fettuccini
2 shallots
Course-ground salt
Pepper

For the pistachio pesto, in a mortar, crush 3 1/2 oz rocket, 2/5 oz basil and garlic to a smooth paste, then add a dash of olive oil and another dash of lemon juice. Add the chopped pistachios and 1 3/4 oz parmesan. Season to taste and set aside. Slice the tomatoes in half and dress with Modena balsamic vinegar, olive oil, course-ground salt and pepper. Bake at 320 °F for 45 minutes. Allow to cool, chop lengthways again and set aside. Boil the pasta al dente, strain and set aside. Finely chop 7/10 oz rocket, 4/10 oz basil, the shallots and baked tomatoes. Steam in a saucepan with olive oil over a very low heat, together with the pistachio pesto, but without overheating the pesto, so that it does not turn bitter. Add the pasta and mix with the sauce. As soon as everything is hot, add the lemon juice and 3 1/2 oz parmesan.
Serve the pasta and sprinkle with course-ground salt to taste.

120 g frischer Rucola
20 g Basilikum
2 Knoblauchzehen
Olivenöl
50 ml Zitronensaft
50 g Pistazien
150 g geriebener Parmesan
6 Birnentomaten
Balsamico di Modena
500 g Fettuccini
2 Schalotten
Grobes Salz
Pfeffer

Für das Pistazienpesto in einem Mörser 100 g Rucola, 10 g Basilikum und den Knoblauch zerstampfen, bis sich eine homogene Paste bildet, und einen Schuss Olivenöl, sowie einen Schuss Zitronensaft zugeben. Die gehackten Pistazien und 50 g Parmesan zufügen. Nach Geschmack würzen und beiseite stellen. Die Tomaten halbieren und mit dem Balsamico di Modena und Olivenöl, grobem Salz und Pfeffer anmachen. Im Ofen 45 Minuten bei 160 °C backen. Erkalten lassen, nochmals längs durchschneiden und beiseite stellen. Die Nudeln al dente kochen, abgießen und beiseite stellen. 20 g Rucola, 10 g Basilikum, die Schalotten und die gebackenen Tomaten fein schneiden. In einem Topf mit Olivenöl zusammen mit dem Pistazienpesto bei ganz niedriger Flamme dünsten, ohne das Pesto zu stark zu erwärmen, damit es nicht bitter wird. Die Nudeln zugeben und mit der Soße mischen. Wenn alles heiß ist, den Zitronensaft und 100 g Parmesan zufügen.
Die Nudeln anrichten und mit grobem Salz nach Geschmack würzen.

120 g de roquette fraîche
20 g de basilic
2 gousses d'ail
Huile d'olive
50 ml de jus de citron
50 g de pistaches
150 g de parmesan râpé
6 tomates Roma
Vinaigre balsamique de Modène
500 g de fettuccini
2 échalotes
Gros sel
Poivre

Pour le pesto de pistaches, piler dans un mortier 100 g de roquette, 10 g de basilic et l'ail jusqu'à obtenir une masse homogène, y ajouter un filet d'huile d'olive et un filet de jus de citron. Incorporer les pistaches pilées et 50 g de parmesan. Assaisonner à volonté et réserver. Couper en deux les tomates et assaisonner avec le vinaigre balsamique de Modène, l'huile d'olive, le gros sel et le poivre. Glisser au four pendant 45 minutes à 160 °C. Laisser refroidir, couper à nouveau les tomates dans la longueur et réserver. Faire cuire les pâtes al dente. Égoutter et réserver. Couper finement 20 g de roquette, 10 g de basilic, les échalotes et les tomates braisées. Dans une casserole, mettre un peu d'huile d'olive et faire revenir à feu très doux avec le pesto de pistaches, sans trop le réchauffer afin d'éviter toute amertume. Incorporer les pâtes et mélanger à la sauce. Une fois réchauffées, ajouter le jus de citron et 100 g de parmesan. Servir les pâtes et saler avec le gros sel à volonté.

120 g de rúcula fresca
20 g de albahaca
2 dientes de ajo
Aceite de oliva
50 ml de zumo de limón
50 g de pistachos
150 g de parmesano rallado
6 tomates de pera
Vinagre balsámico de Módena
500 g de fettuccini
2 chalotas
Sal gruesa
Pimienta

Para el pesto de pistacho, majar en un mortero 100 g de rúcula, 10 g de albahaca y el ajo hasta obtener una pasta homogénea y añadir un chorrito de aceite de oliva y otro de zumo de limón. Incorporar los pistachos picados y 50 g de parmesano. Sazonar al gusto y reservar. Partir por la mitad los tomates y aliñar con el vinagre balsámico de Módena y el aceite de oliva, sal gruesa y pimienta. Hornear a 160 °C durante 45 minutos. Enfriar, volver a cortar a lo largo y reservar. Hervir la pasta al dente. Colar y reservar. Cortar finamente 20 g de rúcula, 10 g de albahaca, las chalotas y los tomates horneados. En un cazo con aceite de oliva, rehogar a fuego muy lento junto con el pesto de pistacho, sin recalentar demasiado este último para no quedar amargo. Incorporar la pasta y mezclar con la salsa. Una vez caliente, añadir el zumo de limón y 100 g de parmesano. Servir la pasta y salpimentar con sal gruesa al gusto.

120 g di rucola fresca
20 g di basilico
2 spicchi d'aglio
Olio d'oliva
50 ml di succo di limone
50 g di pistacchi
150 g di parmigiano grattugiato
6 pomodori a pera
Aceto balsamico di Modena
500 g di fettuccine
2 scalogni
Sale grosso
Pepe

Per il pesto al pistacchio, in un mortaio pestare 100 g di rucola, 10 g di basilico e l'aglio fino ad ottenere una pasta omogenea, dopodiché aggiungere un filo d'olio d'oliva e un altro di succo di limone. Unire i pistacchi tritati e 50 g di parmigiano. Condire secondo i gusti e mettere da parte. Tagliare a metà i pomodori e condirli con l'aceto balsamico di Modena, l'olio d'oliva, il sale grosso e il pepe. Infornare per 45 minuti a 160 °C. Farli raffreddare, tagliarli nuovamente per lungo e rimetterli da parte. Far cuocere la pasta al dente. Colare e mettere da parte. Tagliare finemente 20 g di rucola, 10 g di basilico, gli scalogni e i pomodori cotti al forno. In una pentola con dell'olio d'oliva, rosolare a fuoco molto lento assieme al pesto di pistacchio; quest'ultimo non va riscaldato in eccesso per evitare che diventi troppo amaro. Incorporare la pasta e mescolare con la salsa. Una volta calda, aggiungere il succo di limone e 100 g di parmigiano. Servire la pasta, salare con sale grosso e pepare secondo i gusti.

Omega

Design: Mike Hanna of Curve 9 | Chef: Peter Conistis

161 King Street | Sydney, 2000 | Central Business District
Phone: +61 2 9223 0242
www.omegarestaurant.com.au
Opening hours: Mon–Fri lunch from noon to 2:30 pm, dinner from 6 pm until late, Sa
dinner from 6 pm until late
Average price: Starters A$ 21–32, main courses A$ 35–41, desserts A$ 6–22
Cuisine: Modern Australian with Greek influences
Special features: Fine dining in modern opulence

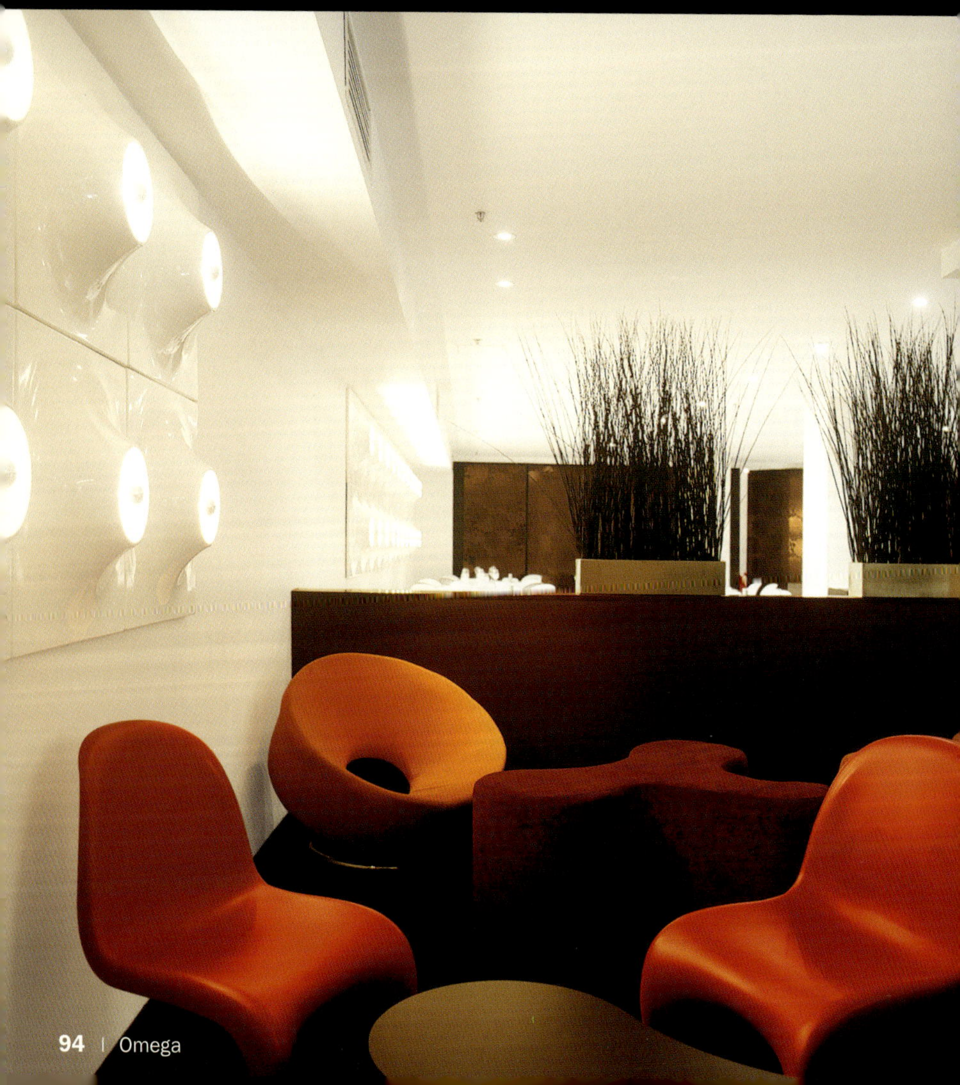

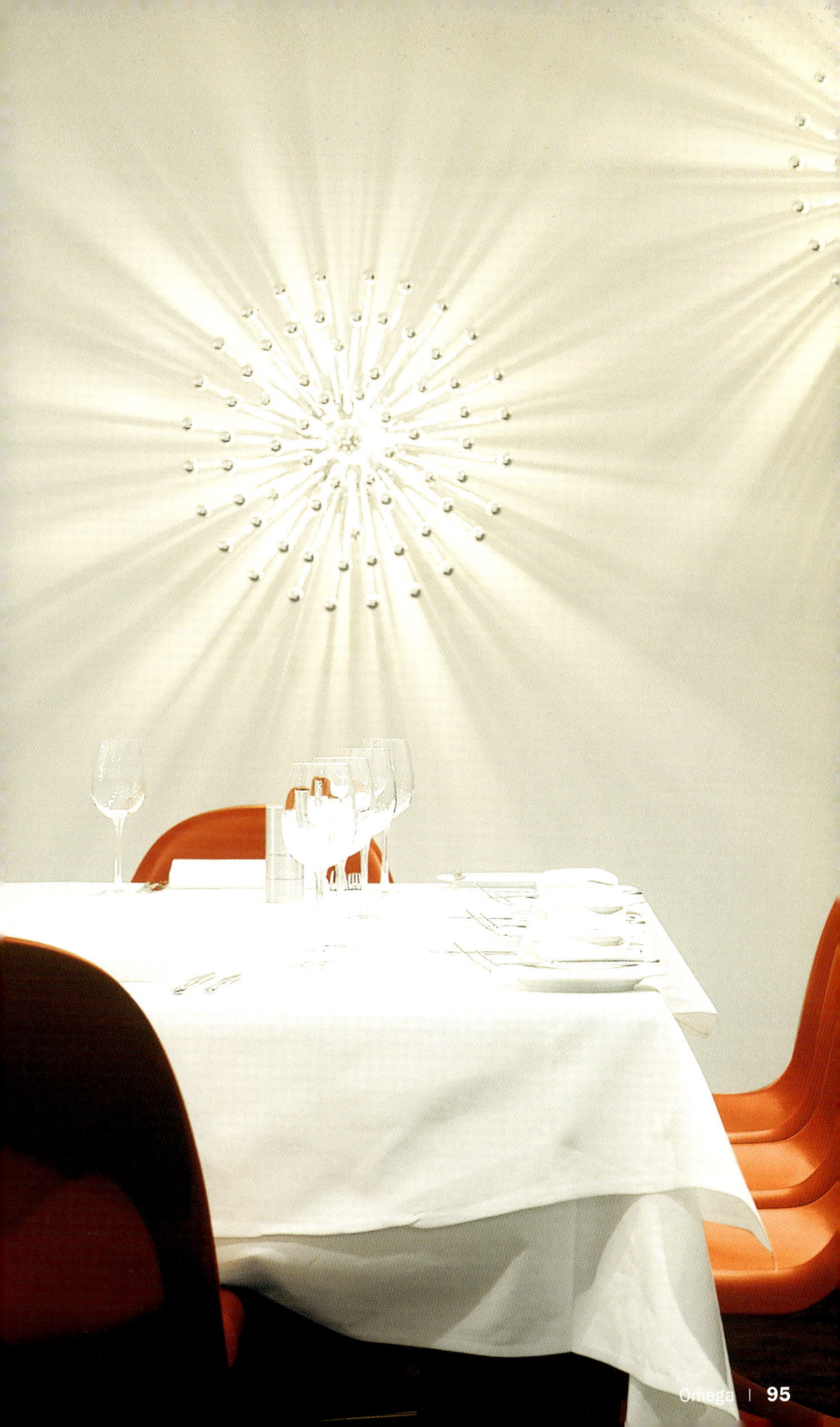

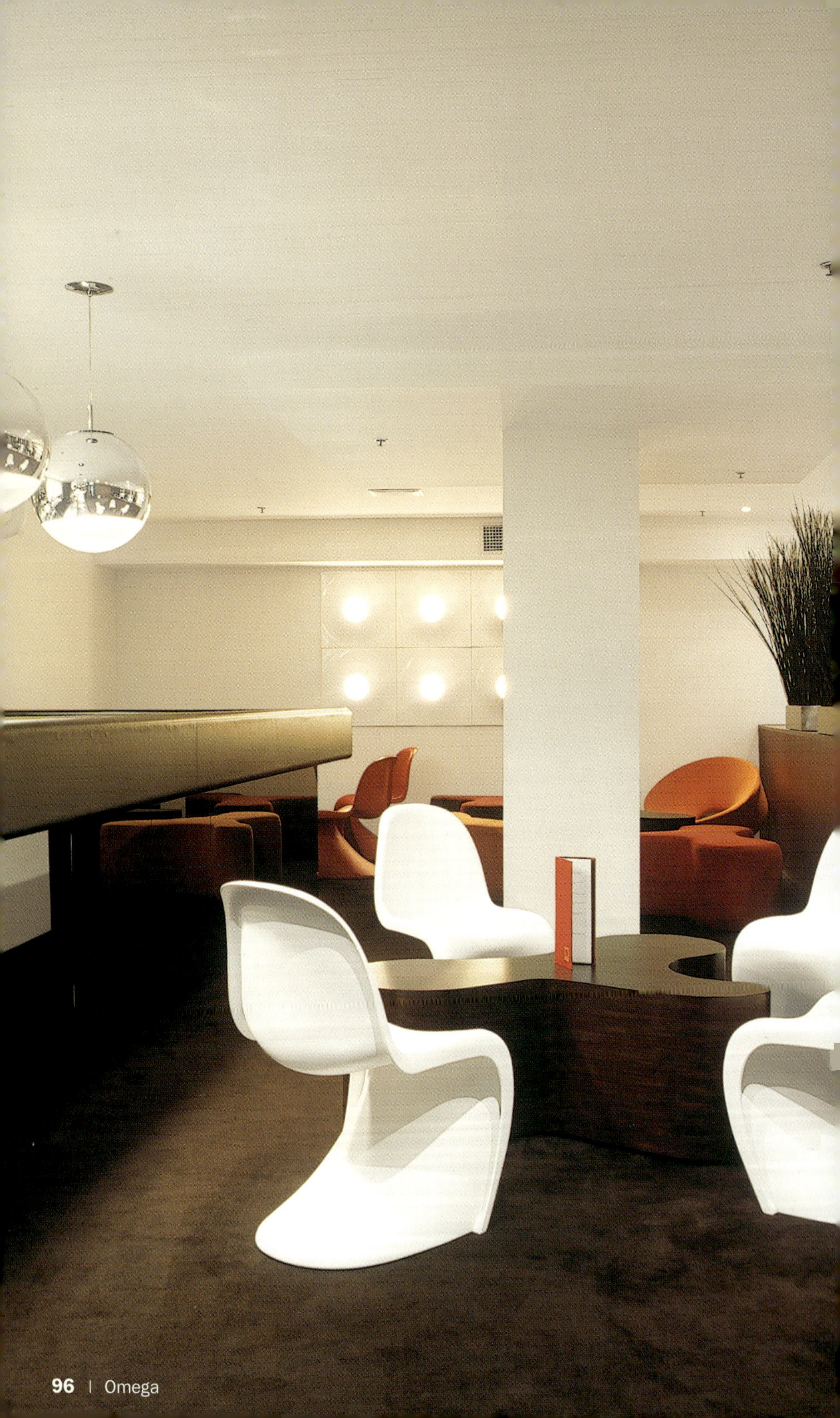

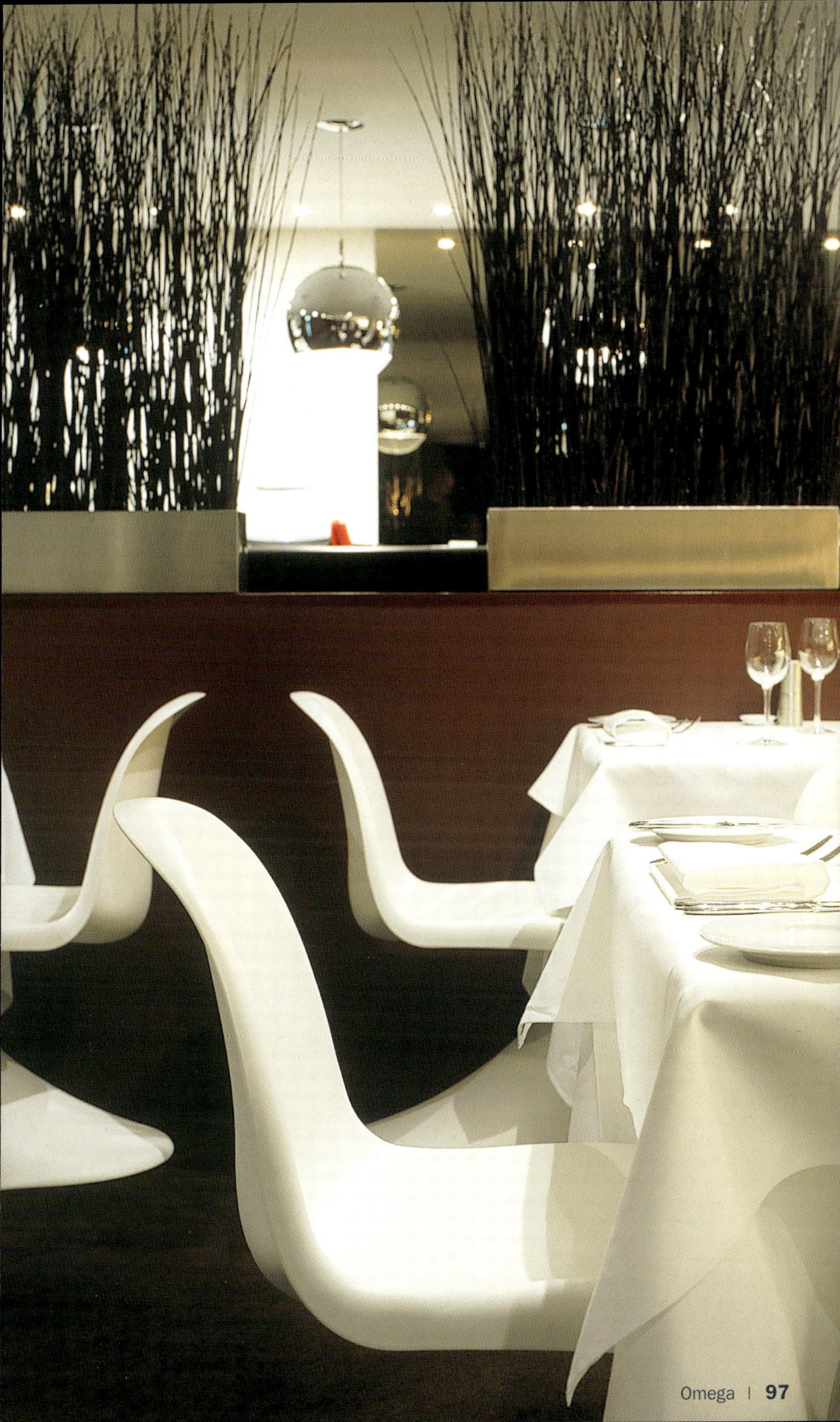

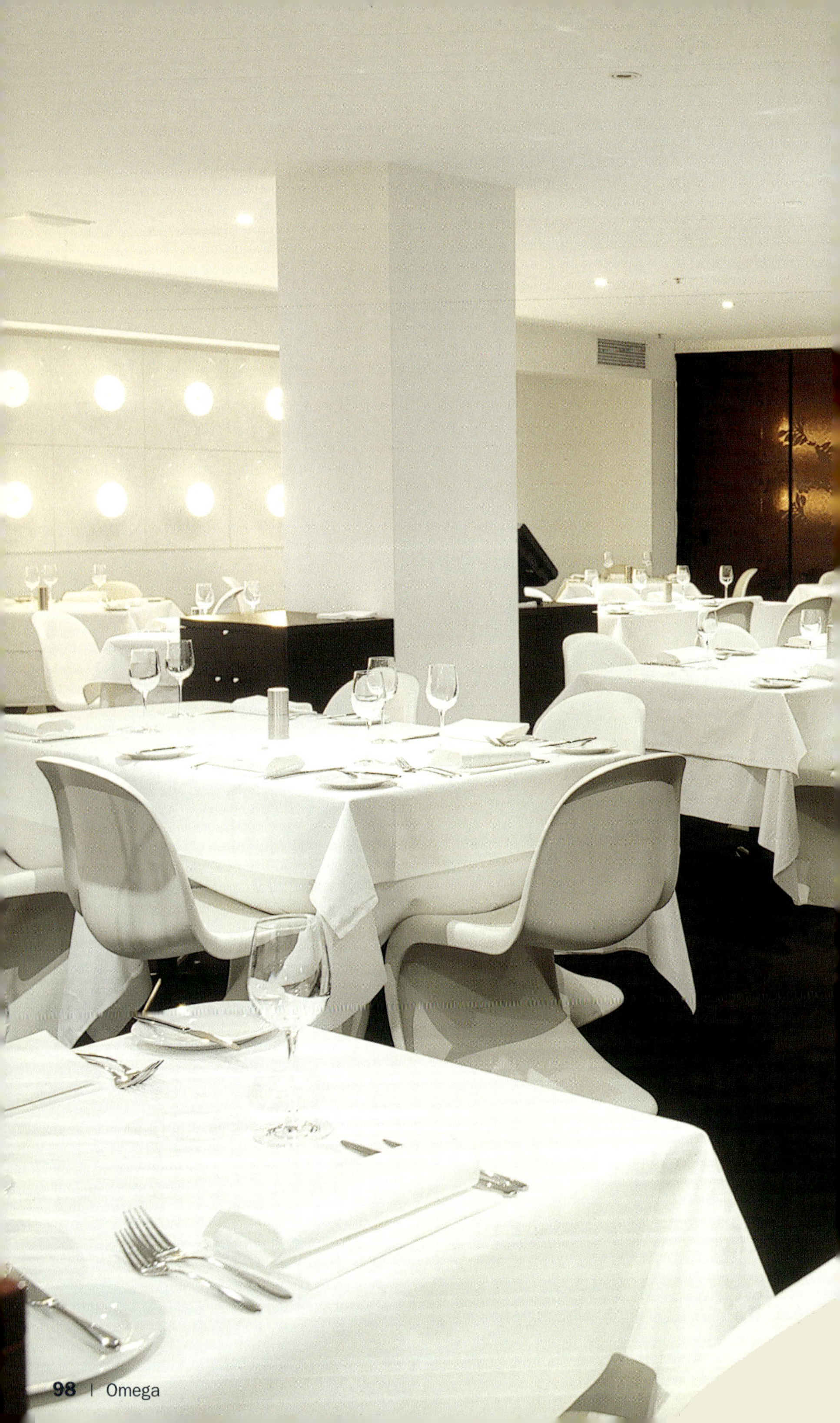

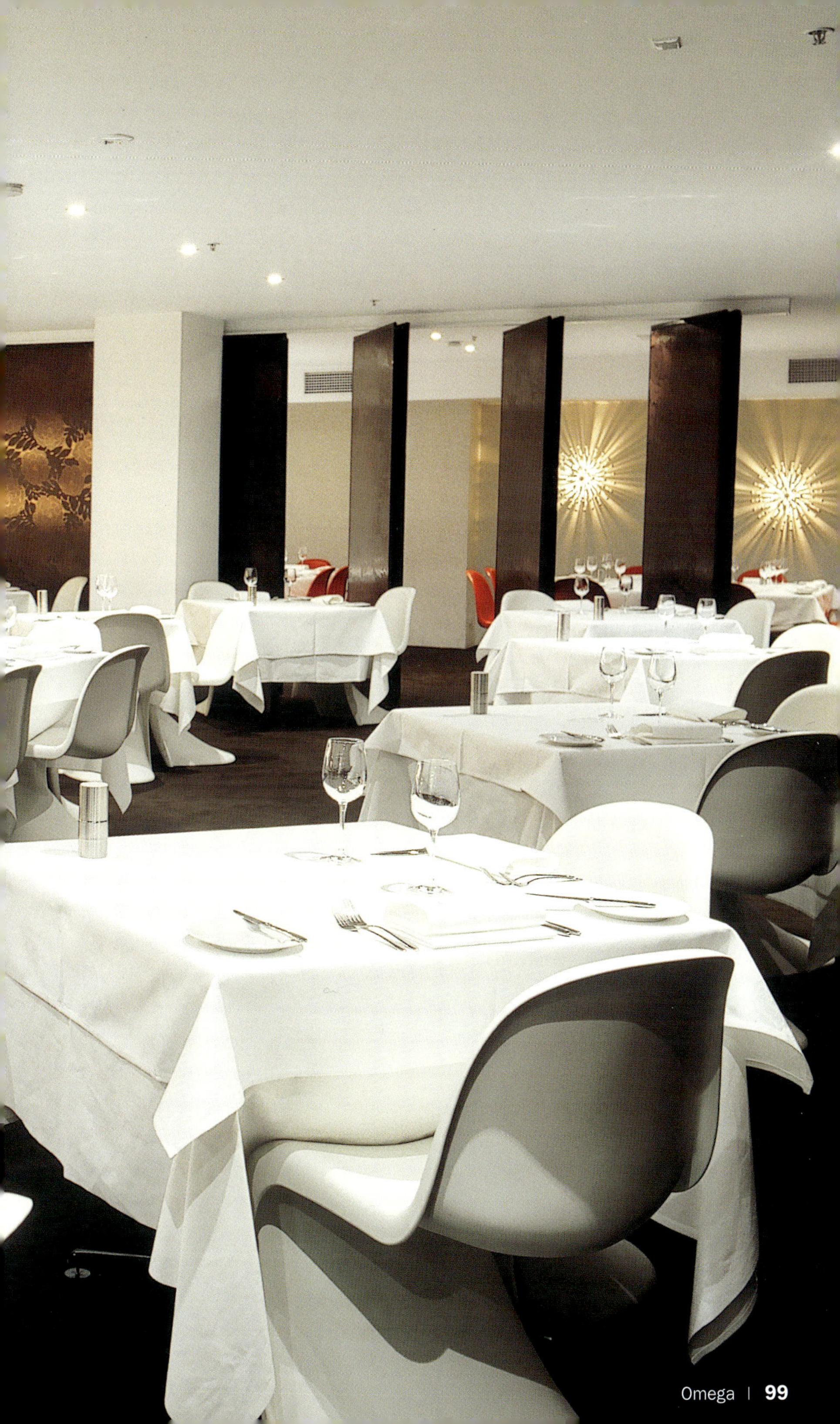

Sky Phoenix

Design: 3R Design | Chef: Tom Leung and Keung Chau

77 Castlereagh Street, Level 3, Skygarden | Sydney, 2000 | Central Business District
Phone: +61 2 9223 8822
www.skyphoenix.com.au
Opening hours: Every day from 11 am to 3 pm, from 5:30 pm to 10:30 pm
Average price: Starters A$ 12–16, main courses A$ 18–26
Cuisine: Southern Chinese
Special features: From traditional Chinese banquet menu to relaxing brunch

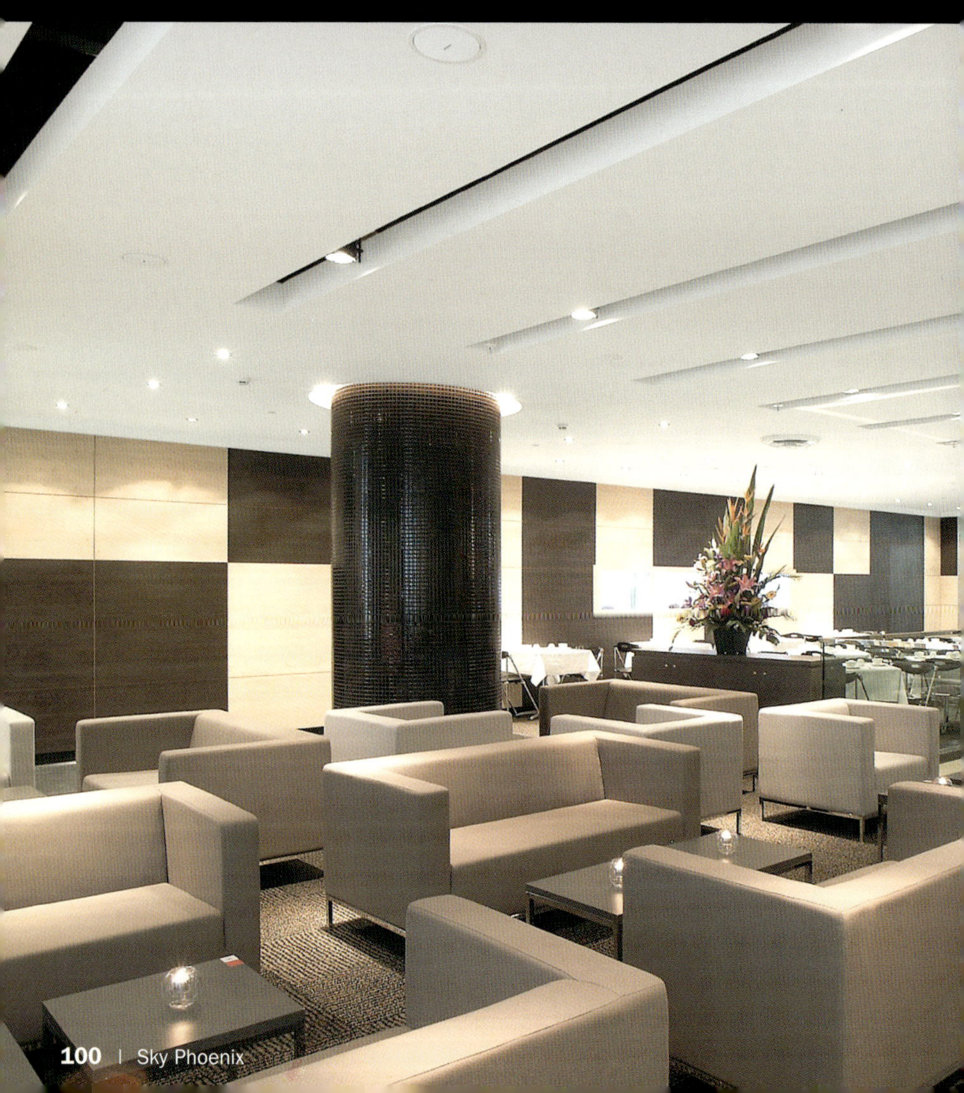

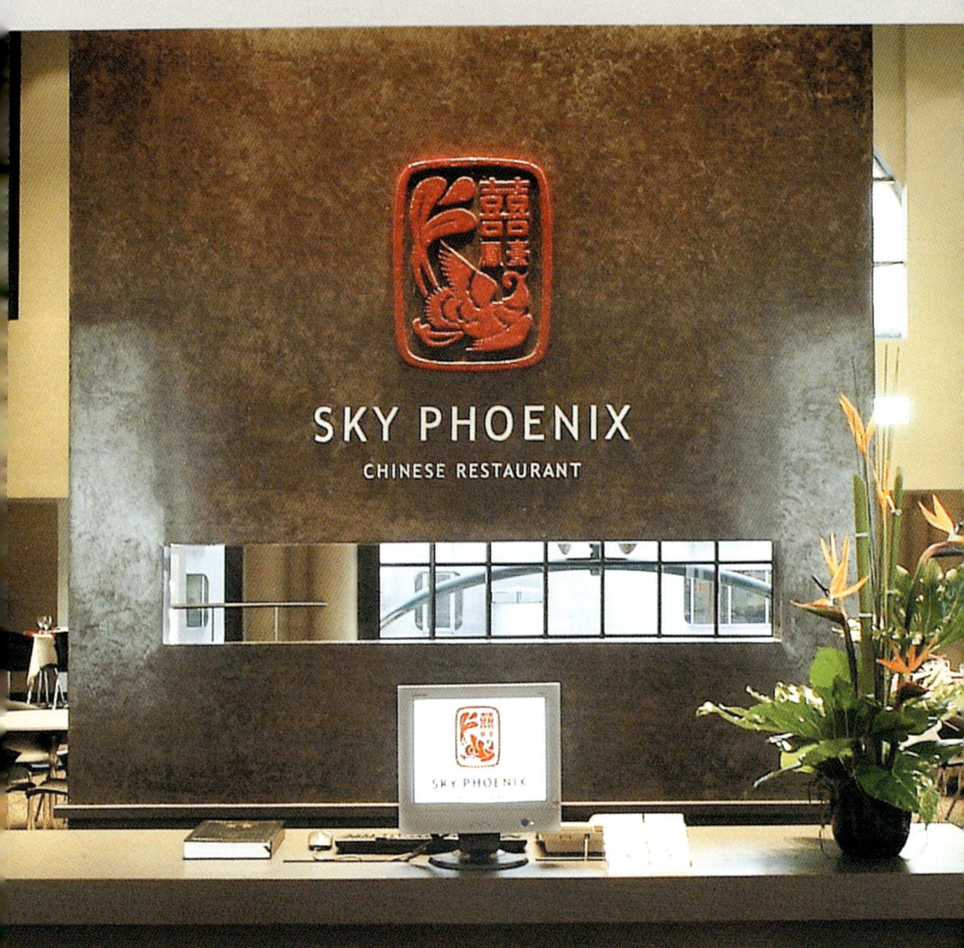
SKY PHOENIX
CHINESE RESTAURANT
SKY PHOENIX

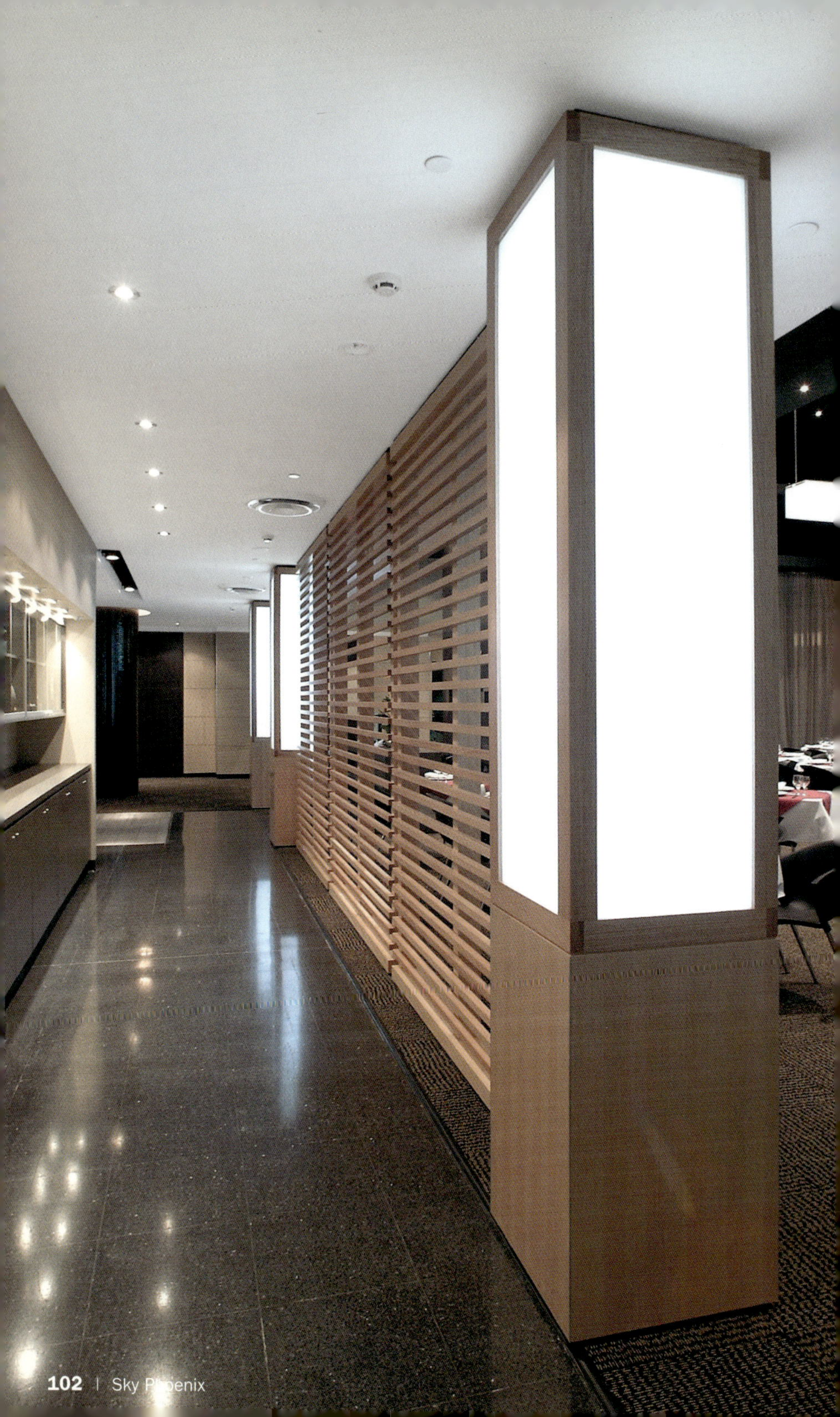

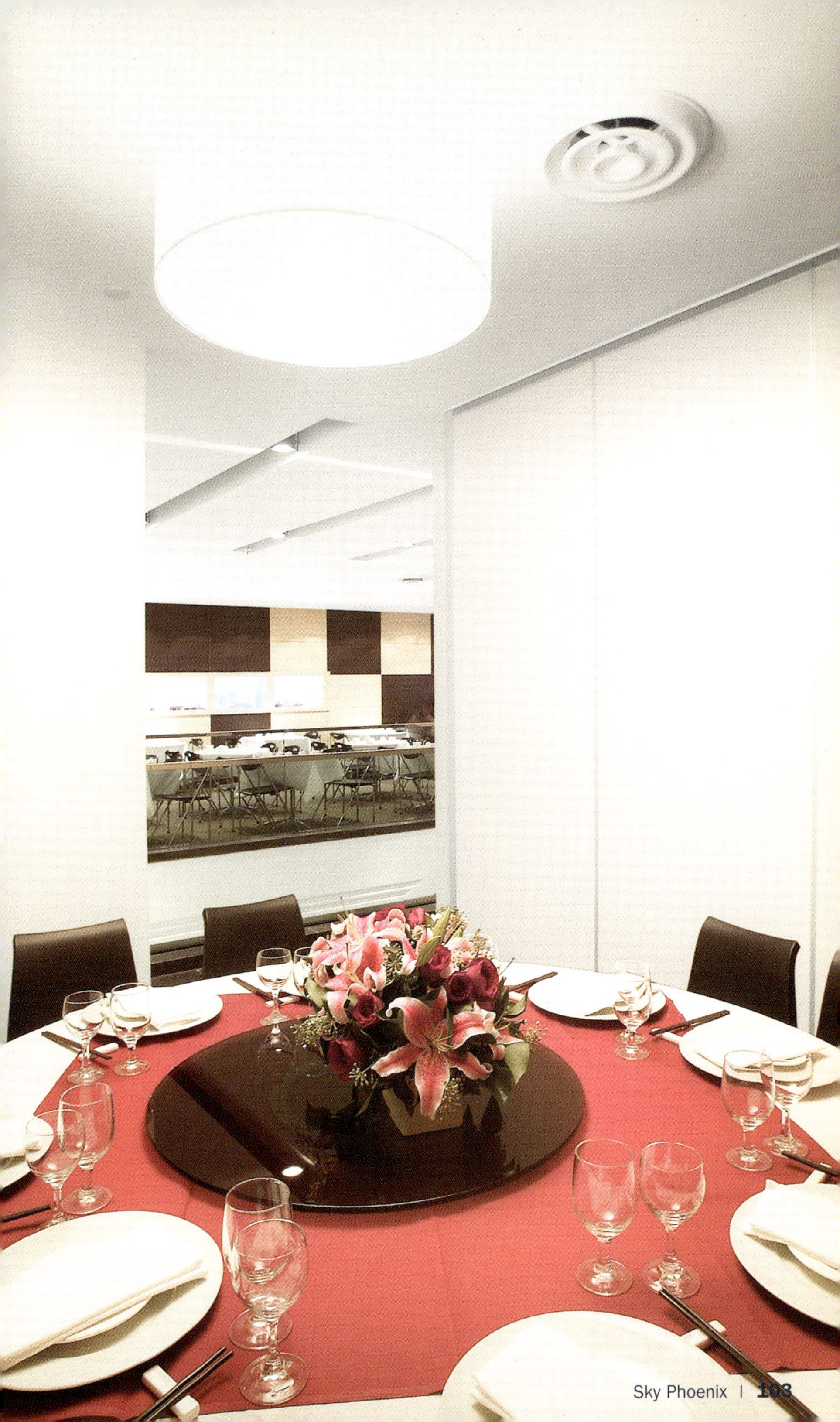

Langoustine
and Noodle Casserole

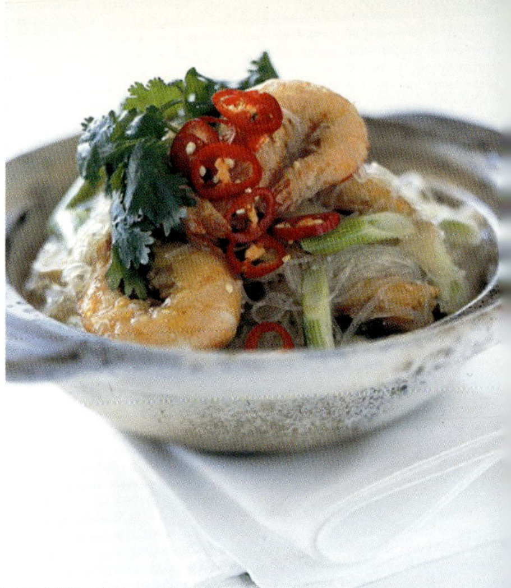

Schmortopf von Langustinen mit
Suppennudeln

Casserole de langoustines aux vermicelles

Cazuela de langostinos y fideos

Casseruola di gamberetti e fidelini

10 langoustines
5 1/4 oz noodles
20 ml olive oil
1 small onion
2 garlic cloves
5 ml oyster sauce
1/5 oz sugar
1/5 oz grated ginger
5 ml soy sauce
200 ml Chinese Shaoshing wine
350 ml chicken stock
2/5 oz wheat flour
1 chili
Salt

Make an incision along the back of the langoustines and sauté in a frying pan with oil until they split open. Set aside. Boil the noodles. Heat 20 ml oil in a wok and sauté the noodles, finely chopped onion, 2 crushed garlic cloves, oyster sauce, sugar, ginger and soy sauce for 1 minute. Add the Shaoshing wine, langoustines and chicken stock. Finally, add the flour, season to taste with salt and boil for 15 minutes.
Preheat an earthenware dish in the oven for 5 minutes. Pour the soup into the dish and garnish with some finely diced chili.

10 Langustinen
150 g Suppennudeln
20 ml Öl
1 kleine Zwiebel
2 Knoblauchzehen
5 ml Austernsoße
5 g Zucker
5 g geriebener Ingwer
5 ml Sojasoße
200 ml chinesischer Shaoshing-Wein
350 ml Geflügelbrühe
10 g Weizenmehl
1 Chili
Salz

Die Langustinen am Rücken entlang einschneiden und sie in einer Pfanne mit Öl anbraten, bis der Rücken sich öffnet. Beiseite stellen. Die Suppennudeln kochen. In einem Wok 20 ml Öl erhitzen und mit den Nudeln die feingehackte Zwiebel, die 2 Knoblauchzehen zerdrückt, die Austernsoße, den Zucker, Ingwer und die Sojasoße 1 Minute lang anbraten. Den Shaoshing-Wein, die Langustinen und die Geflügelbrühe zugeben. Zum Schluss das Mehl zufügen, mit Salz abschmecken und 15 Minuten kochen lassen.
Eine Tonschüssel im Ofen 5 Minuten vorwärmen. Die Suppe da hineingießen und mit etwas kleingeschnittenem Chili dekorieren.

10 langoustines
150 g de vermicelles
20 ml d'huile
1 petit oignon
2 gousses d'ail
5 ml de sauce aux huîtres
5 g de sucre
5 g de gingembre râpé
5 ml de sauce soja
200 ml de vin de Shaoshing
350 ml de bouillon de volaille
10 g de farine de blé
1 chili
Sel

Trancher le dos des langoustines et les faire frire dans une poêle avec de l'huile jusqu'à ce que le dos s'ouvre. Réserver. Faire bouillir les vermicelles. Dans un wok, faire chauffer 30 ml d'huile et faire revenir pendant 1 minute, avec les vermicelles, l'oignon coupé fin, les 2 gousses d'ail écrasées, la sauce aux huîtres, le sucre, le gingembre et la sauce soja. Ajouter le vin Shaoshing, les bouquets et le bouillon de volaille. Ajouter enfin la farine, équilibrer avec du sel et faire bouillir pendant 15 minutes.
Préchauffer au four un plat en terre pendant 5 minutes. Y verser la soupe et décorer avec un peu de chili coupé en petits morceaux.

10 langostinos
150 g de fideos
20 ml de aceite
1 cebolla pequeña
2 dientes de ajo
5 ml de salsa de ostras
5 g de azúcar
5 g de jengibre rallado
5 ml de salsa de soja
200 ml de vino chino Shaoshing
350 ml de caldo de ave
10 g de harina de trigo
1 chile
Sal

Practicar un corte en el lomo de los langostinos y freírlos en una sartén con aceite hasta que el lomo se abra. Reservar. Hervir los fideos. En un wok calentar 20 ml de aceite y freír durante 1 minuto, junto con los fideos, la cebolla cortada finamente, los 2 dientes de ajo machacados, la salsa de ostras, el azúcar, el jengibre y la salsa de soja. Añadir el vino Shaoshing, los langostinos y el caldo de ave. Agregar por último la harina, rectificar de sal y hervir durante 15 minutos.
Precalentar una cazuela de barro en el horno durante 5 minutos. Verter en ella la sopa y decorar con un poco de chile cortado en trozos pequeños.

10 gamberetti
150 g di fidelini
20 ml di olio
1 cipolla piccola
2 spicchi d'aglio
5 ml di salsa di ostriche
5 g di zucchero
5 g di zenzero grattugiato
5 ml di salsa di soia
200 ml di vino cinese Shaoshing
350 ml di brodo di pollo
10 g di farina di grano
1 peperoncino piccante
Sale

Praticare un taglio sul dorso dei gamberetti e friggerli in una padella con olio fino a che il dorso non si apra. Mettere da parte. Cuocere i fidelini. In un wok riscaldare 20 ml d'olio e per 1 minuto, assieme ai fidelini, friggere la cipolla tagliata finemente, i 2 spicchi d'aglio schiacciati, la salsa di ostriche, lo zucchero, lo zenzero e la salsa di soia. Aggiungere il vino Shaoshing, i gamberetti e il brodo di pollo. In ultimo unire la farina, correggere di sale e cuocere per 15 minuti.
Preriscaldare una scodella di terracotta nel forno per 5 minuti. Versarvi la zuppa e decorare con dei pezzettini di peperoncino.

Sticky + Moo

Design: 3R Design | Chef: Leigh Hudson

747 Botany Road, Shop 251 | Sydney, 2018 | Rosebery
Phone: +61 2 9699 2353
www.stickyandmoo.com
Opening hours: Mon–Fri from 7 am to 4 pm
Average price: A$ 9-21
Cuisine: Italian
Special features: Easygoing atmosphere and outdoor seating

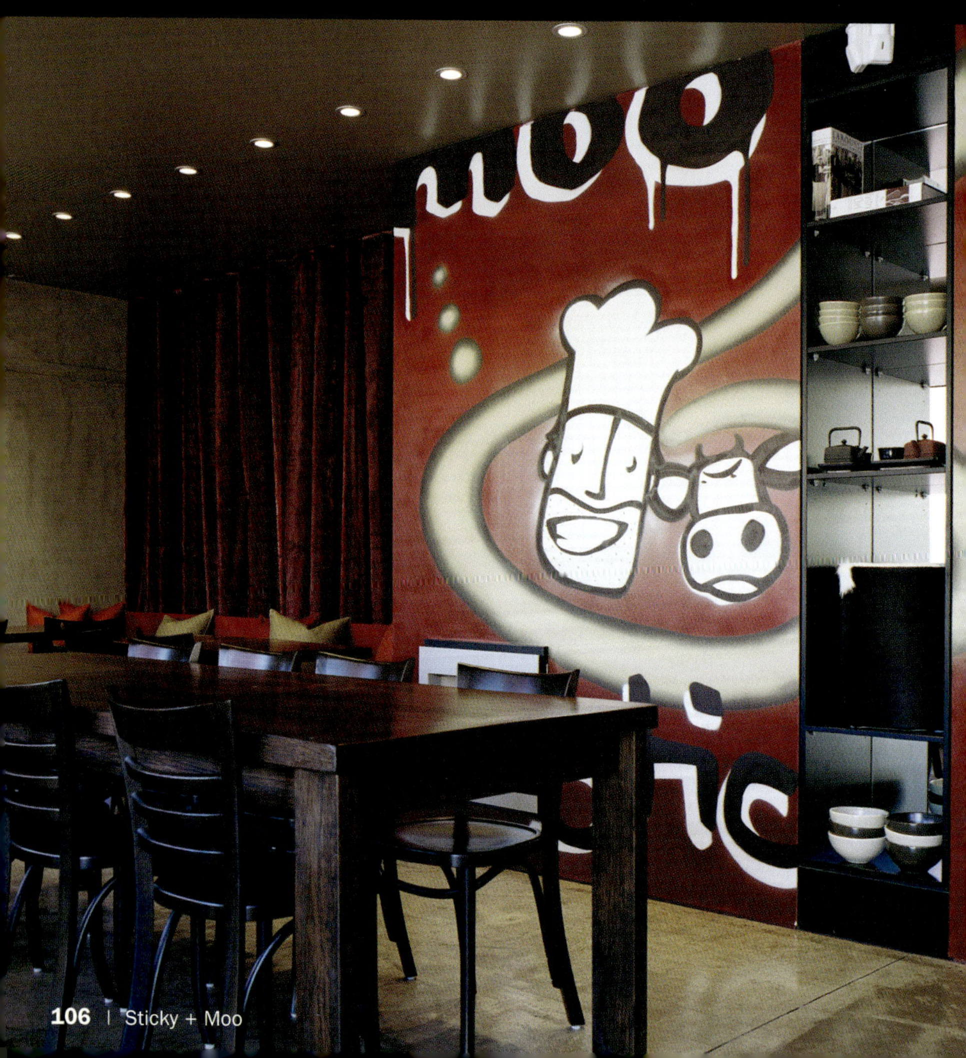

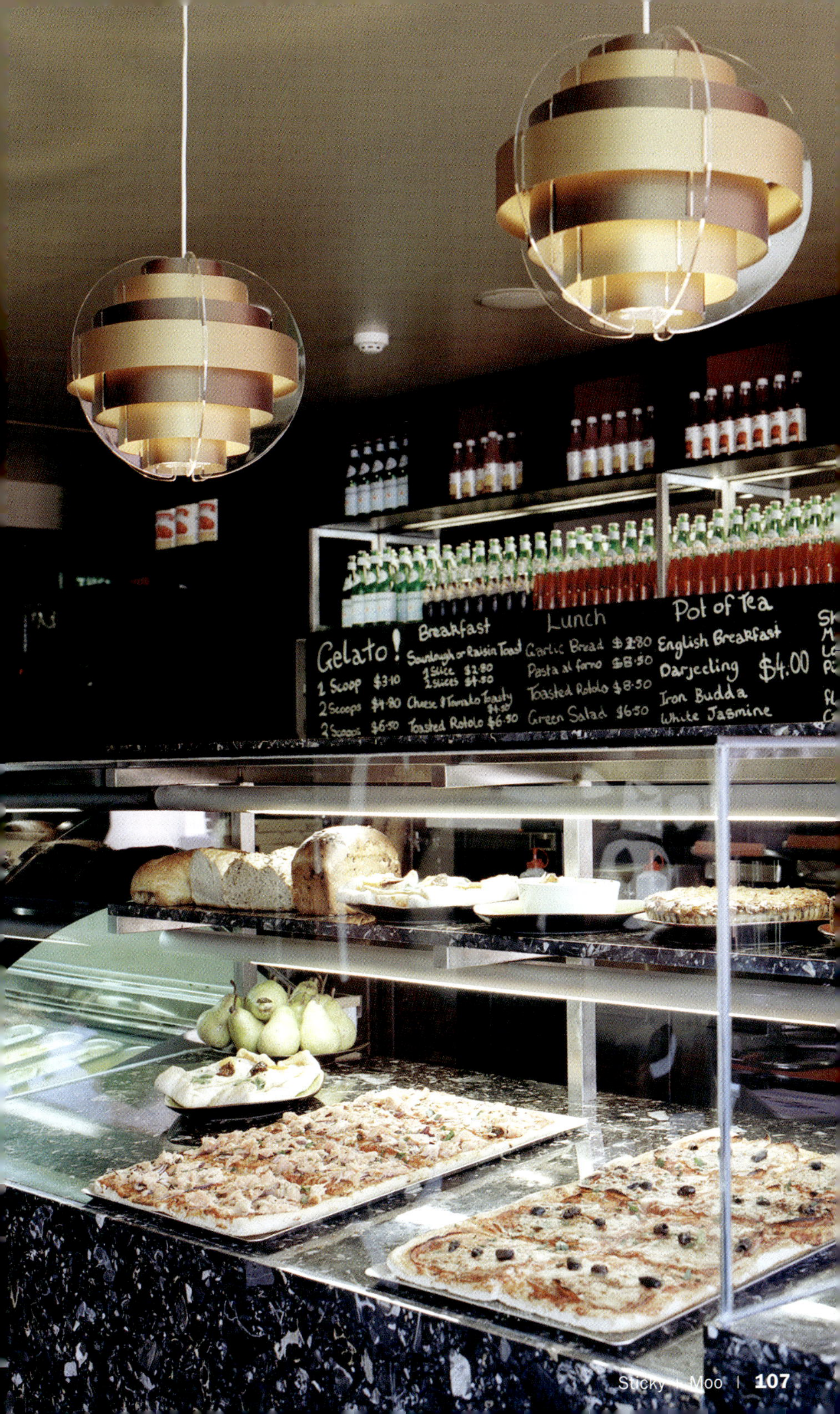

Gelato!
Breakfast
Lunch
Pot of Tea
1 Scoop $3.10
Sourdough or Raisin Toast
1 Slice $2.80
2 Slices $4.50
Garlic Bread $2.80
Pasta al forno $8.50
English Breakfast
Darjeeling $4.00
2 Scoops $4.80
Cheese & Tomato Toasty $4.50
Toasted Rotolo $8.50
Iron Budda
2 Scoops $6.50
Toasted Rotolo $6.50
Green Salad $6.50
White Jasmine

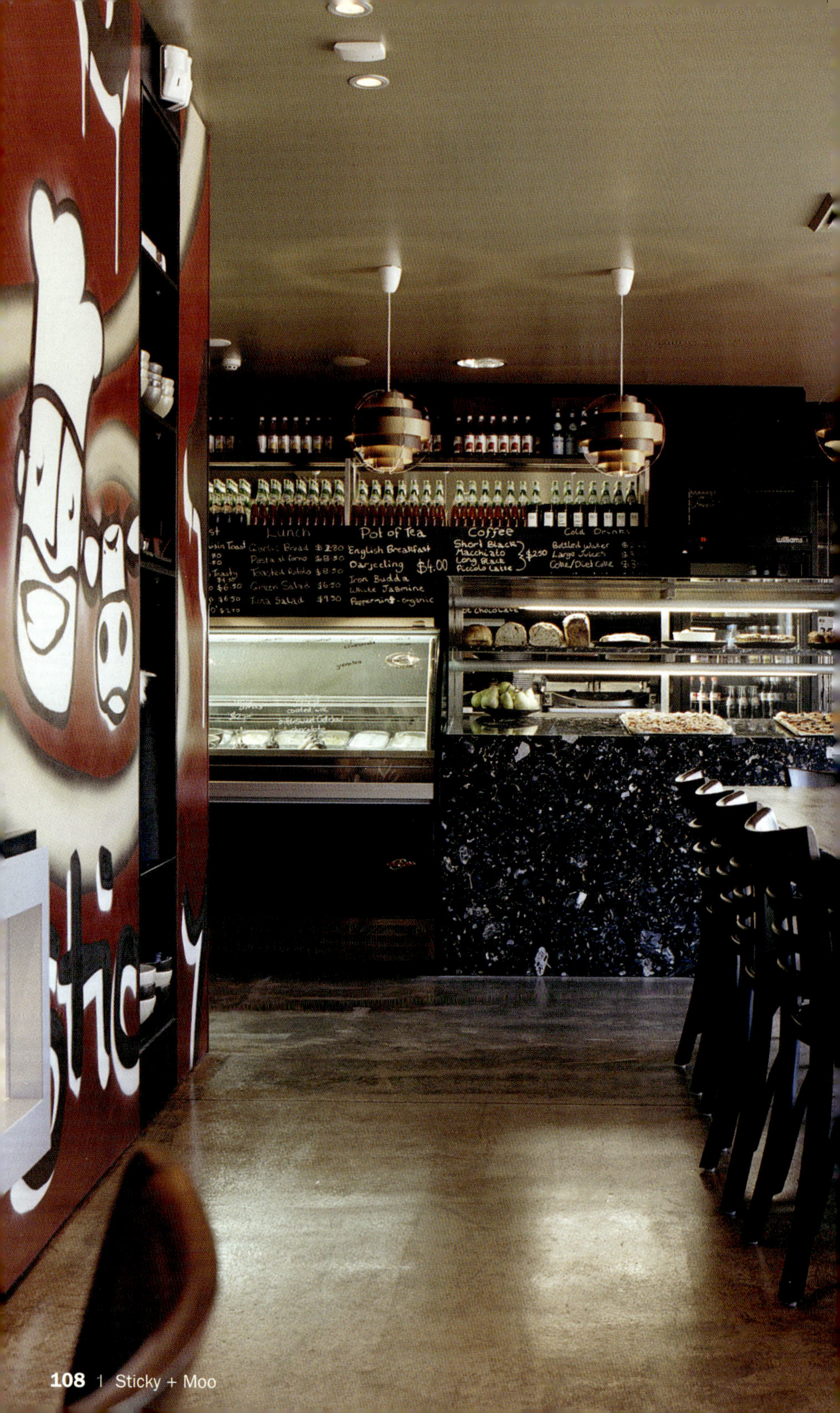
Lunch
Garlic Bread $2.80
Pasta al forno $8.50
Toasted Ciabatta $8.50
Green Salad $6.50
Tuna Salad $9.50
Pot of Tea
English Breakfast
Darjeeling $4.00
Iron Budda
White Jasmine
Peppermint - organic
Coffee
Short Black
Macchiato
Long Black
Piccolo Latte
Cold Drinks
Bottled Water
Large Juice
Coke/Diet Coke

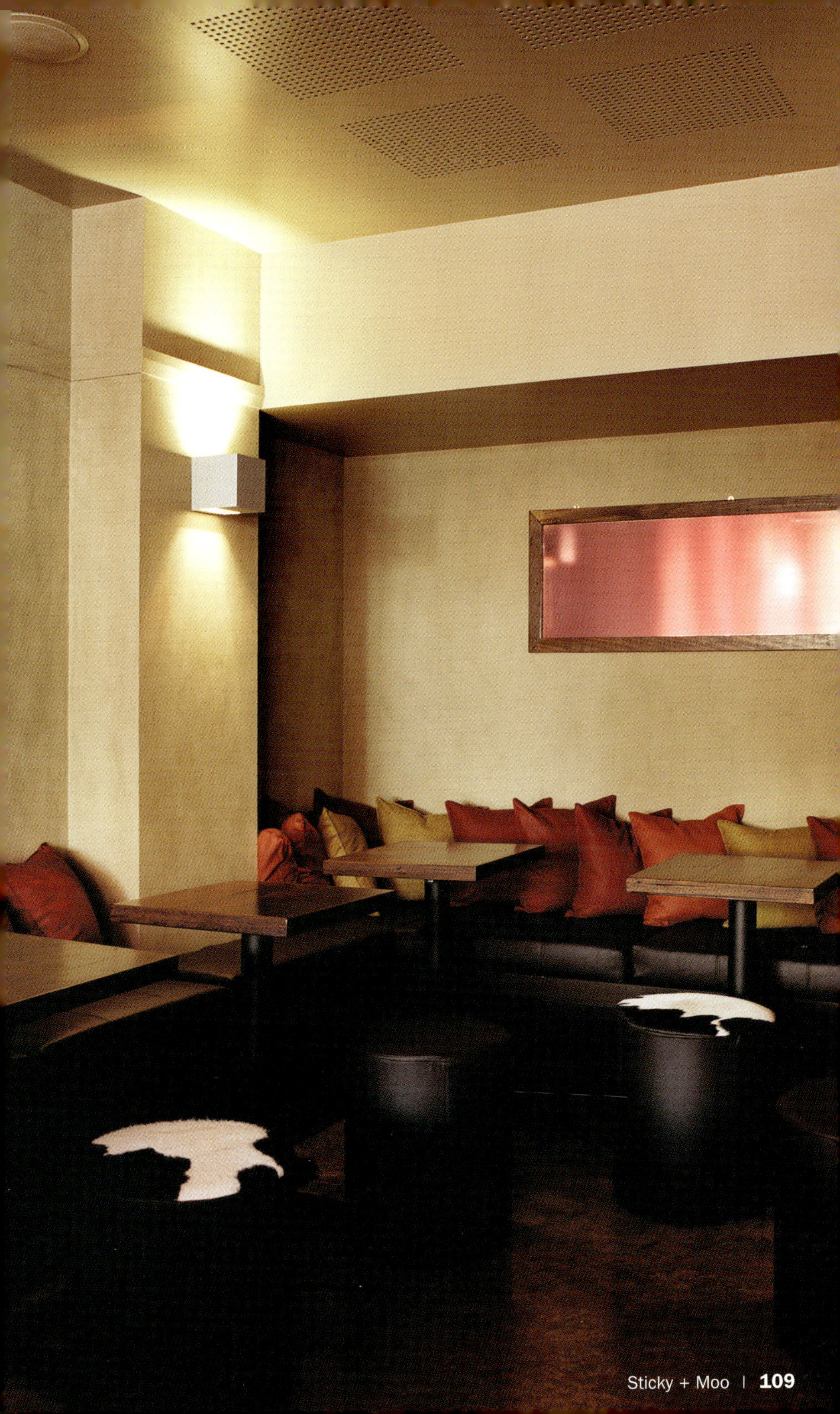

Rotolo Breakfast

Frühstück Rotolo

Déjeuner Rotolo

Desayuno Rotolo

Colazione Rotolo

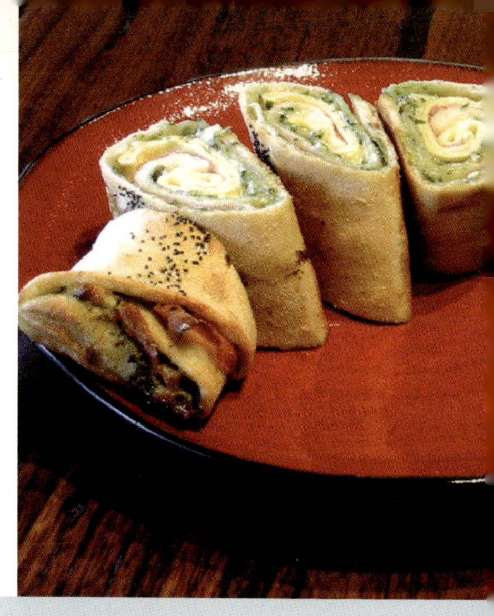

400 ml water
9/10 oz yeast
4 tbsp olive oil
1 lb 9 1/5 oz flour
2 garlic cloves
7/10 oz pine nuts
1 2/5 oz basil
1 3/4 oz parmesan
13 eggs
3 mozzarella balls
12 slices of boiled ham
Salt

Pour 400 ml water into a bowl, add the yeast and some salt. Add 1 tbsp of oil and the flour and knead for 8 minutes. Chill in the refrigerator for 12 hours. For the pesto, crush the garlic and pine nuts.
Add salt and chopped basil and stir, adding 3 tbsp oil until a smooth paste forms. Place in a bowl and add grated parmesan. Set aside. Remove the dough from the refrigerator and shape into 6 dough balls, each weighing 5 3/5 oz. Roll out to patties measuring 7 4/5 inches in diameter and allow to stand for 15 minutes. Prepare 6 2-egg omelets and sprinkle with parmesan. Spread the pesto over the dough, but leaving a 2/5 inch border around the edge. Cover each dough base with sliced mozzarella, an omelet and two slices of boiled ham. Roll together and glaze with a little beaten egg. Bake for 12 minutes at 320 °F.

400 ml Wasser
25 g Hefe
4 EL Olivenöl
720 g Mehl
2 Knoblauchzehen
20 g Pinienkerne
40 g Basilikum
50 g Parmesan
13 Eier
3 Kugeln Mozzarella
12 Scheiben gekochter Schinken
Salz

400 ml Wasser in eine Schüssel gießen, die Hefe und etwas Salz dazugeben. 1 EL Öl und Mehl zufügen und 8 Minuten lang kneten. Im Kühlschrank 12 Stunden ruhen lassen. Für das Pesto den Knoblauch und die Pinienkerne zerstampfen.
Salz und gehacktes Basilikum dazu und unter Zugabe von 3 EL Öl verrühren, bis eine homogene Paste entsteht. In ein Gefäß gießen und den geriebenen Parmesan dazugeben. Beiseite stellen. Den Teig aus dem Kühlschrank nehmen und 6 Kugeln von 160 g formen. Zu Scheiben von 20 cm Durchmesser ausrollen und 15 Minuten ruhen lassen. 6 Omelettes aus je 2 Eiern zubereiten und mit Parmesan bestreuen. Die Teigplatten mit dem Pesto bestreichen, dabei rundherum 1 cm Rand lassen. Jede Teigplatte mit in Scheiben geschnittenem Mozzarella, einem Omelette und 2 Scheiben gekochtem Schinken bedecken. Einrollen und mit etwas verquirltem Ei bestreichen. 12 Minuten bei 160 °C backen.

400 ml d'eau
25 g de levure
4 c. à soupe d'huile d'olive
720 g de farine
2 gousses d'ail
20 g de pignons de pin
40 g de basilic
50 g de parmesan
13 œufs
3 boules de mozzarella
12 tranches de jambon cuit
Sel

Verser 400 ml d'eau dans un bol, ajouter la levure et un peu de sel. Incorporer 1 c. à soupe d'huile et la farine et pétrir pendant 8 minutes.

Laisser reposer au réfrigérateur pendant 12 heures. Pour le pesto, piler l'ail et les pignons de pin.
Ajouter le sel et le basilic et remuer tout en ajoutant 3 c. à soupe d'huile jusqu'à obtention d'une pâte homogène. Verser dans un récipient et ajouter le parmesan râpé. Réserver. Sortir la pâte du réfrigérateur et faire 6 boules de 160 g chacune. Étaler en galettes de 20 cm de diamètre et laisser reposer pendant 15 minutes. Préparer 6 omelettes de 2 œufs chacune et les saupoudrer de parmesan. Napper les galettes de pâte avec le pesto en laissant une marge de 1 cm autour. Disposer sur chaque galette des rondelles de mozzarella, 1 omelette et 2 tranches de jambon cuit. Enrouler et badigeonner d'œuf battu. Glisser au four pendant 12 minutes à 160 °C.

---

400 ml de agua
25 g de levadura
4 cucharadas de aceite de oliva
720 g de harina
2 dientes de ajo
20 g de piñones
40 g de albahaca
50 g de parmesano
13 huevos
3 bolas de mozarela
12 lonchas de jamón dulce
Sal

Verter 400 ml de agua en un bol, añadir la levadura y un poco de sal. Incorporar 1 cucharada de aceite y la harina y amasar durante 8 minutos.

Dejar reposar en la nevera durante 12 horas. Para el pesto, majar el ajo y los piñones.
Añadir la sal y la albahaca picada y remover añadiendo 3 cucharadas de aceite hasta conseguir una pasta homogénea. Verter en un recipiente y añadir el parmesano rallado. Reservar. Sacar la masa de la nevera y hacer 6 bolas de 160 g cada una. Aplanar en rodajas de unos 20 cm de diámetro y dejar reposar durante 15 minutos. Preparar 6 tortillas de 2 huevos cada una y espolvorearlas con parmesano. Untar las rodajas de masa con el pesto dejando 1 cm de margen en el borde. Cubrir cada rodaja con la mozarela cortada en rodajas, 1 tortilla y 2 lonchas de jamón dulce. Enrollar y pintar con un poco de huevo batido. Hornear durante 12 minutos a 160 °C.

---

400 ml d'acqua
25 g di lievito
4 cucchiai di olio d'oliva
720 g di farina
2 spicchi d'aglio
20 g di pinoli
40 g di basilico
50 g di parmigiano
13 uova
3 bocconcini di mozzarella
12 fette di prosciutto cotto
Sale

Versare 400 ml d'acqua in una ciotola, aggiungere il lievito e un po' di sale. Incorporare 1 cucchiaio d'olio, la farina e impastare per 8 minuti.

Far riposare in frigo per 12 ore. Per il pesto, pestare l'aglio e i pinoli.
Aggiungere il sale e il basilico tritato e rimescolare aggiungendo 3 cucchiai d'olio fino ad ottenere una pasta omogenea. Versare in un recipiente e aggiungere il parmigiano grattugiato. Mettere da parte. Estrarre l'impasto dal frigo e formare 6 palle da 160 g ciascuna. Spianare in rondelle di circa 20 cm di diametro e far riposare per 15 minuti. Preparare 6 omelette di 2 uova ciascuna e spolverizzarle con il parmigiano. Ungere le rondelle di impasto con il pesto lasciando 1 cm di margine nel bordo. Coprire ogni rondella con la mozzarella tagliata a rondelle, 1 omelette e 2 fette di prosciutto cotto. Avvolgere e ungere con un po' di uovo sbattuto. Infornare per 12 minuti a 160 °C.

Sugaroom

Design: Neil Bradford | Chef: Greg Anderson

1 Harris Street, Shop 2 | Sydney, 2009 | Pyrmont
Phone: +61 2 9571 5055
www.sugaroom.com.au
Opening hours: Tue–Sun lunch from noon to 3 pm, Mon–Sat dinner from 6 pm until late
Average price: Starters A$ 12, main courses A$ 23
Cuisine: Modern Australian
Special features: Perfect place to enjoy the afternoon alongside the water

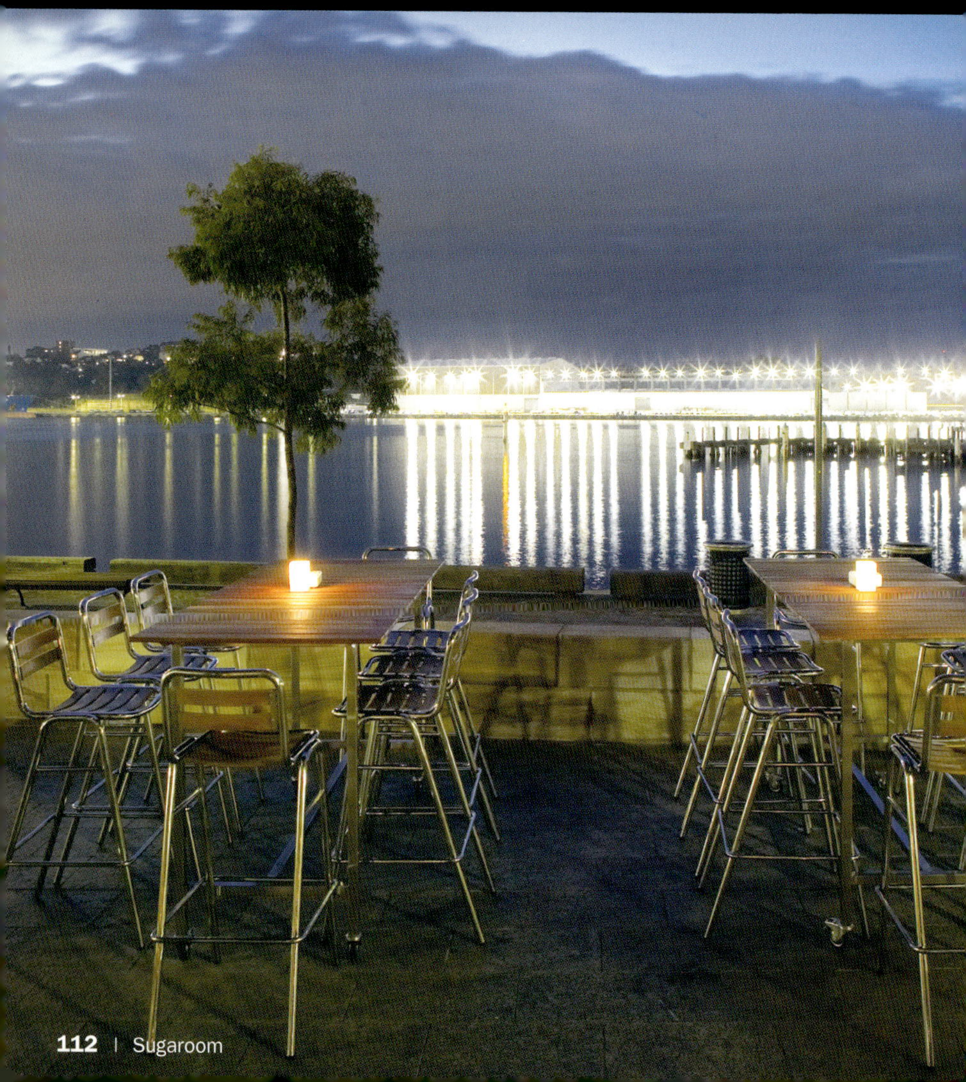

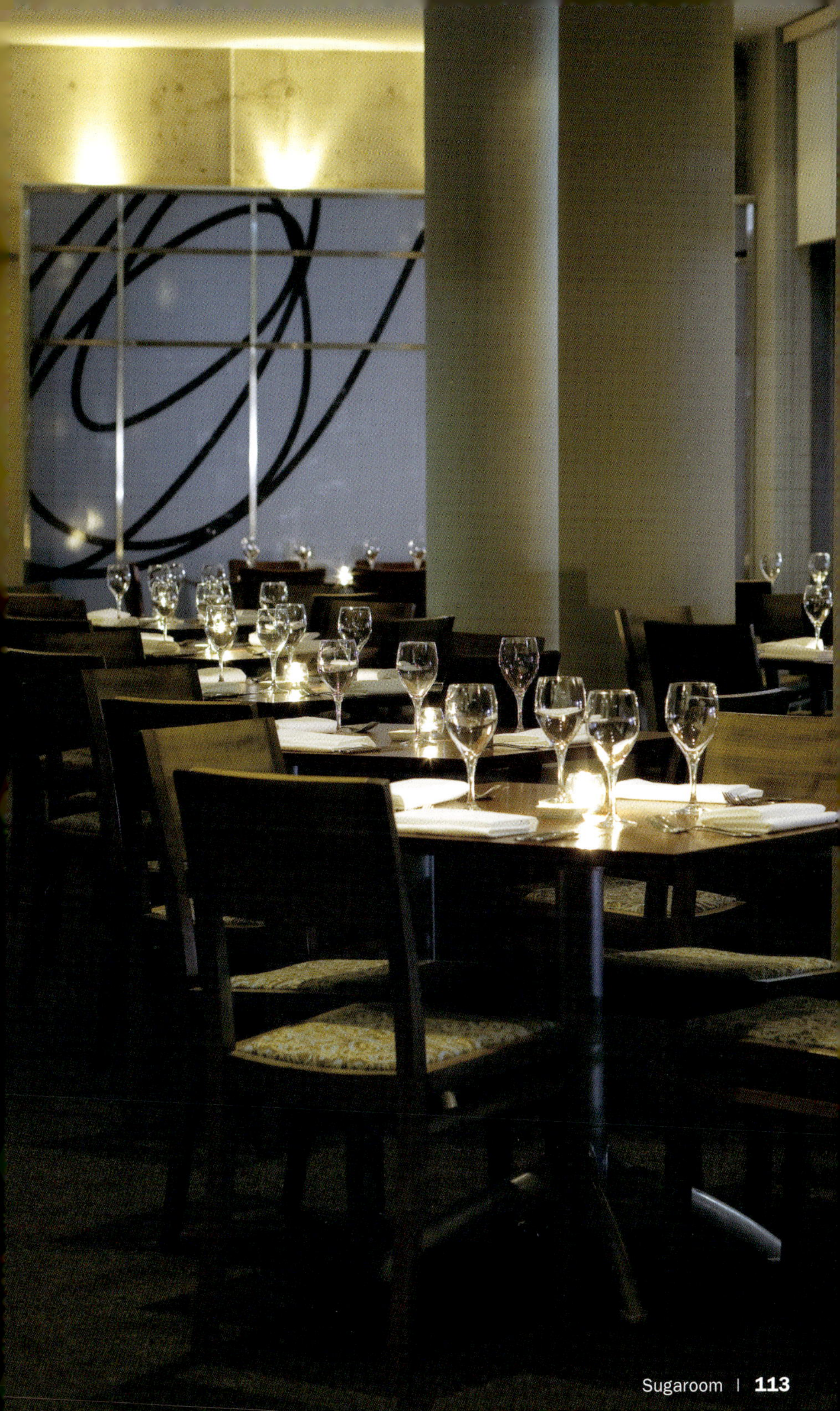

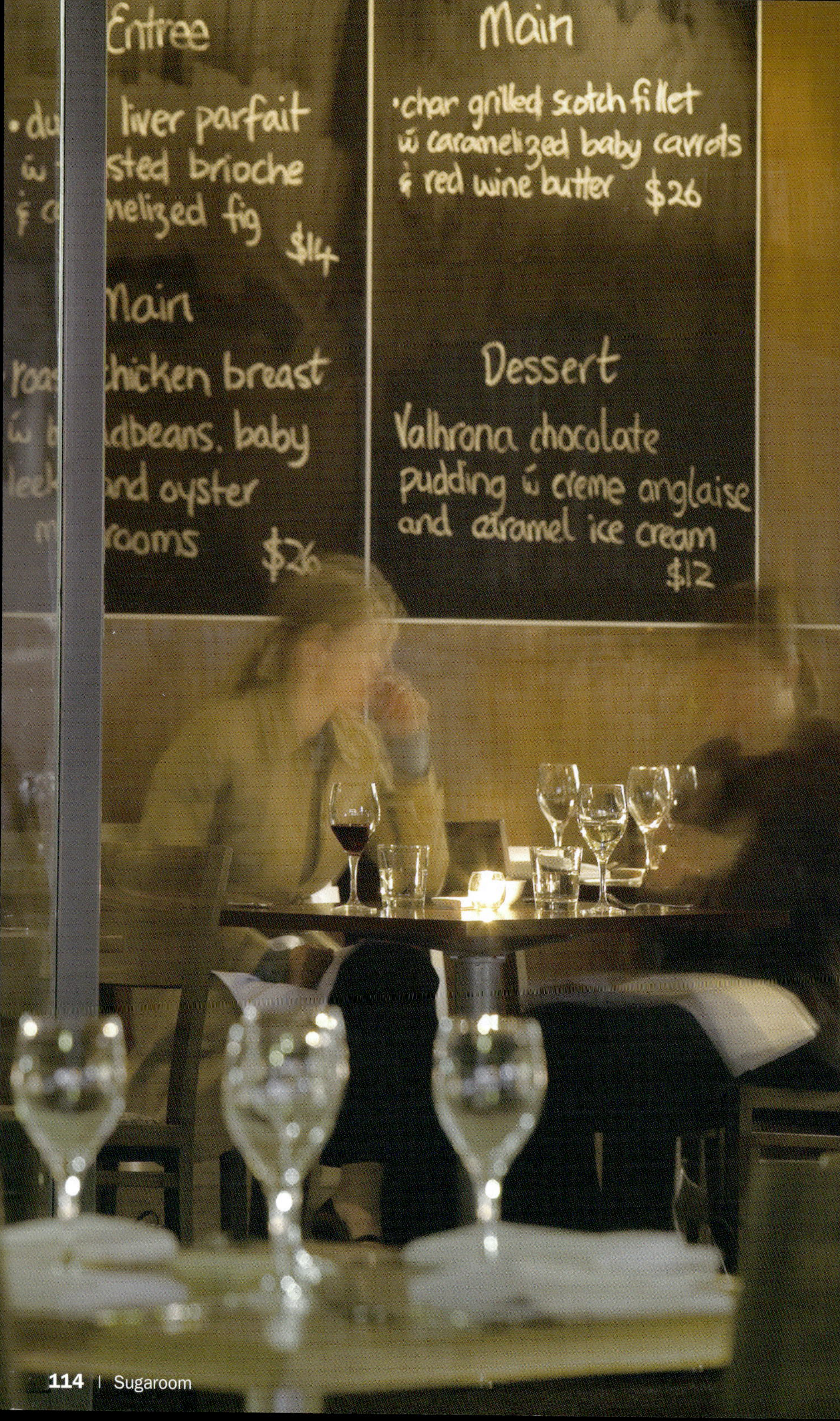

Entree
Main
· du liver parfait
ü   sted brioche
ç ca melized fig $14
·char grilled scotch fillet
ü caramelized baby carrots
ç red wine butter $26
Main
roas chicken breast
ü   dbeans. baby
eek nd oyster
m   rooms $26
Dessert
Valhrona chocolate
pudding ü creme anglaise
and caramel ice cream
$12

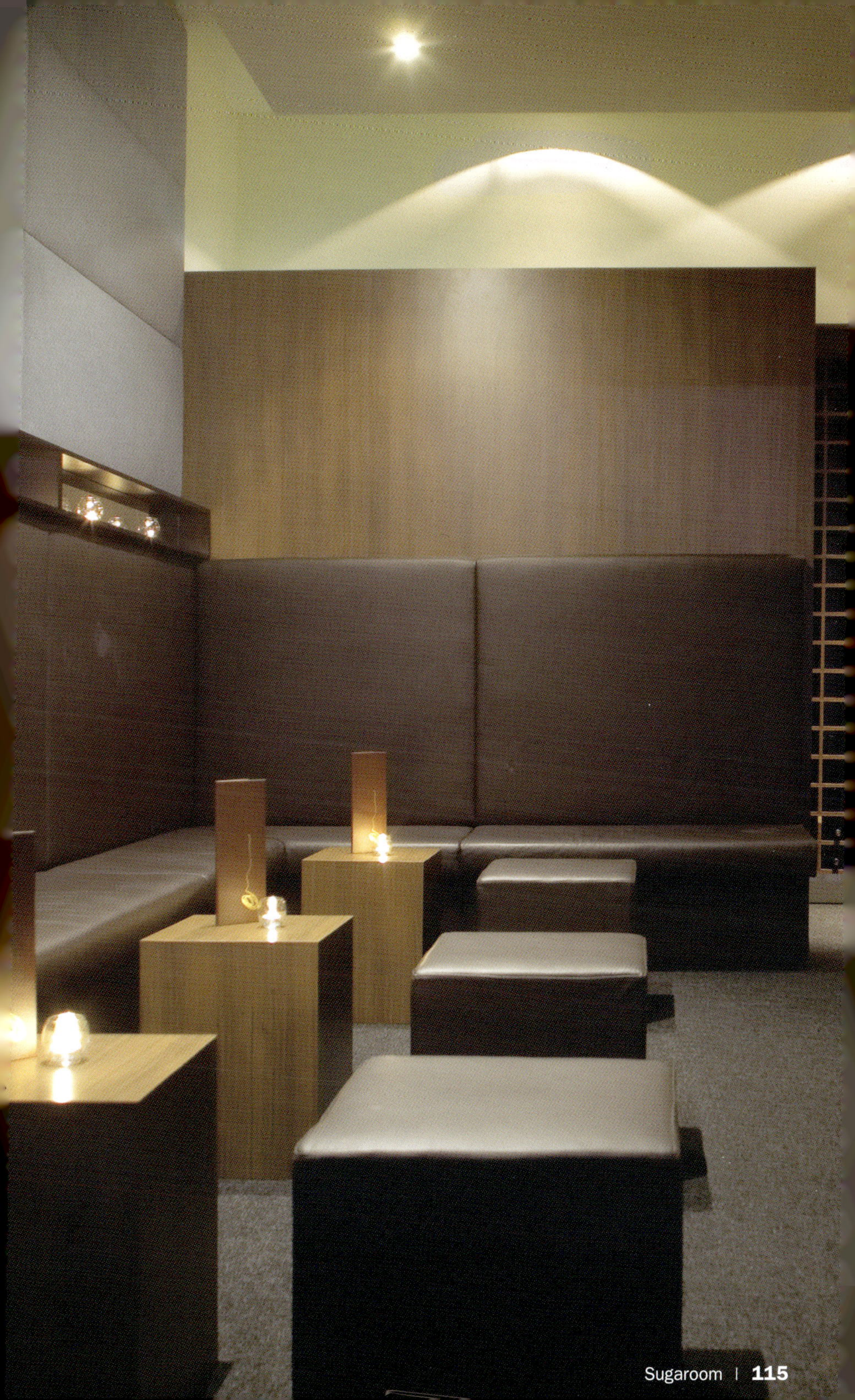

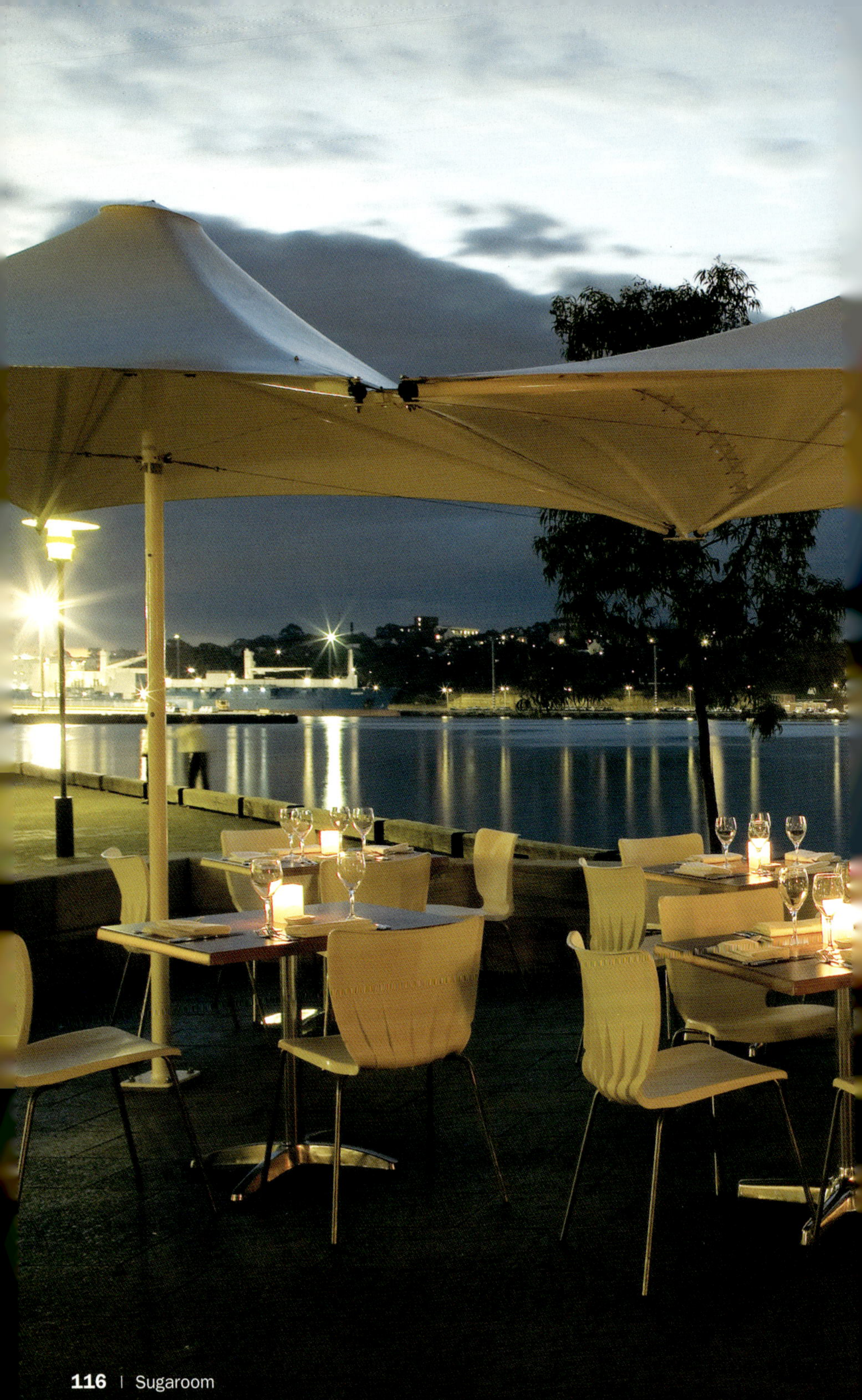

Mandarin Cocktail

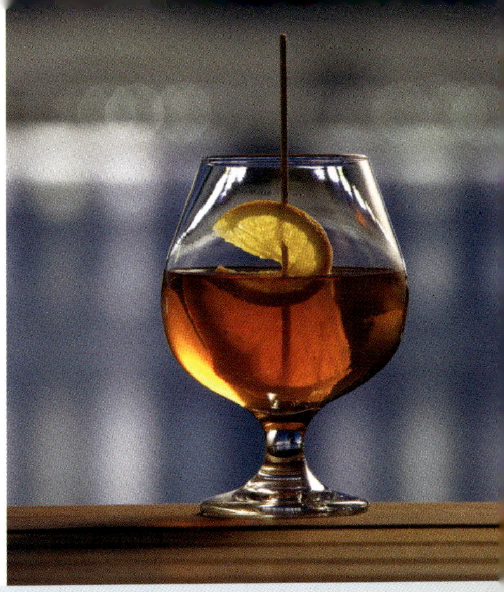

45 ml Cointreau
15 ml Grand Marnier
30 ml mandarin syrup

Pour the liquors and mandarin syrup into a cocktail shaker and blend. Serve the contents in a cocktail glass

45 ml Cointreau
15 ml Grand Marnier
30 ml Mandarinensirup

Die Liköre und den Mandarinensirup in einen Cocktailshaker gießen und mixen. Den Inhalt in einem Cocktailglas servieren.

45 ml de Cointreau
15 ml de Grand Marnier
30 ml de sirop de mandarine

Verser les liqueurs et le sirop de mandarine dans le shaker et agiter. Servir le mélange dans un verre à cocktail.

45 ml de Cointreau
15 ml de Grand Marnier
30 ml de jarabe de mandarina

Verter los licores y el jarabe de mandarina en la coctelera y agitar. Servir el contenido en una copa de cóctel.

45 ml di Cointreau
15 ml di Grand Marnier
30 ml di sciroppo di mandarino

Versare i liquori e lo sciroppo di mandarino nello shaker ed agitare. Servire il contenuto in un bicchiere da cocktail.

Summit

Design: Burley Katon Halliday | Architect: Harry Seidler |
Chef: Michael Moore

264 George Street, Level 47 | Sydney, 2000 | Australia Square
Phone: +61 2 9247 9777
www.summitrestaurant.com.au
Opening hours: Sun–Fri lunch from noon to 3 pm, every day dinner from 6 pm until late
Average price: Menus from A$ 39–68
Cuisine: Modern Australian
Special features: 360 degree uninterrupted views of Sydney, revolving panorama
of city skyline

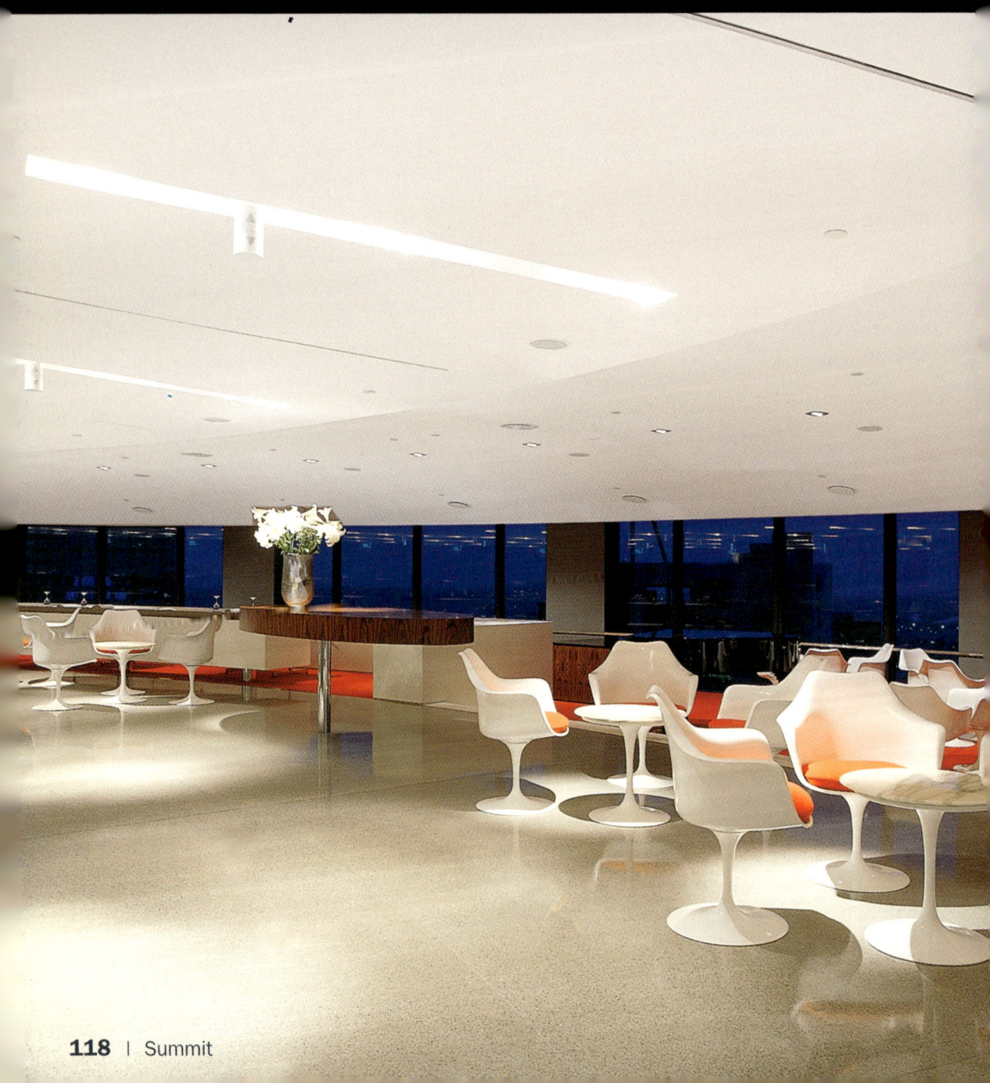

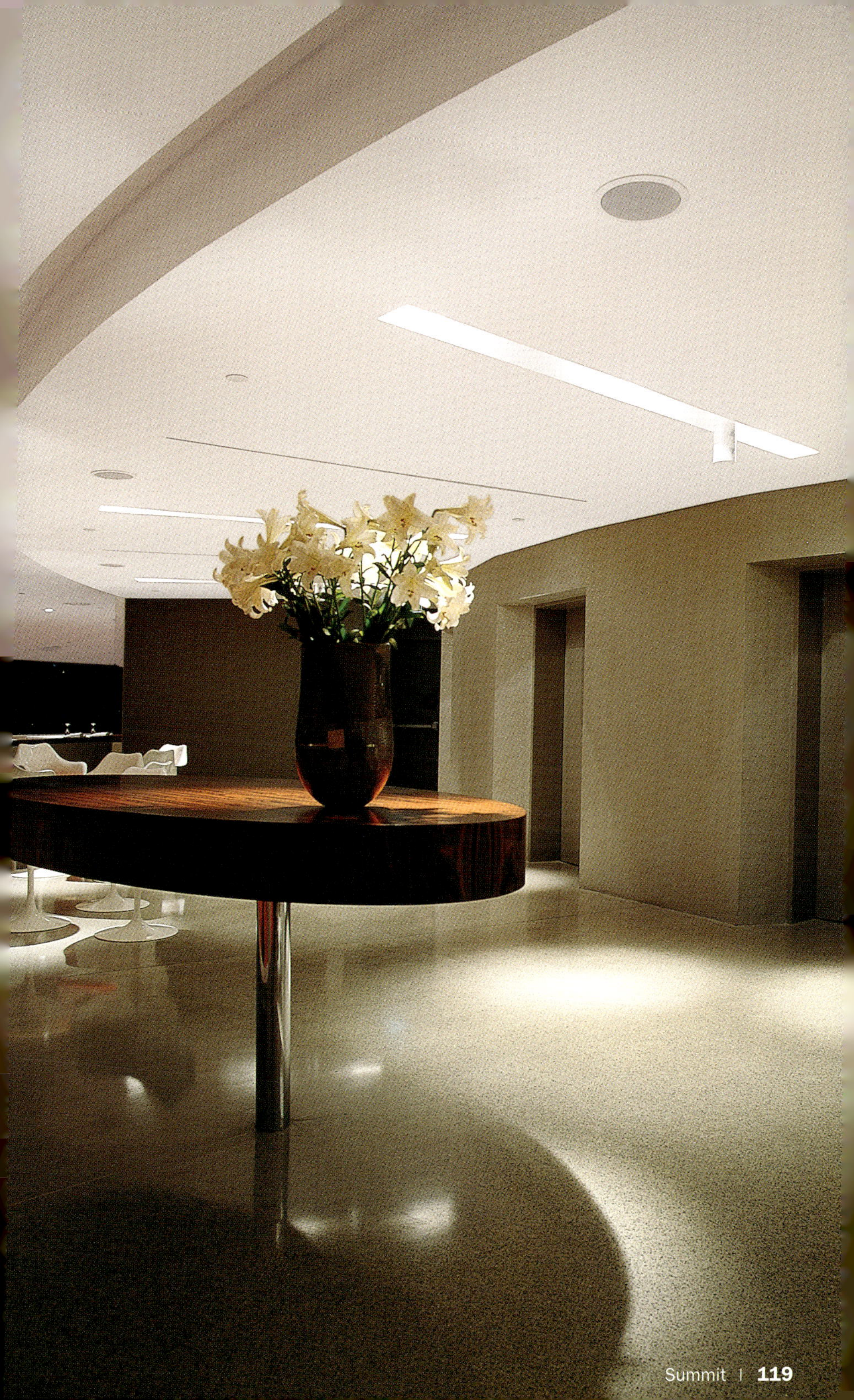

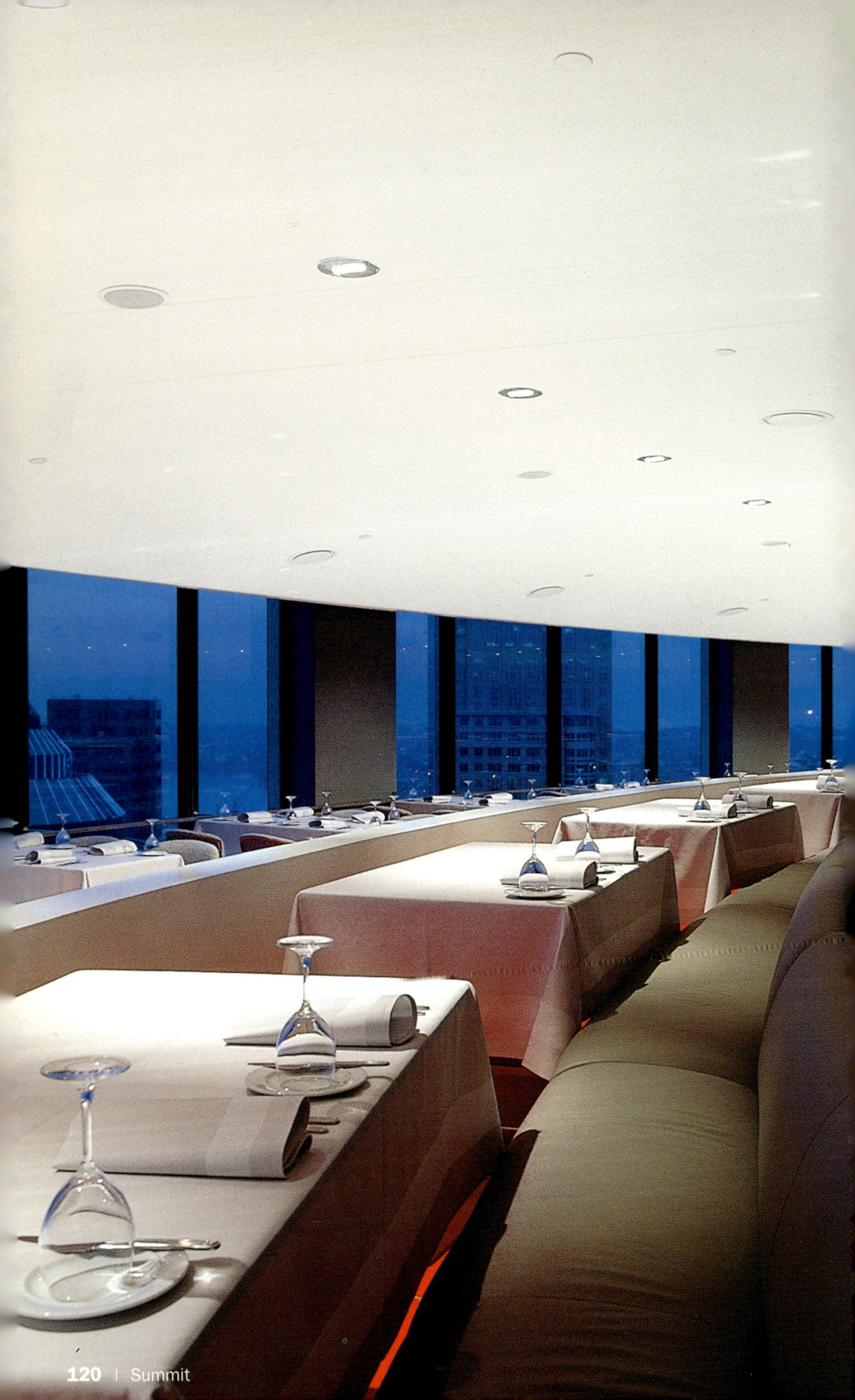

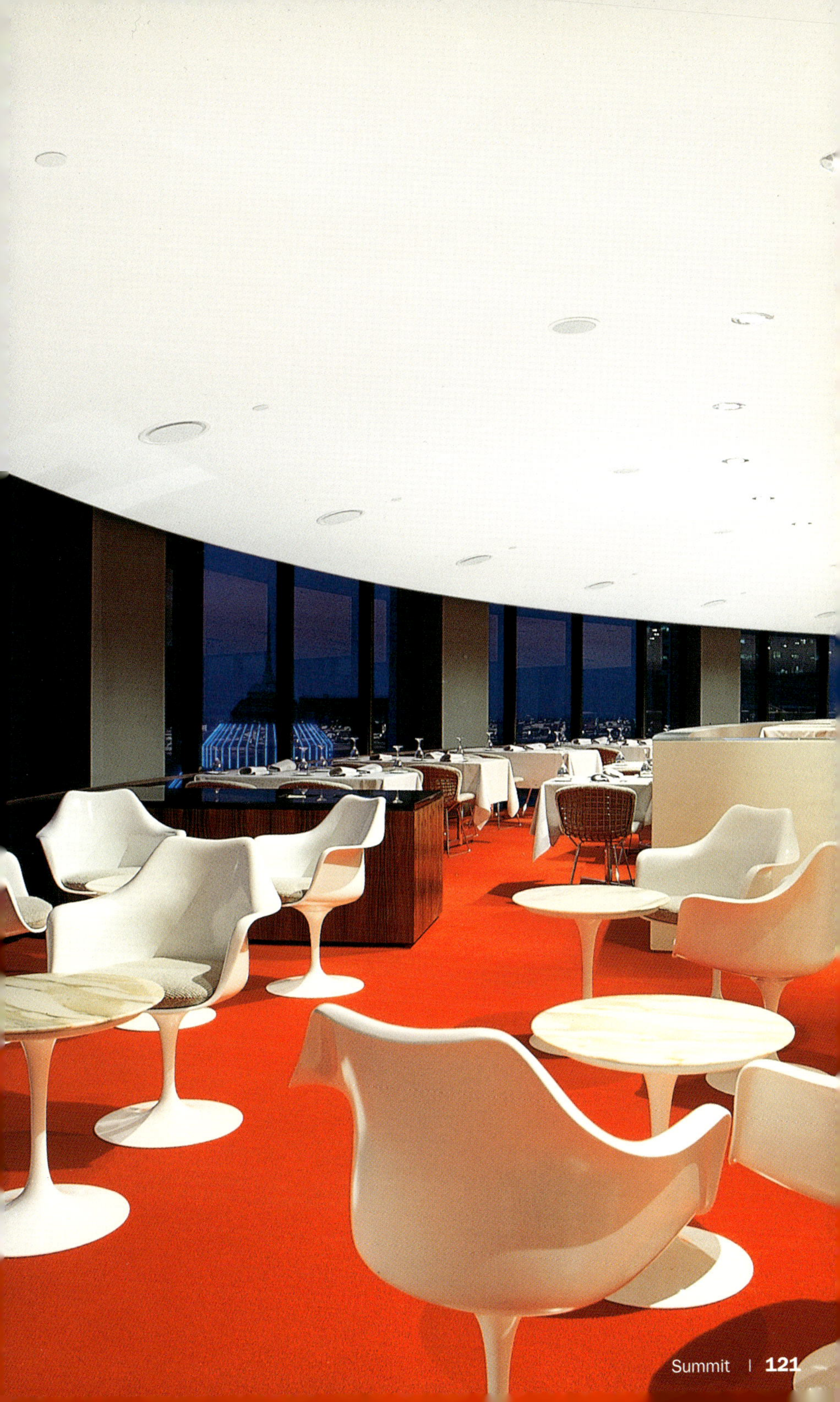

Cream of Parsnip
and Mushroom Soup

Cremesuppe von Pastinaken und
Champignons

Crème de panais et de champignons
de Paris

Crema de chirivías y champiñones

Crema di pastinache e champignon

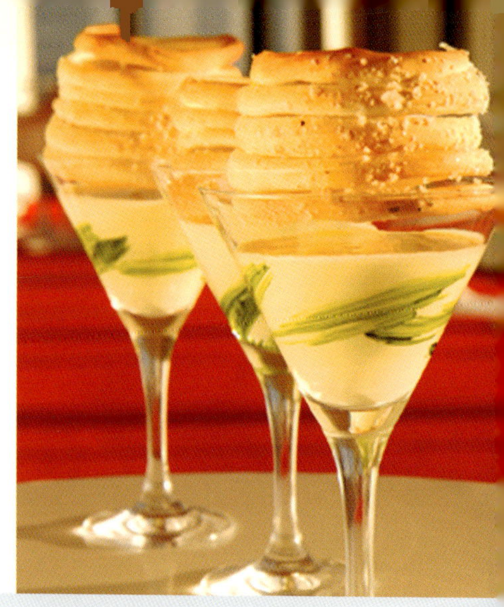

3 parsnips
3 tbsp honey
1 oz butter
3 1/2 oz cauliflower
1 garlic clove
1 onion
3 1/2 oz mushrooms
250 ml white wine
400 ml vegetable stock
150 pouring cream
2/5 oz ground mushrooms
Salted bread sticks in shape of snails
Salt
Pepper

Clean and chop the parsnips lengthways, coat them in butter and honey and bake in the oven for 20 minutes until they are golden brown. Finely chop the cauliflower, garlic and onion and cook in a saucepan with a little butter over a low heat for 5 minutes. Add the sliced mushrooms and boil for a further 10 minutes. Add the parsnips and white wine and, after 2 minutes, pour in the vegetable stock. Simmer over a low heat for another 15 minutes. Purée the mixture in the blender, add the pouring cream and season with the ground mushrooms, salt and pepper.
Serve in cocktail glasses and decorate with the salted sticks.

3 Pastinaken
3 EL Honig
30 g Butter
100 g Blumenkohl
1 Knoblauchzehe
1 Zwiebel
100 g Champignons
250 ml Weißwein
400 ml Gemüsebrühe
150 ml flüssige Sahne
10 g gemahlene Pilze
Gedrehte Salzstangen
Salz
Pfeffer

Pastinaken putzen und längs durchschneiden, mit Butter und Honig bestreichen und im Ofen 20 Minuten goldbraun backen. Den Blumenkohl, den Knoblauch und die Zwiebel fein schneiden und in einem Topf mit etwas Butter auf niedriger Flamme 5 Minuten dünsten. Die in Scheiben geschnittenen Champignons hinzufügen und weitere 10 Minuten kochen. Die Pastinaken und den Weißwein zugeben und nach 2 Minuten mit der Gemüsebrühe auffüllen. Weitere 15 Minuten bei schwacher Hitze köcheln. Die Mischung im Mixer fein pürieren, die flüssige Sahne zugeben und mit den gemahlenen Pilzen, Salz und Pfeffer würzen.
In Cocktailgläsern anrichten und mit den Salzstangen dekorieren.

3 panais
3 c. à soupe de miel
30 g de beurre
100 g de chou-fleur
1 gousse d'ail
1 oignon
100 g de champignons de Paris
250 ml de vin blanc
400 ml de bouillon de légumes
150 ml de crème liquide
10 g de champignons secs en poudre
Petites baguettes salées de pain grillé en spirale
Sel
Poivre

Laver et couper dans la longueur les panais, les napper de beurre et de miel et faire dorer au four 20 minutes. Couper finement le chou-fleur, l'ail, l'oignon et cuire à feu doux dans un peu de beurre pendant 5 minutes. Ajouter les champignons de Paris coupés en rondelles et faire encore bouillir pendant 10 minutes. Incorporer les panais et le vin blanc puis, passées 2 minutes, couvrir avec le bouillon de légumes. Laisser encore cuire pendant 15 minutes. Mixer le mélange jusqu'à ce qu'il soit très fin, ajouter la crème liquide et assaisonner avec les champignons en poudre, le poivre et le sel.
Servir dans des verres à cocktails et décorer avec les petites baguettes salées.

3 chirivías
3 cucharadas de miel
30 g de mantequilla
100 g de coliflor
1 diente de ajo
1 cebolla
100 g de champiñones
250 ml de vino blanco
400 ml de caldo vegetal
150 ml de nata líquida
10 g de setas molidas
Barritas saladas de pan tostado con forma de caracol
Sal
Pimienta

Limpiar y cortar longitudinalmente las chirivías, untarlas con mantequilla y miel y dorarlas en el horno durante 20 minutos. Cortar finamente la coliflor, el ajo y la cebolla, y cocer a fuego lento en un recipiente con un poco de mantequilla durante 5 minutos. Agregar los champiñones cortados en láminas y hervir 10 minutos más. Incorporar las chirivías y el vino blanco y, pasados 2 minutos, cubrir con el caldo vegetal. Seguir cociendo a fuego lento durante 15 minutos. Pasar la mezcla por la batidora hasta que quede muy fina, añadir la nata líquida y sazonar con las setas molidas, la pimienta y la sal.
Servir en copas de cóctel y decorar con las barritas saladas.

3 pastinache
3 cucchiai di miele
30 g di burro
100 g di cavolfiore
1 spicchio d'aglio
1 cipolla
100 g di champignon
250 ml di vino bianco
400 ml di brodo vegetale
150 ml di panna liquida
10 g di funghi trifolati
Barrette salate di pane tostato a forma di chiocciola
Sale
Pepe

Pulire e tagliare per lungo le pastinache, ungerle con burro e miele e farle dorare in forno per 20 minuti. Tagliare finemente il cavolfiore, l'aglio e la cipolla e cuocere a fuoco lento in un tegame con un po' di burro per 5 minuti. Unire gli champignon tagliati a listelle e far cuocere per altri 10 minuti. Incorporare le pastinache e il vino bianco e, trascorsi 2 minuti, ricoprire con il brodo vegetale. Continuare a far cuocere a fuoco lento per 15 minuti. Passare il composto al frullatore fino a che diventi molto fine, aggiungere la panna liquida e condire con i funghi trifolati, il pepe e il sale.
Servire in appositi bicchieri per cocktail e decorare con le barrette salate.

The Bourbon

Design: Artazan | Chef: Colin Holt

24 Darlinghurst Road | Sydney, 2011 | Kings Cross
Phone: +61 2 9358 1144
www.thebourbon.com.au
Opening hours: Every day from noon to 10 pm
Average price: Main courses A$ 13–28
Cuisine: Bistro with an Italian touch
Special features: Eating and having fun in one of Sydney's most desired
party destinations

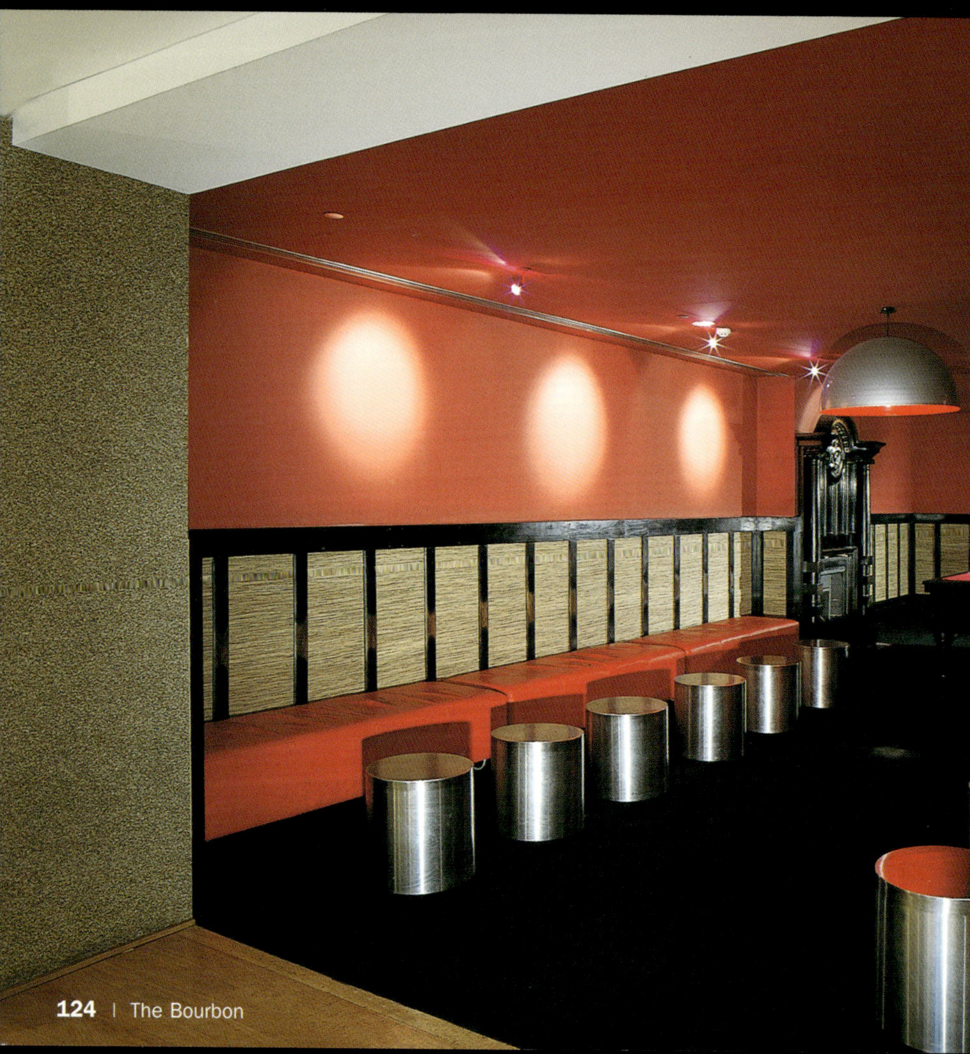

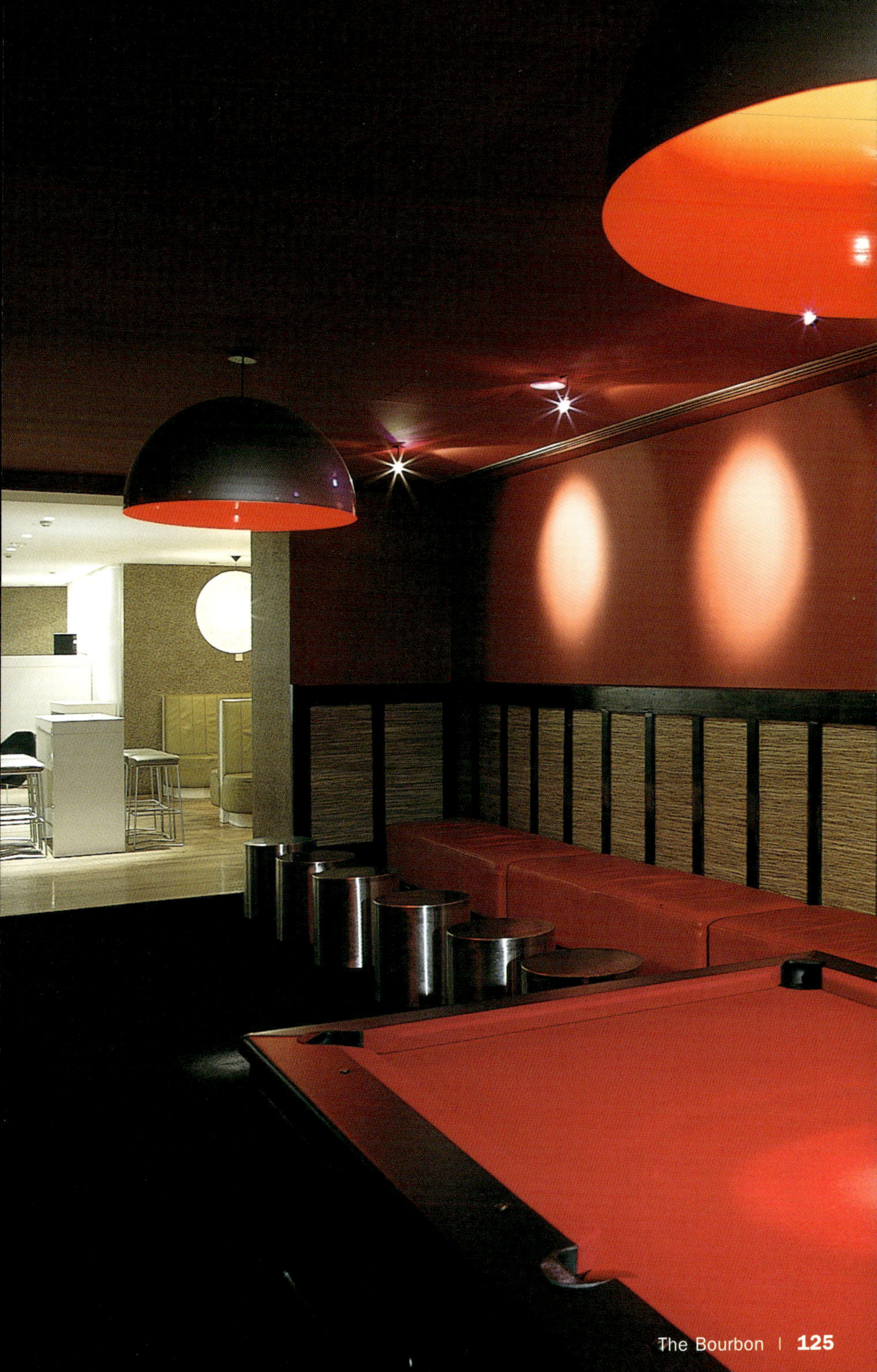

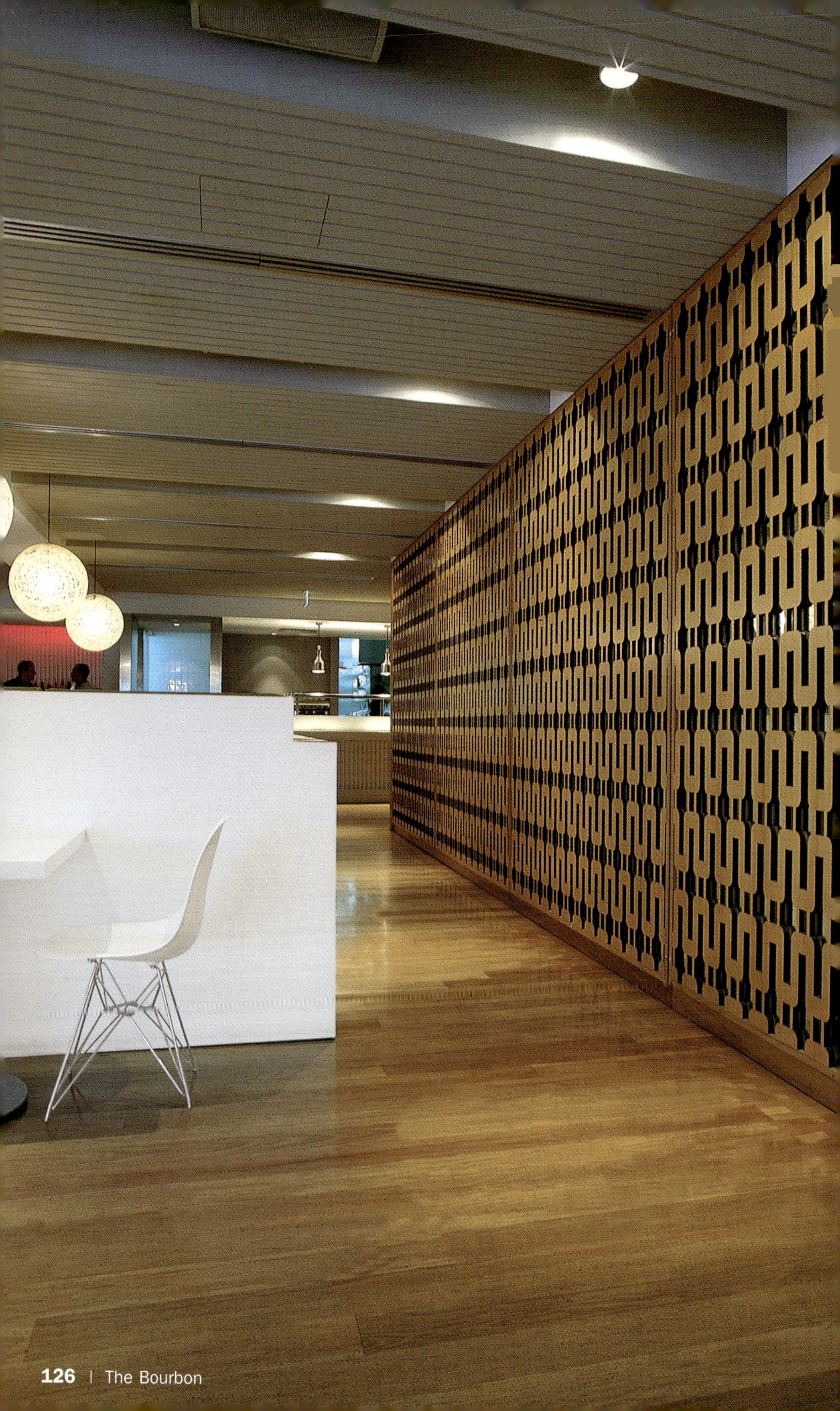

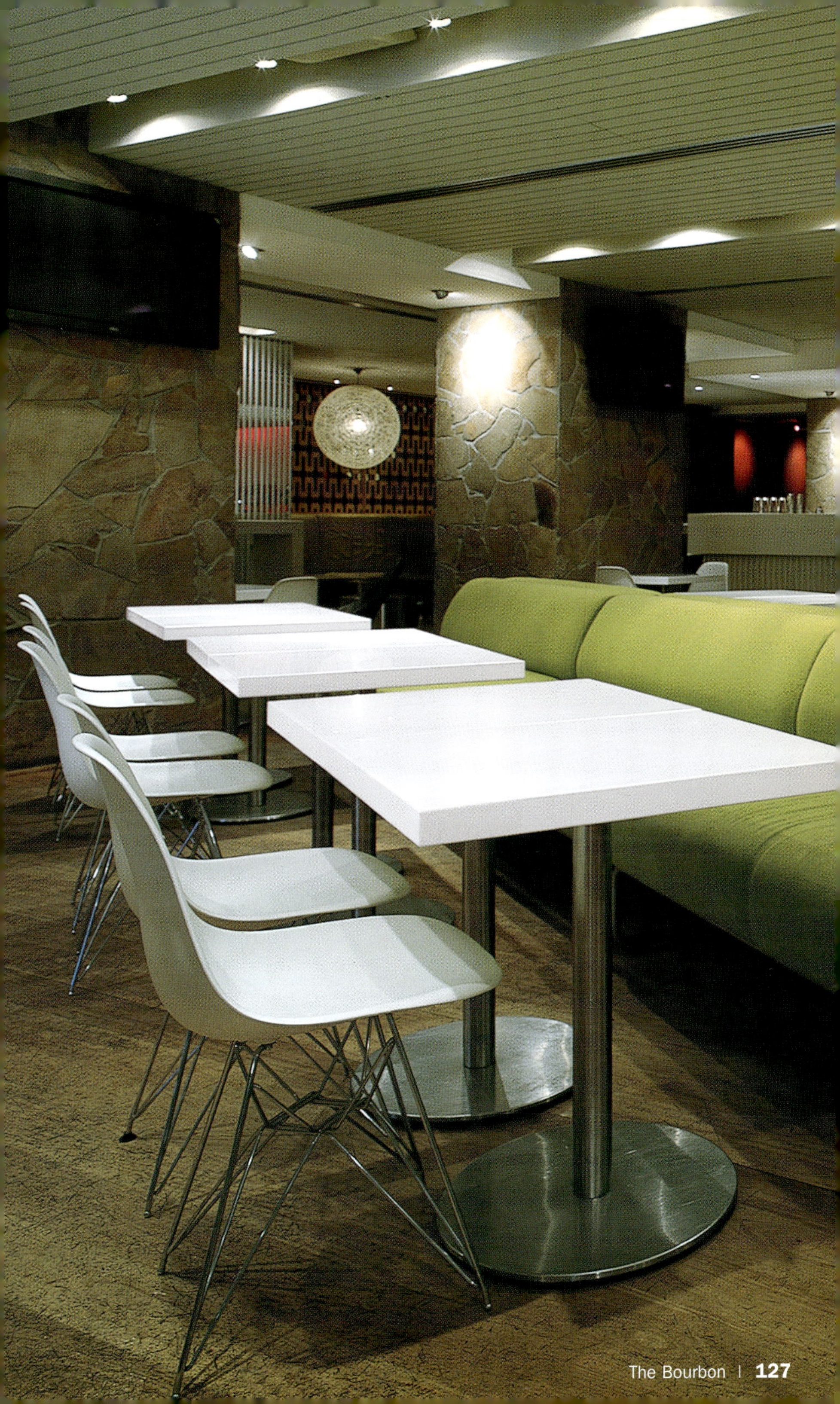

The Wharf Restaurant

Design: Tim Pak Poy | Chef: Aaron Ross & Tim Pak Poy

Pier 4 Hickson Road | Sydney, 2000 | Walsh Bay
Phone: +61 2 9250 1761
www.thewharfrestaurant.com.au
Opening hours: Lunch Mon–Sat from noon to 3 pm, dinner Mon–Sat from 6 pm until late
Average price: Starters A$ 19, main courses A$ 32, desserts A$ 13
Cuisine: Modern Australian
Special features: Relaxed and comfortable ambience with unrivalled views of the
Harbour Bridge. Original Arne Jacobsen dining room chairs

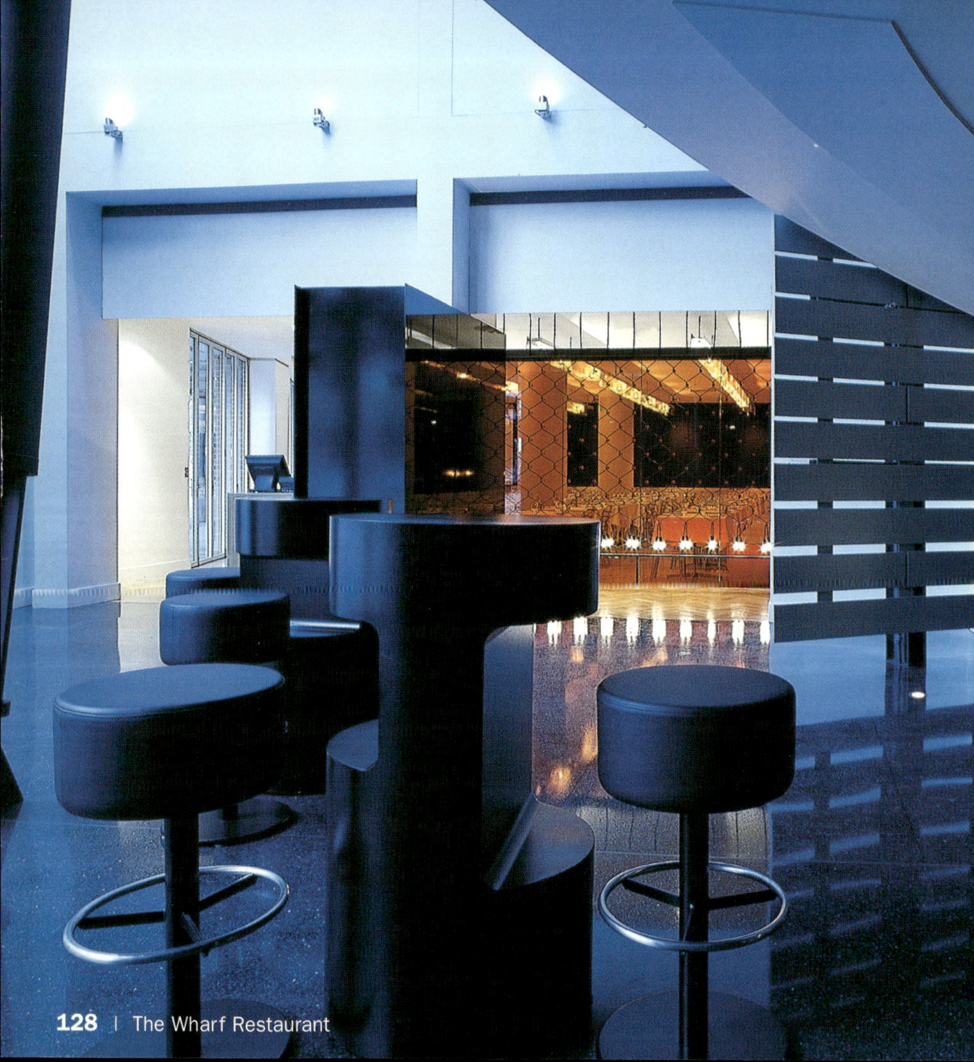

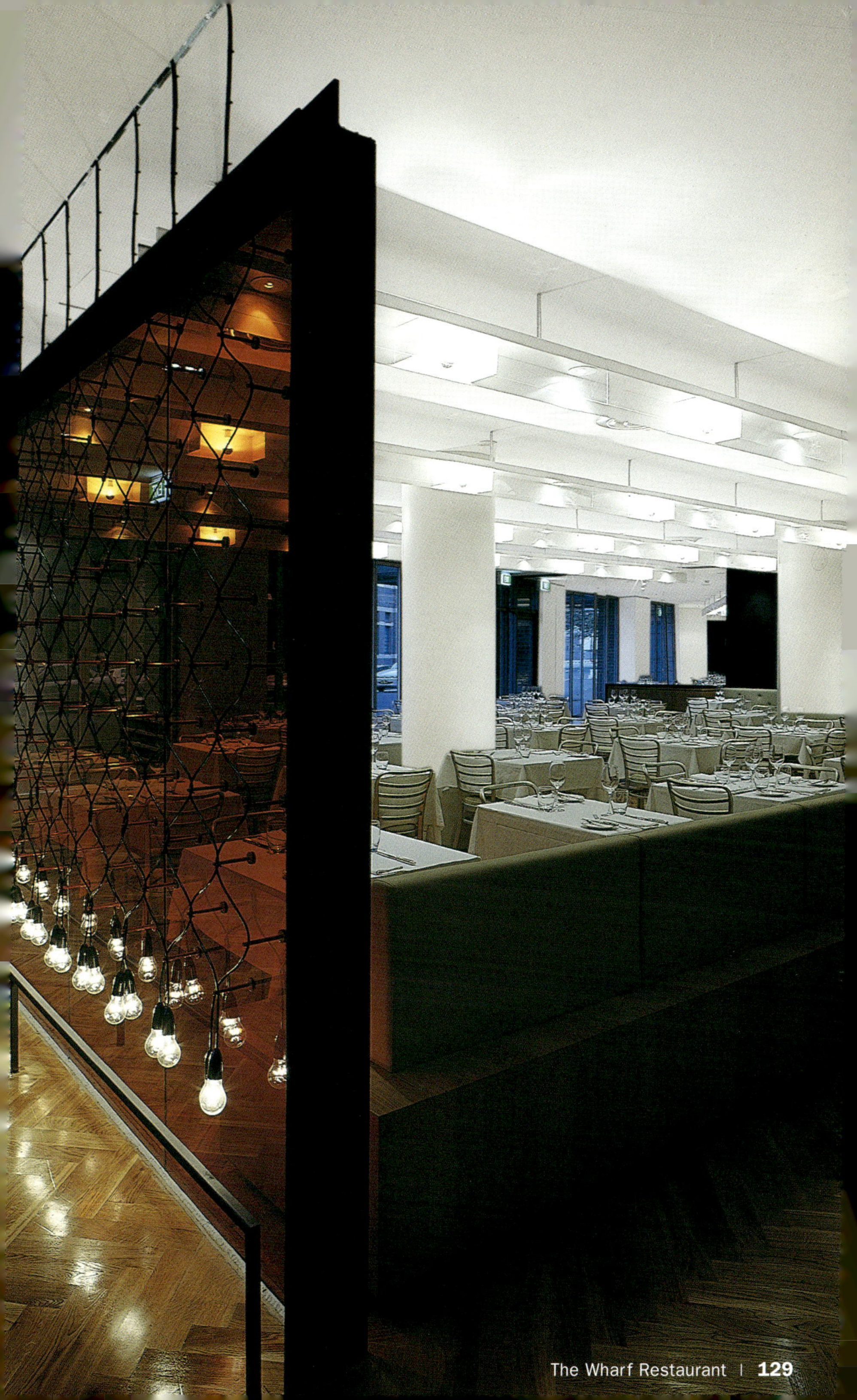

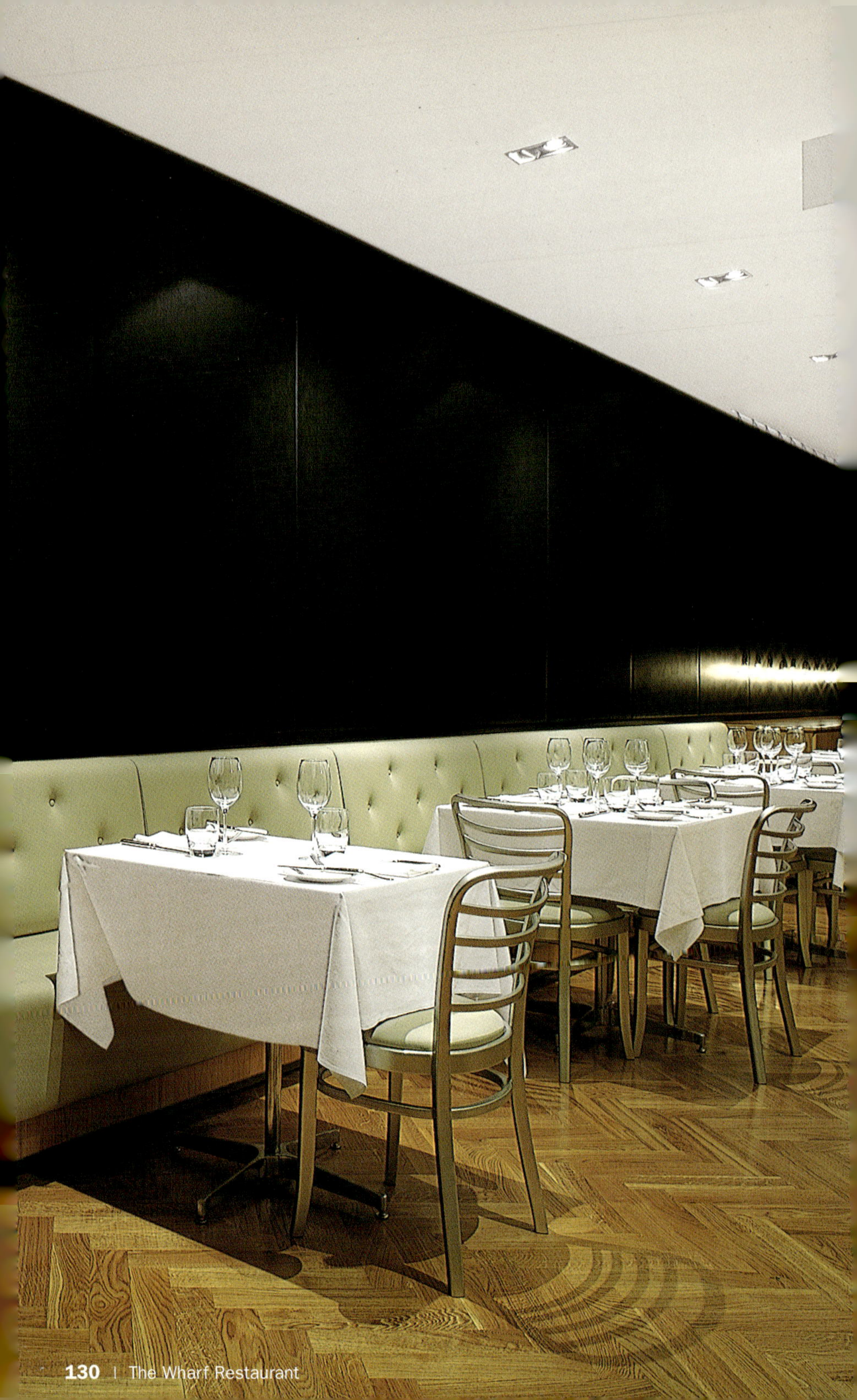

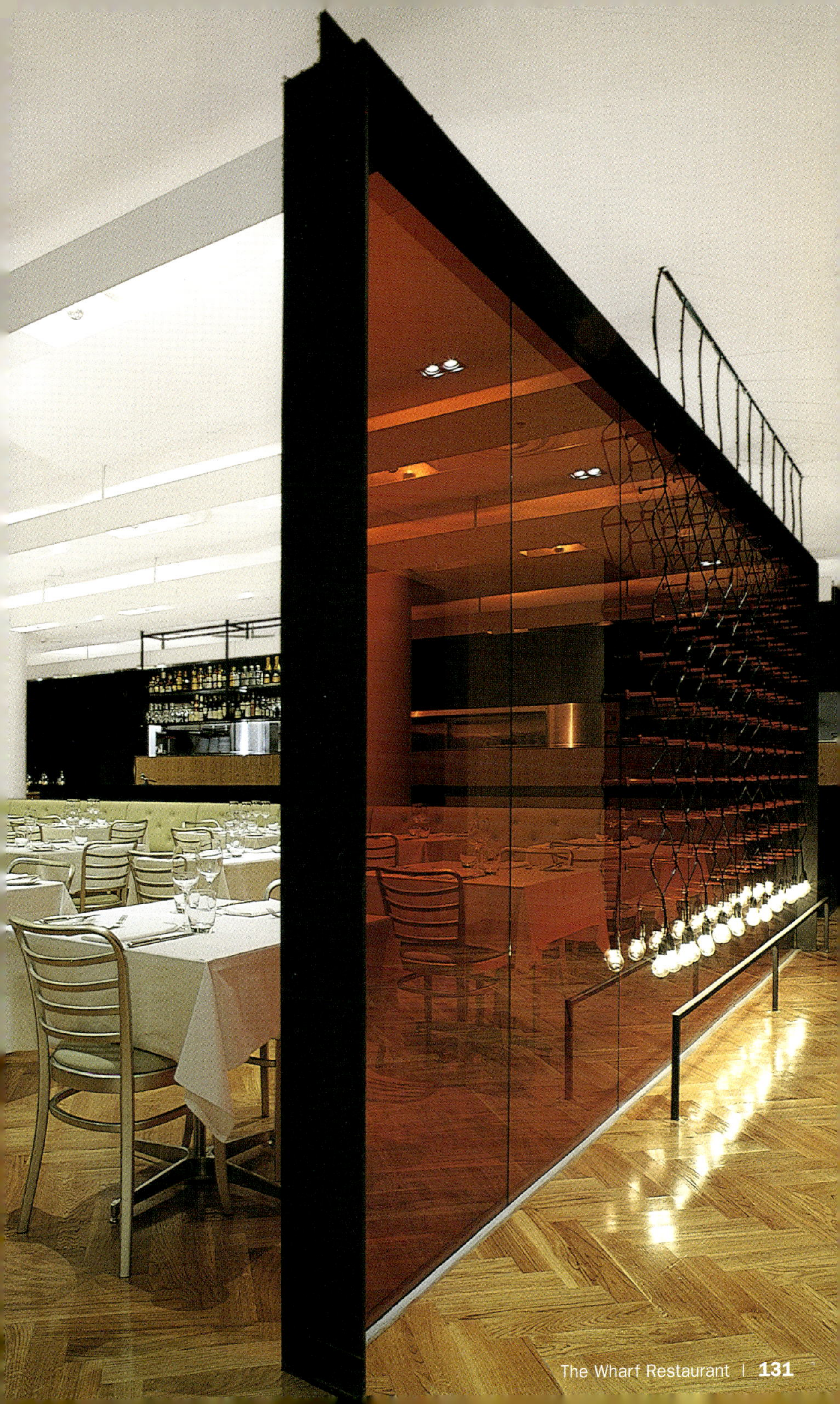

Chilled Oysters
with Salmon Caviar

Geeiste Austern mit Lachskaviar
Huîtres glacées au caviar de saumon
Ostras heladas con caviar de salmón
Ostriche gelate con caviale di salmone

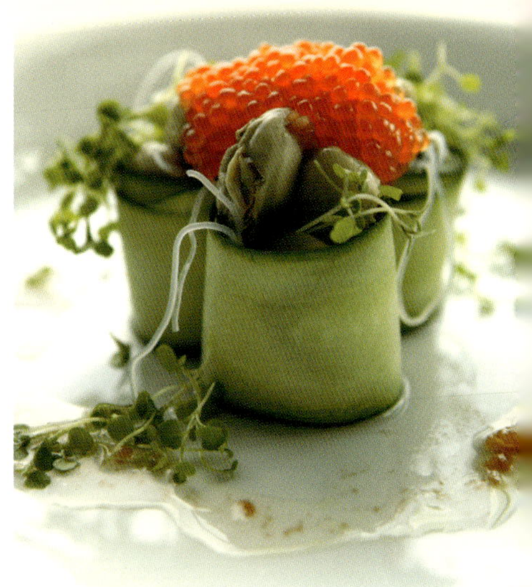

12 oysters
1 cucumber
30 ml olive oil
10 ml vinegar
1/5 oz diced shallots
3 1/2 oz salmon caviar
1 bunch of watercress

Blanch the oysters with boiling water for 10 seconds and immediately cool off with very cold water. With a potato peeler, shred the cucumber into very fine strips. For the dressing, mix the olive oil with the vinegar and shallots.
On each dish, arrange 3 oysters and a few cucumber strips into a ring shape, drench with the oil, vinegar and shallot dressing, and top with salmon caviar and some finely chopped watercress.

12 Austern
1 Gurke
30 ml Olivenöl
10 ml Essig
5 g gehackte Schalotten
100 g Kaviar vom Lachs
1 Bund Kresse

Austern mit kochendem Wasser 10 Sekunden abbrühen und sofort in sehr kaltem Wasser abschrecken. Mit einem Kartoffelschäler die Gurke in sehr feine Streifen hobeln. Für das Dressing Olivenöl mit Essig und Schalotten mischen. Auf jedem Teller 3 Austern und einige Gurkenstreifen ringförmig anordnen, mit der Essig-Öl-Schalotten-Mischung anmachen und mit dem Lachskaviar und ein wenig feingehackter Kresse krönen.

12 huîtres
1 concombre
30 ml d'huile d'olive
10 ml de vinaigre
5 g d'échalote hachée
100 g de caviar de saumon
1 bouquet de cresson

Ébouillanter les huîtres pendant 10 secondes puis les refroidir immédiatement dans de l'eau très froide. À l'aide d'un couteau économe, couper le concombre en lamelles très fines. Pour l'assaisonnement, mélanger l'huile, le vinaigre et l'échalote.

Dans chaque assiette, disposer 3 huîtres et quelques lamelles de concombre en forme de cercle, assaisonner avec le mélange d'huile, de vinaigre et d'échalote puis couronner avec le caviar de saumon et un peu de cresson finement haché.

12 ostras
1 pepino
30 ml de aceite de oliva
10 ml de vinagre
5 g de chalota picada
100 g de caviar de salmón
1 ramillete de berro

Escaldar las ostras en agua hirviendo durante 10 segundos y refrescarlas inmediatamente en agua muy fría. Con un pelador de patata, cortar el pepino en tiras muy finas. Para el aliño, mezclar el aceite, el vinagre y la chalota.

En cada plato, disponer 3 ostras y unas tiras de pepino en forma de anillo, aliñar con la mezcla de aceite, vinagre y chalota, y coronar con el caviar de salmón y un poco de berro finamente picado.

12 ostriche
1 cetriolo
30 ml di olio d'oliva
10 ml d'aceto
5 g di scalogno tritato
100 g di caviale di salmone
1 mazzetto di crescione

Scottare le ostriche in acqua bollente per 10 secondi e subito dopo fare raffreddare in acqua molto fredda. Con un pelapatate, tagliare il cetriolo a rondelle molto sottili. Per il condimento, mescolare l'olio, l'aceto e lo scalogno.

Su ogni piatto, disporre 3 ostriche e delle rondelle di cetriolo, condire con il composto d'olio, aceto e scalogno e coronare con il caviale di salmone e un po' di crescione finemente tritato.

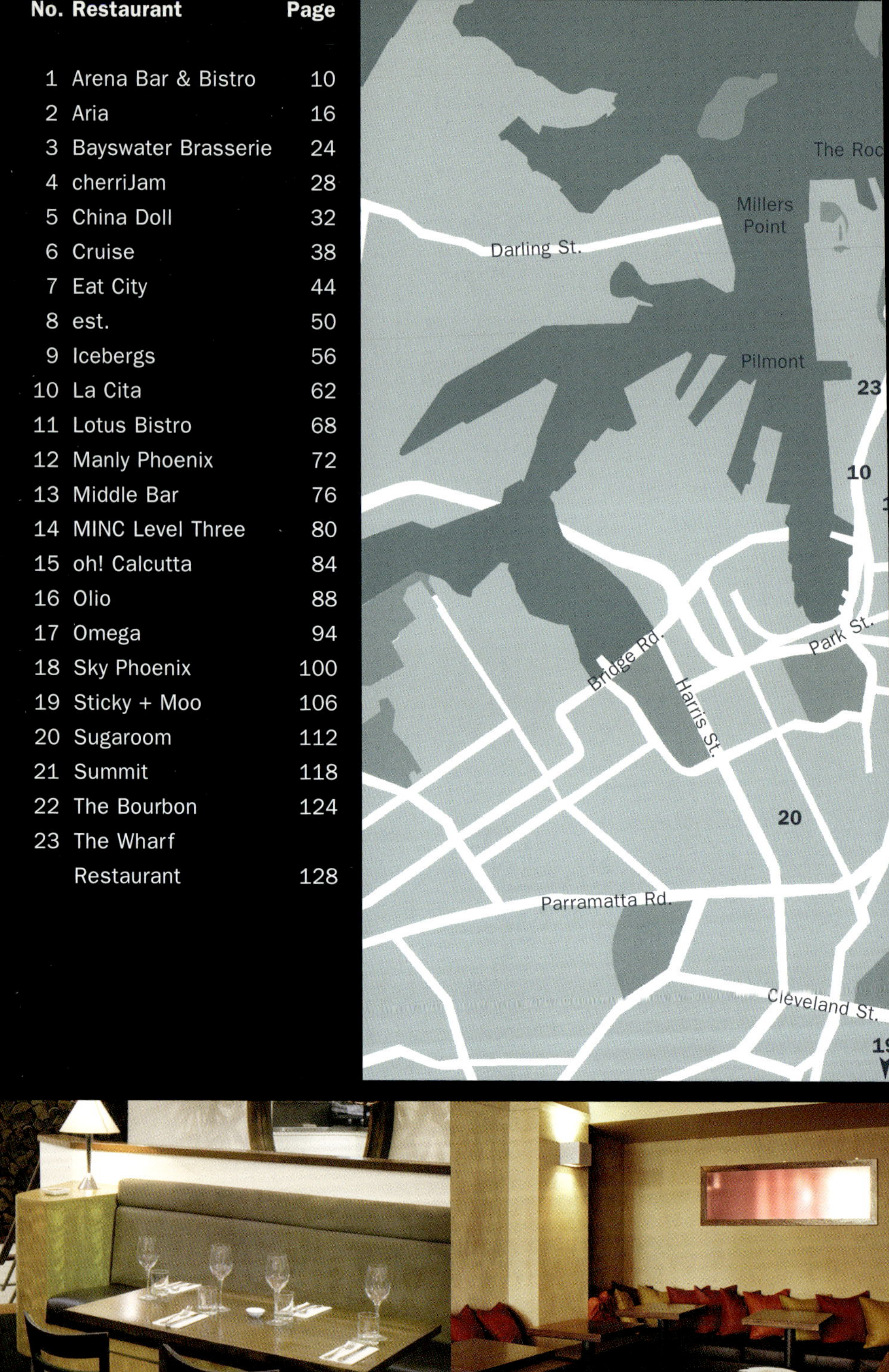

The Roc
Millers
Point
Darling St.
Pilmont
23
10
Bridge Rd.
Harris St.
Park St.
20
Parramatta Rd.
Cleveland St.
19

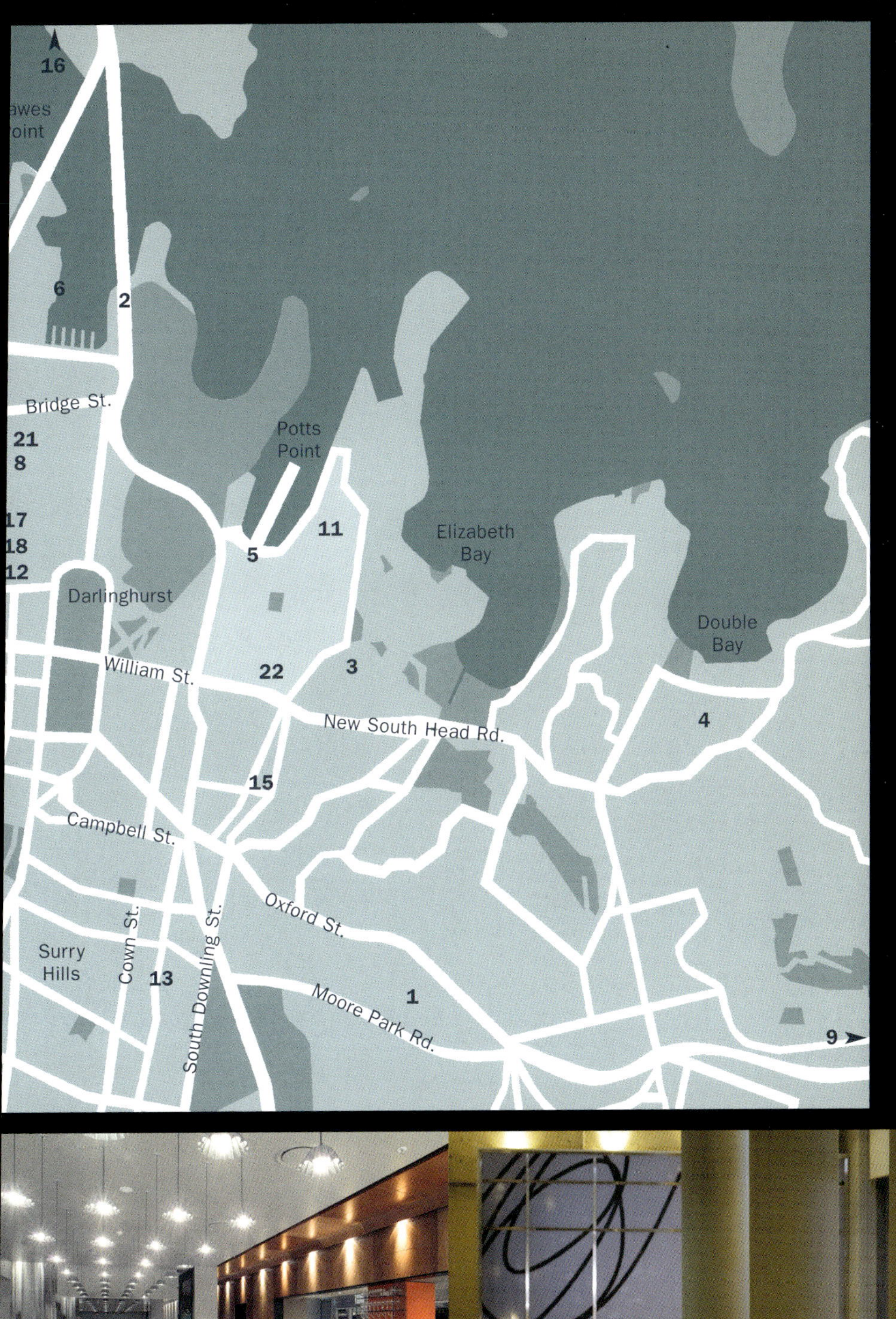

16
awes
oint
6
2
Bridge St.
21
8
17
18
12
Darlinghurst
Potts
Point
11
5
Elizabeth
Bay
Double
Bay
William St.
22
3
New South Head Rd.
4
15
Campbell St.
Surry
Hills
Cown St.
South Downling St.
Oxford St.
13
Moore Park Rd.
1
9

Cool Restaurants

Size: 14 x 21.5 cm/ 5 $^1/_2$ x 8 $^1/_2$ in.
136 pp, Flexicover
c. 130 color photographs
Text in English, German, French,
Spanish, Italian or (*) Dutch

Other titles in the same series:

Amsterdam
ISBN 3-8238-4588-8

Barcelona
ISBN 3-8238-4586-1

Berlin
ISBN 3-8238-4585-3

Brussels (*)
ISBN 3-8327-9065-9

Cape Town
ISBN 3-8327-9103-5

Chicago
ISBN 3-8327-9018-7

Cologne
ISBN 3-8327-9117-5

Côte d'Azur
ISBN 3-8327-9040-3

Frankfurt
ISBN 3-8327-9118-3

Hamburg
ISBN 3-8238-4599-3

Hong Kong
ISBN 3-8327-9111-6

Istanbul
ISBN 3-8327-9115-9

Las Vegas
ISBN 3-8327-9116-7

London 2nd edition
ISBN 3-8327-9131-0

Los Angeles
ISBN 3-8238-4589-6

Madrid
ISBN 3-8327-9029-2

Mallorca / Ibiza
ISBN 3-8327-9113-2

Miami
ISBN 3-8327-9066-7

Milan
ISBN 3-8238-4587-X

Munich
ISBN 3-8327-9019-5

New York 2nd edition
ISBN 3-8327-9130-2

Paris 2nd edition
ISBN 3-8327-9129-9

Prague
ISBN 3-8327-9068-3

Rome
ISBN 3-8327-9028-4

San Francisco
ISBN 3-8327-9067-5

Shanghai
ISBN 3-8327-9050-0

Tokyo
ISBN 3-8238-4590-X

Toscana
ISBN 3-8327-9102-7

Vienna
ISBN 3-8327-9020-9

Zurich
ISBN 3-8327-9069-1

To be published in the same series:

Copenhagen
Dubai
Geneva

Moscow
Singapore
Stockholm

teNeues